THE MORMON MIRAGE

THE MORMON MIRAGE

*A Former Mormon
Tells Why She Left the Church*

Latayne Colvett Scott

ZONDERVAN
PUBLISHING HOUSE   OF THE ZONDERVAN CORPORATION
GRAND RAPIDS, MICHIGAN 49506

Bible quotations are taken from the King James Version unless otherwise indicated.

THE MORMON MIRAGE
© 1979 by The Zondervan Corporation
Grand Rapids, Michigan

Zondervan Books are published by Zondervan
Publishing House, 1415 Lake Drive, S.E.,
Grand Rapids, MI 49506.

Library of Congress Cataloging in Publication Data

Scott, Latayne Colvett, 1952-
   Mormon mirage.

   Bibliography: p.
   1. Mormons and Mormonism—Doctrinal and controversial works—Church of Christ
authors.
2. Scott, Latayne Colvett, 1952-   I. Title.
BX8645.S35   230'.9'33   79-17717
ISBN 0-310-38911-9

Printed in the United States of America

88 89 90 91 92 93 / / 18 17 16 15 14 13 12 11 10 9

Thank you, God, for leading me to Dan.
Thank you, Dan, for leading me to God.

Contents

Acknowledgments

Three groups of people helped immensely with the preparation of this book. Sandra Tanner, Dave Wilkins, and David and Donna Lusk were kind enough to read and comment on each chapter as it was prepared. They, along with my concerned typist, Carol Allen, were invaluable mentors.

Carol Jantz, Raylie Lusk, Virginia Lykins, Melissa Harding, and Rhonda Varley served lovingly as substitute mommies during the last stages of this book.

Ray Smith, who recently left Mormonism after being active in it all his life, was instrumental in bringing to my attention many changes in doctrine and practice that occurred since this book first appeared in 1979. I have incorporated many of his suggestions in this revised edition.

Most special thanks, though, goes to my wonderful husband, Dan, and to my two precious children, Ryan and Celeste, who with patience and understanding did without wife and mother for a while so that the cause of Christ could in some small way be proclaimed.

Preface

For over two years, this book has been the focus of my life activity. The more I researched, the more I have realized that I know little about Mormonism. And, though I lived it as a religion faithfully for almost ten years, I never knew it then, either. The Christian world as a whole owes much to such researchers as Jerald and Sandra Tanner, those pioneer ex-Mormons who have published many original Mormon documents which show the false nature of the Church of Jesus Christ of Latter-day Saints.

Accuracy is so important in a book of this sort that footnotes are included making it possible for Mormon friends to research sources for themselves. Though I make no pretensions to being a historian, I have relied heavily upon Mormon history, from Mormon sources.

The real doctrines of a religion, however, are not written in books or creeds, but in the hearts of its believers. My life as a devout, believing Mormon is the one "primary source" of this book. The last few years that I was a Mormon, I kept a journal daily. I also took notes on 3 by 5 cards of every meeting, conference, and fireside I attended. Since the Mormons teach that whatever their leaders speak is doctrine, these cards and my journal reflect the day-to-day instructions by which I, as a faithful Mormon, lived.

Some might say that I have been too hard on the Mormons and their doctrine. It must be remembered, above all, that the Mormon leaders claim that they speak for God, and much of what they have spoken is false. Others, like some ex-Mormons, would say that there is nothing good about Mormonism. Besides being in error, such a statement compromises the credibility of anyone who would say this. Many Mormons, as outsiders know, are honorable people, sincerely trying to do what they believe is pleasing to God. It is not their devotion that I would challenge; it is the object of that devotion which needs to be changed.

The most persistent question that my Mormon friends have asked me is, "Why, Latayne? How could you leave the Church?" This book is my answer to them, and my challenge to all other Mormons.

First of all, I have not left Christ's church. I have found it—I have united myself with that group of people, the believers that Christ called His body. This group of believers isn't limited to those who have a sign with a certain name on it outside the building where they worship. They are bound together by love for each other and gratitude to a Savior who did for them what they could not do for themselves.

I have found in true Christianity turmoil and great peace. I have found spirituality and doubt. I have found life as it is—with no false promises of godhood as a reward for virtue—but just the elementals of living the Christian life and praising God each day that He cared enough to send His Son to die for even the sins I've forgotten.

I know now that I can't "earn" my home with God by attendance at meetings, or offerings, or prayers, or even good deeds—no matter how many or how much. I realize now that these things and the many more that characterize the life of a Christian are the *result* of gratitude for salvation, not the means of achieving it. Praise God for showing me the way, and may many more Mormons find it as I have.

Note on the Revised Edition

Since this book was first released in 1979, many stories have been circulated, especially by Mormon missionaries, about why I was excommunicated from the Mormon Church. I had been an active member of a Christian body in Albuquerque for six years when I myself initiated the proceedings. Since I did not recognize the authority of the LDS "court" over me, I did not attend it. I was excommunicated from the Mormon Church at my own request in Albuquerque on Thursday, December 20, 1979, on the grounds of apostasy.

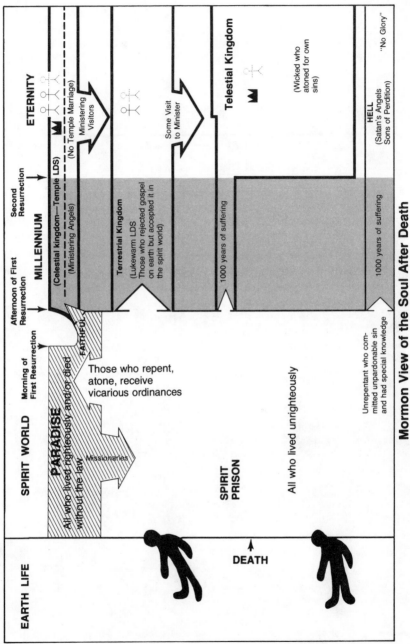

Mormon View of the Soul After Death

1
A Gentle Apostasy

Not that I have already obtained all this, or have already been made perfect, but I press on to take hold of that for which Christ Jesus took hold of me. Brothers, I do not consider myself yet to have taken hold of it. But one thing I do: Forgetting what is behind and straining toward what is ahead, I press on toward the goal to win the prize for which God has called me heavenward in Christ Jesus. All of us who are mature should take such a view of things. And if on some point you think differently, that too God will make clear to you. Only let us live up to what we have already attained.

—Philippians 3:12-16 NIV

Every Mormon, when he or she is about twelve years old, goes before a man of the Mormon community who is revered for his wisdom and experience. Such a man is known as the Stake Patriarch. He alone can give what is called a "patriarchal blessing."

I was about thirteen when I went before Garland F. Bushman, the patriarch of the stake, or area, in which I lived. Patriarch Bushman placed his hands on my head and said: "In the pre-existence, you were one of the choice souls of heaven noted by Father Abraham. Your ancestors were noble people, of the tribe of Ephraim. You yourself have a great destiny—to become a leader of women in the Church and in the state where you will reside. You will meet a fine young man, be married in a temple of our Lord, and raise up righteous children. Finally, you will arise in the morning of the first resurrection, surrounded by your family."

These wonderful predictions made me weep for joy. The patriarch warned me, however, that Satan wanted my soul very much—so much, in fact, that he would try hard to deceive me. All the blessings promised me would therefore be conditional upon my resisting Satan, and my obedience to the precepts of Mormonism.

Now it is thirteen years later. I have left Mormonism—and feel so strongly about it that I am writing a book telling why I have left.

It wasn't easy to leave. I owed, and still owe, the Mormon church and its members a great debt of gratitude. But I am regarded by them as a traitor and an apostate. I left Mormonism after tasting some of its sweetest fruits.

Through the tumultuous years of adolescence—those years of being too tall, too clumsy, and having pimples and glasses—the Mormon church was security. Teachers and counselors in the church were compassionate and truly interested in me. These people were bound together by great love for their families (how rare in this day!), the church, and each other.

The excellent youth programs (including track meets, road shows, supervised dances, cookouts, camps, sports activities, firesides, work and service projects, and much more) filled a gap in my life that might otherwise have been filled with early dating and associations in unsavory places. Through Mormonism I found a concrete way to express my fervent love for God and my desires to serve Him. I gave love freely, and had it returned one hundredfold.

Some of Mormonism's blessings were even more tangible. I received an education of the highest quality at Brigham Young University (BYU), and through writing contests I was awarded scholarships that made it easier for me to attend. The part-time jobs I held while in school (dorm resident assistant, staff writer for the university's weekly magazines, translation and public relations work for the Latin-American Studies department, and counter work at the basketball arena's concession stand) were provided by the BYU board of trustees, who were deeply interested in the welfare of its students.

Once, even the food I ate was provided by the Mormon Church. My father had undergone extensive surgery, and when the church officials heard of this, they brought hot meals to our home for several days and assessed our grocery supply to determine what we needed. They returned with sacks and sacks of staple grocery items, and even offered to make car, house, and utility payments if needed.

I loved Mormonism for these things, and returned my love by living and serving as a "good Mormon." Each time that I was interviewed by my bishop and asked about such things as my attendance at meetings, my payment of tithing, observance of the Word of Wisdom (health laws), sexual purity, and support of church doctrines and leaders, I was awarded a coveted "temple recommend" which allowed me as a faithful member to enter any Mormon temple to participate in sacred ordinances there.

During my young adulthood, I served as a teacher in Sunday school, Relief Society (ladies' organization), and Primary (children's organization). I was active as a speaker in Sacrament meetings and was often called on to prepare programs for MIA (youth organization) and for special occasions. For a while, I worked as my ward's (congregation's) media aids supervisor, and in various other church "jobs."

I was never lukewarm. What I believed, I lived. I say all this because I believe that someone who has not lived a doctrine has no grounds to criticize it—just as a grade-school science student cannot reasonably speak with authority on nuclear physics. I lived Mormonism; I loved it—and I left it.

My "apostasy" did not happen overnight. Once the process began, however, it moved quickly. When I returned to my home in Albuquerque, New Mexico, for summer vacation in 1973, my plans were set. I would work at the International Airport, earn the money that, along with a partial scholarship for poetry, would pay for my fourth and final year at BYU. I had begun the process of revising *El Gaucho,* a Spanish textbook written by Sid Shreeve, the head of BYU's Latin-American Studies department. I regarded the summer away from BYU as a necessary evil, and I was anxious to return to that Mormon microcosm.

I was annoyed when my mother, who played ragtime piano at a local pizza parlor, suggested that I date non-Mormons that summer. A missionary I was "waiting for" was due to return that fall, and I just wasn't interested. Besides, I was kept busy between my summer job and the book revision. One night, though, when I went to pick Mother up at work, she introduced me to a young man she had described in glowing terms (which had fallen on disinterested ears).

Dan Scott, the object of her praises, started off our introductory conversation by saying, "So you're a Mormon. I've read the *Book of Mormon.* It was, uh, interesting." Immediately I thought to myself, "Maybe he could be converted."

Then, more cautious, I stalled, searching for a reply. Everyone I'd ever known who'd read the whole *Book of Mormon* had been converted to the Mormon church. In fact, I reflected, I'd known plenty of "faithful" Mormons who had never read the whole thing unless and until required to do so in a religion class or while on a mission. Perhaps, I thought, this would be a good time to terminate this discussion, and I left quickly.

A few weeks later, a voice on the phone said, "Hi! Bet you don't know who this is!" His Tennessee accent had betrayed him. I said, "Yes—Dan Scott." He was crushed, his surprise foiled, but not crushed enough to forget to ask me out. I accepted against my better judgment.

Our first date was a disaster. He took me to midweek services at his church where he announced, "She's a Mormon." I was stared at as if I were from another planet. (Mormons get accustomed, to a degree, to such treatment from curious non-Mormons. Once when I was in junior high, a sincere classmate asked me if something her mother told her was true: that Mormons didn't have navels. We quickly went into the girls' room, and I dispelled that myth with a tug of my blouse!)

Nonetheless, I was attracted by Dan's openness and decided to date him again if he asked, and he did.

He was understanding and compassionate when I learned, early that summer, that a girl I had counseled in the dorms at BYU had drowned while tubing in the treacherous Provo River. I soon found Dan to be a true and warm friend with a sense of humor he could aim at himself as well as at others.

Our only disagreements came when we discussed religion. He was so transparently shocked when I answered his questions about baptism for the dead, polygamy, and Negroes and the Mormon priesthood that we made an agreement. He would study the *Book of Mormon* and other Mormon scripture with me if I would study the Bible with him. I felt this to be a personal triumph, because I'd never studied Mormonism with anyone (except my mother) who did not join the Mormon church.

Soon Dan and I had to admit to ourselves the love that was growing between us. One thing we both agreed on: we could not take the chance of becoming more deeply involved with our hearts so near and our souls so far apart. Our discussions usually put me on the defensive. I was knowledgeable about my religion, and what was more, I was stubborn. Add to that a strong dose of love for the doctrines and people of Mormonism, and you have an idea of the battle Dan had to fight. He didn't fight it alone, though; he had several powerful weapons.

One was his brother-in-law, Charles Williamson, a preacher of great intelligence and patience. One day Charles and I agreed to sit down and talk only about religion. We sat on opposite sides of a table, me with my Bible, *Book of Mormon, Doctrine and Covenants, Pearl of Great Price,* and *Principles of the Gospel;* he with his Bible. Dan soon left the room, a scene he described as a "verbal ping-pong game." Both Charles and I were exhausted after about two hours of table-slamming debate. I was on the verge of anger. I learned later that Charles told Dan in confidence that I knew more than any Mormon elder he'd ever spoken with, and frankly he didn't know if there was any hope for me.

My recurring headaches signaled tension that had begun to grow as my doubts had. Dan and Charles didn't think their talks had served any purpose. I was filled with a sick dread that I then thought was a godly sorrow for the lost souls of people like Dan and Charles. Actually, I was beginning to fear that *my* soul might be lost, and I dared not voice this fear—not even to myself.

Another of the mighty weapons used by Dan in the battle for my soul was the literature he somehow managed to find. These books dealt objectively and factually with Mormonism, from the view of non-Mormons. I was lucky that Dan chose the books he did for me to read. Most anti-Mormon literature I had previously read had had very little effect on me.

There are many books and magazine articles written to convince Mormons of their doctrinal errors. Some of these, however, make two major mistakes. One is underestimating the intelligence, integrity, or character of the Mormon people. Many times when I was a Mormon I had read some otherwise factual literature against Mormonism which by its bitter or berating tone "turned me off." The doctrinal point the writer was making never sank in. Such literature implies that Mormons believe as they do because they are stupid, or narrow-minded, or satanic. Since I considered myself and other Mormon friends to be intelligent, open-minded children of God seeking to do His will, I would toss such offensive literature into the nearest trash can. Then I would offer a prayer to God for the soul of anyone who would tell such lies in print where it might be accepted as fact by someone who'd never met a good Mormon.

The other great error committed by many writers on Mormonism is that of not checking their facts. Like the girl who asked me about my navel, such writers discredit themselves with inaccuracies. Some writers, carried away in their enthusiasm, embellish facts—it's easy to do—but when I would run upon such stretching or bending of the truth in anti-Mormon literature, I would dismiss as also erroneous anything else I read there that didn't agree with Mormon doctrines I had been taught.

This is vitally important to remember when teaching Mormons! Much of their doctrine has been changed radically since the days of Joseph Smith and Brigham Young, but Mormons are taught that *nothing* doctrinal ever changes in their church. When you confront them with, say, copies of the original 1830 edition of the *Book of Mormon,* or strange prophecies made by Joseph Smith which never came true, Mormons are dumbfounded. Such things are suppressed and unavailable to them through any church channels. If, therefore, a book errs when talking to them of things they *do* know about, how can they trust new information on things they have never heard of?

The most effective weapon of all in Dan's armory was three-pronged. First was his overwhelming faith and confidence in the Word of God, the Bible. Second was the prayer that he continually offered for my soul's enlightenment. Third, and most penetrating, was the love he had for me. Had we not loved each other, I don't believe I would have had the courage to leave the comfortable Mormon way of life. Had he ceased loving me before my conversion was completed, I fear I would have returned to the womb of Mormonism and lived ever an infant, frightened and dependent, but secure in my deliberate ignorance.

I finally came to an impasse in my spiritual progress. I was struggling against the bonds of Mormonism—tradition and heritage, doctrinal comfort, and love. Yet I felt that something was terribly wrong there—why did my teachings and background in Mormonism conflict so sharply with my new knowledge of the Bible? Why the inconsistencies in LDS (Latter-day Saint) historical accounts and early documents?

One final acid test remained at the end of the summer. Since I had a scholarship and a writing job waiting for me at BYU, I decided to return, promising Dan that we would marry—if I came back in December feeling about Mormonism as I did then in August. As I was packing, I felt as if the summer had been a dream. Or was it the real part, and the rest of my past life the illusion? I was unhappy about leaving Dan, but I knew I must make my decision alone. No matter how much I loved him, my eternal soul, and my relationship with God, was more important to me.

I was putting my books into boxes when, tired, I sat down with my *Doctrine and Covenants.* Always it had been my favorite book of scripture because of its practical commandments, like the Word of Wisdom, which had purified and uplifted the lives of millions of Mormons. Also commonly bound in the same volume with the *Doctrine and Covenants* is another book of scripture called the *Pearl of Great Price,* which includes two books the Mormons believe were written by Moses and Abraham. These scriptures are unique in that they have what purport to be illustrations by Abraham himself. These illustrations, reproduced by woodcuts, are in the ancient Egyptian style. I have always loved Egyptology, though I have no more than an avid layperson's knowledge of the subject.

I was looking idly through these familiar woodcuts when I was struck by an incongruity that upset me. Two of the women had been labeled in the woodcut by Joseph Smith as men! Egyptian women are easily identified in ancient documents by their distinctive strapped, ankle-length dresses.

Why I had never noticed this before, I do not know. I had studied and read about these woodcuts for years. I knew from reading standard authorities on Egyptology that Egyptian women in history had dressed as men and acted as Pharaoh (Queen Hatshepsut, for example) but no Egyptian man would have been caught dead in a woman's clothing, especially to be preserved for posterity on a papyrus roll!

It was with this discovery that my most concrete doubts about Mormonism began to multiply. No anti-Mormon writer had pointed this out; no hater of the LDS church could have falsified or altered these prints; they were in my own personal copy of scripture. I found myself crushed and exultant, all at the same time.

On the plane trip to Utah, I was shaken and lonely. I had left Dan behind; he was my bulwark of support and I was conscious that the events of the next few months would change my life. I brooded over this frightening thought (for who truly welcomes change?) and tried to keep my mind occupied by reading a paperback book on Mormonism that Dan had given me. I was so absorbed in reading that I hardly noticed a young woman sit down in the seat next to mine. She had a clean-scrubbed, open, friendly face. She smiled and began our conversation by asking about the book I was reading.

I could hardly formulate my thoughts; first, because of the fear that she might be a Mormon and might question my motives in reading such literature; and second, because I didn't quite know how to explain my situation.

"It's about Mormonism," I finally blurted out, pointing to the book.

She smiled. "Are you thinking about becoming a Mormon?" she asked.

"No. I mean—I am one. I mean, I was—I'm thinking about leaving it. . . ." On the verge of tears, I was helpless to finish.

She gave me a look of soul-searching compassion. "How hard it must be to make that decision," she said.

And so I told her of my background in the church, and my love for it. Then I explained what had happened when I met Dan, and what I'd learned through reading and prayer, and how confused and muddled and lost I felt. Before I knew it, we had touched down in Grand Junction, Colorado, which was her destination.

As she prepared to leave, she leaned over and touched my arm. "I'll pray for you," she said. "God knows what is in your heart, and He will guide you to make the right decision."

She arose and walked out of my life as quickly as she had entered it, and I was left with a greater peace in my soul than I'd known for many months. She had touched my life with the bare wire of love, and peace had passed from her soul to mine like a transfusion. Then she was gone.

When I arrived in Provo, I set about making myself as busy as possible. Soon old friends began to arrive for the new school year, and I fooled myself by thinking they wouldn't notice the difference in me. I registered for classes, reported for work, and caught up on all the news of who had married whom, who had gone on missions, and whose missionaries had returned.

But I have never been a good deceiver, and soon my feelings about the church began to surface. Close friends made no secret of the fact that they thought I'd gone crazy. Some attributed my change of heart about Mormonism to a broken relationship with a missionary. Many of my Mormon friends, to this day, assume that I wanted to leave Mormonism because of that missionary. An unhappy bargain that would be—to trade my soul's salvation for revenge!

I became even more upset each time I attended church services. My branch (congregation) hadn't really changed. There were new faces, but the same back-to-school jokes about snoring roommates and the excitement of worshiping together with maybe-your-future spouse. Nothing had changed as much as I had, and I was sick at heart. In a letter to Dan in late September, I said,

> I can't explain the feelings I had in church today. I was looking at Mormonism through new eyes. In Sunday School class I listened to a discussion on the Holy Ghost and silently refuted almost everything that was said—by looking in the Bible. Things I've accepted for years seem suddenly strange. I experienced in part the pity that you felt for Mormons. Dan, I don't know what I'm going to do when they call me to a church position—and they surely will. I simply cannot stand up in front of people and teach from the *Book of Mormon* the way I feel now.

The dreaded call came late one afternoon when I was asked to meet with my branch president. Newly appointed to this job, he was nervous and unsure of himself. Everyone in his BYU student branch was to be interviewed and assigned a church job—teaching, visitation, social activity planning—and he seemed anxious to get these assignments over.

He began by congratulating me on my past service in the church (he had my records before him) and asked me about the kind of job I'd be willing to do.

"I'd like to work on an activities committee," I said, "or work on clean-ups—I'm really good at that, and honestly, I don't mind. In fact, I'd love it."

He looked at me, confused. What did someone with teaching and leadership experience want with a clean-up job? Then a smile broke across his face. He had solved the puzzle—I was trying to be modest! He laughed, relieved, and then asked a question he thought would put us on common ground.

"Well, Latayne," he said, leaning back in his chair, "how do you feel about the Prophet?"

Just that week, Harold B. Lee, the "Prophet, Seer, and Revelator of the Church," had come to BYU. When I had seen 25,000 students rise to their feet and sing through tear-choked throats the song, "We Thank Thee, Oh God, for a Prophet," I had felt faint and ill. How could I now tell this branch president of my feelings?

I looked away and said, "I don't think he *is* a prophet."

The young president sat up so suddenly that the back of his chair snapped forward. He acted as if he had had a bad day and I was pulling a very, very poor joke on him. I tried to explain that I hadn't come to a decision about the church, that I wanted to avoid talking about it publicly, but still wanted to attend services and work in the church.

He only shook his head, his disbelief turning to anger. "How can you think such things?" he asked. "Don't you know that if you leave the church you'll never be able to reach the Celestial Kingdom? *You will never be happy again!"*

Never to be happy again! What a load to put upon a young mind already troubled with uncertainty and fear of displeasing God! I left that interview with a dread in my soul. I went back to my apartment. That night I called Dan, and the next day disenrolled from Brigham Young University, telling only a few of my decision. My roommates were incredulous, my landlady tearful and reproachful, and all but one school official unsympathetic. A similar conflict, this registrar told me, had faced him when he was young. He had taken the part of Mormonism with few regrets, but his experience made him understanding, and concerned with my best interests.

When I arrived back in Albuquerque, little of the pressure was relieved. I received many letters, most anonymous and many cruel, which persuaded and threatened, pleaded and rejected. All had one object in mind—my return to Mormonism. Many pleaded, saying that my leaving would affect those I had taught and helped to convert, or those weak in the faith. (I pray to God it may be so!) Some of the letters told of the punishments awaiting apostates, and one ended by saying, "Don't you realize that you'll *NEVER see the inside of a temple again?"*

Phone calls, too, didn't diminish for several months. Most were from friends who had "heard and just couldn't believe it." Close friends called one night and said several dozen other friends would be fasting and praying together the next day for me. On that day, I, too, fasted and prayed for my soul, for though I felt that I should leave Mormonism, I wasn't sure that Dan's teachings were any more reliable. Once you've found the tenets you most trusted and believed in to be false, you're not anxious to embrace a substitute.

Of only one thing was I certain: however I might begin to comprehend God, I knew that He loved me and knew my anguish, and would show me the way through His Son. This, and no more, could I be sure of.

Even Dan, much as I loved him, could not be the basis of my faith. I knew that if a group of people as dedicated and as sincere as most Mormons could be so wrong, then so could Dan, and his teachings. I have never felt more alone in my life.

I labored in agony with the great questions that left me sick at heart, and spiritually weakened. I pulled this burden along behind me, pushed it before me, and tried to take it upon my shoulders. When I found that I *could not* move it alone—it was too heavy—I gave up and did what I should have done long before. I put it in God's hands, and wondered why I had taken so long to make that wisest of decisions in my life.

I spent a lot of time reading everything I could get my hands on that dealt objectively with Mormonism. I was fascinated and repelled the more I realized my errors. A near-physical sickness would engulf me when I stopped to realize how I had flirted with hell while thinking I was courting heaven. Only a few doubts, those last barriers to real repentance remained, and I took my questions to Lon Elkins, Dan's minister. I had grown to admire this man's vast knowledge of the Scriptures and of archaeology.

How simply he explained those questions I had been hiding so deep in my heart for so many months! I hadn't dared to ask anyone who it was Christ spoke of when He said, "Other sheep I have, which are not of this fold: them also must I bring, and they shall hear my voice" (John 10:16). The Mormons identified those "other sheep" as the Nephites, or those inhabitants of the Americas who lived at the same time Christ did. They taught that Christ spent part of the time between His death and resurrection in America, teaching those Nephites. Could a Christian offer as reasonable an explanation?

Thank God Lon could and did. After he had explained this and many other questions, I realized how it is that any religious group teaching false doctrine can so easily misinterpret the Scriptures to someone who is unfamiliar with them. The greatest battles a cult can wage over the soul of the ignorant man, I believe, are already won when the proselyte is too lazy, or afraid, or unwilling to seek a more correct interpretation of a Scripture passage that teaches a "new" doctrine. We have nothing to fear *but ourselves* when we ignore the admonition to "search the Scriptures."

I had realized this too late to undo my years in Mormonism. I cannot say that I wish I had never been a Mormon. God richly blessed me during those years. Perhaps they were a preparation for my Christian life. I do not question or doubt the wisdom of God, even though I still sorrow for the wrong things I did and taught.

I knew then as now that I must recommit myself to God—I must become a new creature, as different from my Mormon self as a butterfly from a caterpillar. I had so many doubts—not knowing for certain what to trust, or what doctrine was true. I decided on a course of action that included two things: I would be baptized for the remission of my many sins, and I would depend wholly on the Bible as my spiritual guide.

Dan was a little apprehensive as we prepared for my baptism. He was anxious and happy to baptize me, as I had requested. But he was afraid because he'd never baptized anyone before, and he feared he would let me slip into the water or choke. I could only laugh—I knew I could take care of myself in that situation, because I once had been baptized thirty consecutive times (all within a matter of minutes) while doing ordinances for the dead in the Manti, Utah, Mormon temple!

This baptism was different, though. That still September night, I felt a great sense of the majesty of God, and His mercy so undeserved by me, a sinner.

But that baptism hasn't by any means made life easier. In fact, the first few months of being a Christian were very difficult. I made the mistake of comparing Christians around me to Mormons whose clean and moral lives had long been an example to me, and many times the Christians were found wanting in such an examination. It took me a long, long time to square with myself the fact that just because a man is a good man is not a divine endorsement of the doctrine he teaches.

But once I realized that God had forgiven and forgotten my sins, I was able to forgive myself and begin trusting Him for guidance. I am living a new and different life now. I am no more perfect now than when I was a Mormon—in fact, I realize now more than ever my faults and weaknesses. I feel a debt to Mormonism, and that is why I have written this book.

Mormons may regard a book showing the errors of Mormonism a strange way to repay a debt of gratitude. I only wish that when I was a Mormon someone had told me the things of which I write.

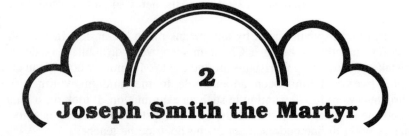

2
Joseph Smith the Martyr

Joseph Smith, the Prophet and Seer of the Lord, has done more, save Jesus only, for the salvation of men in this world, than any other man that ever lived in it.

—President John Taylor
as quoted in
Doctrine and Covenants 135:3

A great statue of St. Peter stands in the Vatican City. This statue, as the story goes, is so adored by Catholic visitors that it was placed on a high pedestal, almost out of reach. But still the pilgrims, in their love, would reach up and touch the only part of the statue they could—the foot of St. Peter. Thousands of pilgrims passed this statue and caressed the foot. Now, many years later, only a smooth, polished, shapeless mass of stone protrudes from the hem of St. Peter's robe.

Did the first pilgrim, who tenderly touched the stone foot of St. Peter, intend this to happen? Did the thousands of subsequent visitors know they were defacing the statue they so adored?

Of course not—but their love, fervently and tenderly applied, had as its end result the blending and muting of the sharp lines the sculptor's chisel had wrought. It is still recognizable as a foot, if only because of its position on the body, but it bears no resemblance to the fine-veined, sandled foot that once supported the statue.

The same thing has happened today to the stories of Joseph Smith, the founder of the Mormon religion. While Joseph Smith was alive, he was seen as he was, with his human imperfections (which we all have) and even his deliberate deceptions. But the eroding forces of time have faded many of these characteristics, and what is left has been lovingly wiped away by Mormon historians. What remains is a cleaned-up and unrealistic picture; a still-life portrait of a little boy who allowed himself to be scrubbed and perfumed and dressed up in a scratchy Sunday suit to be preserved for posterity with a click of the Mormon historian's shutter. This untrue picture is what is presented to, and accepted by, the Mormon people.

While I was a Mormon, I would have regarded the material in these chapters to be heresy. All Mormon leaders, especially the General Authorities, are considered to be above reproach, especially in matters of doctrine. The prophets are considered to be doctrinally infallible, and it seems that the longer a Mormon prophet has been dead, the greater the aura of perfection that surrounds him.

A Mormon song, entitled "Praise to the Man," lyrics by W. W. Phelps,[1] deals with Joseph Smith in a way that exemplifies the Mormon attitude toward him. That he was a martyr to his cause is history, and the testament of his blood to the things he taught charges that history with emotion. Mormons from earliest childhood are taught stories about Joseph Smith interspersed with and undifferentiated from stories of Bible characters like Daniel and David and Timothy, and characters from the *Book of Mormon* such as Alma and Nephi, and Mormon leaders such as Hyrum Smith and David O. McKay. To them, all were great men, all prophets, and all equal. Only two stand above the rest: Christ, and just below Him, Joseph Smith.

The Mormon Story of Their Prophet

Joseph Smith, Junior, was born in Vermont on December 23, 1805. About ten years later his family moved to New York State and settled. By the time they finally homesteaded in Manchester, New York, they were a sizable family: Joseph Smith Sr., his wife Lucy Mack Smith, and their children Alvin, Hyrum, Joseph Jr., Samuel Harrison, William, Don Carlos, Sophronia, Catherine, and Lucy.

It was after they had lived in Manchester about two years that Joseph had some experiences that were to change his life and the lives of millions of others. As recorded in the Mormon scripture, the *Pearl of Great Price*, in the chapter known as Joseph Smith 2, the following things took place.

A great religious revival in the area caused confusion in the mind of young Joseph, who, though he wanted to become a Methodist, felt that the many conflicting doctrines and teachings of different churches made it impossible for him, a practically unschooled youth in his "fifteenth year" to make an intelligent and mature decision concerning his soul. While his mind was in this turmoil, he read a Scripture verse found in James, chapter 1, verse 5: "If any of you lack wisdom, let him ask of God, that giveth to all men liberally, and upbraideth not; and it shall be given him."

Cheered by this, Joseph went into the woods near his house, knelt, and offered his first vocal prayer. No sooner had he begun than "some power" overcame him and bound his tongue—a power so great that it was only by a last desperate cry to God that the evil power was dissolved. A pillar of light, brighter than the sun, then descended upon him, and Joseph saw two glorious Personages, suspended in the air. One called him by name, and identified the other as "My Beloved Son."

Joseph then asked the question that had been troubling him: which church should he join? He was told that, because of the corruption of all existing creeds and their ministers, he was to join none of them. After the second Personage told Joseph many things that he was told not to write down, the Personages departed, leaving Joseph weak and exhausted.

He was greatly persecuted by friends, ministers, and laymen alike whenever he told this story. For the next three years he led a life that, he admitted, though not greatly sinful, was unworthy of someone who had had an experience such as his. He in his own words "frequently fell into many foolish errors, and displayed the weakness of youth, and the foibles of human nature."[2]

Then one evening as he was praying in bed for forgiveness of his sins, a great light shone around him and a person whose face was so bright as to be "like lightning" appeared. Suspended in the air, this person identified himself as Moroni, a messenger from God. God had a great mission in life for Joseph, Moroni said, and it would be one that would make him famous, both beloved and notorious. He told Joseph of a book written upon gold plates that contained the history and origins of early Americans. It contained, he said, "the fulness of the everlasting Gospel."[3] Also deposited with the plates were "seers," two stones in silver bows that were attached to a breastplate, provided to help in translating the golden book. These seers were known as the Urim and Thummim. The messenger quoted Scriptures from Malachi, Isaiah, Acts, Joel, and other Books of the Bible, most just as they appear in a King James Version. He then warned Joseph not to show the plates or seers to anyone unless commanded to do so, and Joseph saw in a vision the hiding place of those objects.

The light in the room seemed to seep back into the person of Moroni, and he ascended into heaven by means of a "conduit." Joseph was left amazed, and as he thought about what had happened to him, the room began to glow again and the messenger returned in the same manner as before. He repeated his prior message verbatim, adding a prophecy of great disaster that would soon occur on earth. Then the messenger ascended to heaven exactly as before. Joseph by this time was wide awake with wonder that increased when the whole scene was repeated a third time—exactly as before, except this time the messenger warned Joseph against succumbing to Satan, who would tempt him to sell the plates.

The three visits had taken all night. Joseph went that morning to work in the fields with his father, who noticed something was wrong. He advised his son to go home and rest. Joseph on his way stumbled from fatigue and lost consciousness. The messenger again appeared, repeated all he had told him the night before, and told Joseph to tell his father of what he had learned. Joseph's father, upon hearing of the visits, agreed that Joseph should do as the messenger said. So Joseph went to the hill he had seen in the vision, the resting place of the plates. There, under a large stone, he found the plates buried in a box of cement or stone. He raised the lid with a lever and looked in. But he was forbidden by the messenger to touch the plates. The messenger said Joseph was to meet him at the same site a year from that date for further instructions.

In fact, at the end of every year's time for several years, Joseph met with Moroni for further instructions regarding the Lord's plans to establish His kingdom. Meanwhile, Joseph worked as a laborer. In 1825 he was hired by a man named Josiah Stoal, who hoped Joseph could help him find the location of an old Spanish silver mine in Pennsylvania. Also during this time Joseph met Emma Hale, with whose father Joseph boarded. They were married when they eloped to New York in January of 1827. This marriage was bitterly opposed by the Hale family, who did not believe Joseph's stories of visions.

In September of that same year Joseph met as usual with Moroni, who turned the golden plates, the seer stones, and the breastplate over to Joseph. The angel warned him that many people would try to take them from him. This prediction proved to be true.

Beginning the Translations

Joseph was ridiculed and persecuted, and finally he and his wife returned to Pennsylvania, aided by a farmer named Martin Harris. Joseph began to copy the inscriptions from the plates and to translate them. At first, his wife acted as his scribe while he dictated. He gave a copy of some of the ancient inscriptions to Mr. Harris, who took them to New York to show to a renowned professor, Dr. Charles Anthon.

At first Professor Anthon said that the inscriptions were indeed authentic, and were of the Egyptian, Chaldaic, Assyrian, and Arabic tongues. He identified Joseph Smith's translation of them as an accurate one, and wrote out a certificate to that effect.

But he took the certificate back and tore it up when Martin Harris told him that the characters had come from golden plates given to Joseph Smith by an angel. Anthon offered to translate the plates himself, but upon hearing that portions of them were "sealed," he said, "I cannot read a sealed book."

Martin Harris returned with this news to Joseph Smith, and then began serving for a short while as scribe to him. Joseph lent him 116 handwritten pages of translation, which Martin lost. These pages were never re-translated for fear that enemies might alter the original translation and ridicule Joseph when a subsequent translation differed from the lost one.

In April of 1829 a young schoolteacher named Oliver Cowdery approached Joseph Smith after hearing of the plates. A short while later he wrote as Joseph dictated the translation of the *Book of Mormon*. On May 15 of that year they came upon a reference to baptism mentioned in the plates, and they decided to go into the woods to pray about the meaning of it.

A messenger of God appeared to them and identified himself as John the Baptist. He laid his hands on Smith and Cowdery and conferred upon them the Priesthood of Aaron, which had been taken from the earth with the death of the last apostle. This priesthood involved the ministering of angels, and repentance and baptism for the remission of sins. It did not, however, involve the laying on of hands for the gift of the Holy Ghost, which would be given later.

Joseph then baptized Oliver, and Oliver baptized Joseph. Joseph gave the Aaronic Priesthood to Oliver, then Oliver laid his hands on Joseph for the same purpose. Following this, they both began to prophesy about the church that would soon be established.

After this glorious experience, their efforts were redoubled in bringing forth the *Book Of Mormon*. Joseph applied for a copyright on the book in June of 1829.

The entire translation of the *Book of Mormon* was completed in 75 working days. Though Joseph admitted that it was a work complete in itself, it was the translation of less than one-half of the plates the angel had delivered to Joseph. The remaining plates remained untranslated, and were sealed and taken back by the angel.

Joseph, in addition to his translation work, had received many revelations. One was a revelation directed at his father concerning missionary work;[4] another referred to the ordination to the Aaronic Priesthood;[5] and several others were directed to Oliver Cowdery and his work with the Prophet.[6] Revelations like this were personal in nature, intended for specific persons, but others dealt with matters of general doctrine and instruction. Almost without exception this latter, general type of revelation had as its purpose the strengthening of the validity of the *Book of Mormon*.

During June and July of 1829, according to Mormon Daniel Ludlow, Joseph showed the plates to eleven persons,[7] and their testimony concerning the plates is recorded in the front part of every modern edition of the *Book of Mormon*. All of these witnesses were honorable men above reproach, and none ever denied their testimony of the plates and their divine origin.

The first three witnesses, Oliver Cowdery, David Whitmer, and Martin Harris, said that God Himself told them that the *Book of Mormon* was true, and that an angel had shown them the plates. The other eight witnesses (Christian Whitmer, Jacob Whitmer, Peter Whitmer Jr., John Whitmer, Hiram Page, Joseph Smith Sr., Hyrum Smith, and Samuel H. Smith) did not mention in their printed testimony anything of God or an angel testifying about the plates. They did, however, claim to have seen and touched the plates themselves.

The year 1830 was a momentous one for Joseph Smith. He received additional revelation on such matters as the suffering of Christ, baptism, duties of officers of the church, the frequency of general conferences, voting in the church, duties of baptized members, blessing of children, the mode of administering the sacrament, and excommunication.

Other revelations received that year dealt with the use of water instead of wine in the Lord's Supper, false prophets and false seer stones being used in the church, the end of the earth and the Millenium, the free agency of man, and the mission to the Lamanites (American Indians).

In March of 1830 the first edition of the *Book of Mormon* was published, financed by Martin Harris. It attracted the notice of many people, but detracting from its impact were the numerous grammatical and typographical errors contained in it. These errors were put there by the printer who hoped thereby to discredit the Prophet Joseph.

Sometime during late 1829 or early 1830 (the exact date is not known), Peter, James, and John appeared to Joseph Smith and Oliver Cowdery. The apostles gave them the keys of the kingdom and a dispensation of the gospel for the last time, and for the fulness of time, in which the Lord promised to gather together everything which was in heaven and on earth.[8]

This bestowal was known as the restoration of the Melchizedek Priesthood, which had been promised the May before by John the Baptist. This ordination to the Melchizedek Priesthood gave Joseph Smith the proper authority to organize the church, which he did on April 6, 1830, in Fayette, New York.

Joseph Smith laid hands on Oliver Cowdery and ordained him an elder in the church, and Oliver did similarly to Joseph. These two elders then laid hands on the six other baptized believers present, bestowing upon them the Holy Ghost, and confirming them members of the only true church.

By mid-May the young church, then known as The Church of Christ, had forty members. Later that year several men who would later become leaders in the new church joined—Orson Pratt, Sidney Rigdon, and Edward Partridge. These men through divine revelation were promised great things and commissioned to teach the gospel.

Undaunted by opposition, apostasy, debt, and even arrest and a court trial, Joseph continued to receive revelations foretelling the future migration of the church westward. Meanwhile, largely through the efforts of men like Sidney Rigdon, the church had also been established in Kirtland, Ohio. In January of 1831 Joseph and Emma traveled there.

In Ohio the Prophet had to combat a further threat of division in the church—many members began to practice their own brand of religion, egged on by "false spirits," and had to be rebuked by the Prophet. The young church, though growing, was continually beset by problems from those who claimed to receive revelation, and Joseph's role as sole revelator for the church had to be continually reaffirmed. False stories about Joseph's past, too, continually surfaced, and prevented many from accepting the *Book of Mormon*.

Still new members poured into Ohio, and preparations were made for the temporary establishment of a city. The 150 converts in Kirtland quickly accepted Joseph's revelation on the establishment of a Biblical type of communal living known as "The United Order of Enoch." They were joined by hundreds of persons investigating the stories of a city of God, where all things were held in common. Things went well for a while, the church growing and Joseph busy, working on an "Inspired Translation" of the New Testament. He hoped with this new version of the Bible to clarify doctrinal obscurities caused in inaccuracies in the King James Version.

Adversity

Financial problems, however, began to plague the United Order, and Joseph received a revelation commanding him and fifty others to go to Missouri, the new "promised land."[9] Others from New York joined them, and the site for a temple was chosen near Independence, Missouri. A new United Order was begun. Joseph then returned to Hiram, Ohio, encouraged by the financial comeback the Kirtland United Order was making, and continued his inspired translation of the Bible.

Persecution, especially from apostates, continued to hamper the Prophet's work. In 1832, he was beaten senseless, tarred and feathered one cold March evening, but the next morning preached a quiet, dignified sermon to a Sunday congregation that included some of his assailants.

Soon Joseph decided to settle in Kirtland, where he received his famous revelation on the Civil War many years before that war took place. A natural athlete, he encouraged dances and athletic contests. He impressed members and non-members alike with his cheerful, friendly manner.

Joseph and Emma had several children who died at or shortly after birth. Joseph's first son who lived past infancy was born on November 6, 1832. He was named after his father, and helped ease Emma's pain at having lost a previous son and a set of twins shortly after they were born.

That month, too, Joseph met a new convert who was to have a great influence on the church. His name was Brigham Young.

In the spring of 1833 work on a temple in Kirtland was begun. Joseph also exhibited his great talent as a city planner, and the city plat he designed was used years later in laying out the well-ordered streets of Salt Lake City.

In Independence, Missouri, though, the Mormons had by their religious fervor and political views (namely, not holding slaves) alienated their Gentile neighbors. A mob had in retaliation for imagined wrongs destroyed the church printing press, injured many church leaders, and demanded that the entire Mormon colony leave the state. Outnumbered, the Saints agreed to leave Jackson County by the next spring.

Mob violence continued, however, and Missouri civil officials were unsympathetic to the Mormon cause. The Lieutenant Governor of Missouri, Liliburn Boggs, gave in to public pressure and tricked the church leaders into surrendering their arms. He then allowed a mob to run wild, raiding Mormon homes, beating the men, and turning the entire Mormon colony out of their homes in the dead of winter. Citizens in nearby Clay County gave asylum to the homeless hundreds, many of whom had spent several days camped in the open beside the frozen Missouri River. The United Order collapsed, and was never again practiced among the church as a whole.

In February of 1834 Joseph Smith received a revelation that Independence, Jackson County, Missouri (known to the faithful as Zion), could be redeemed by force.[10] Under the leadership of Joseph Smith, a two-hundred-man military company called "Zion's Camp" was organized and marched from Kirtland in early May, 1834. News of their coming, which was regarded by Missouri as a military invasion, went before them, however, and alienated much of whatever feeble governmental support the Mormons once had in Jackson County. A cholera epidemic struck Mormons and non-Mormons alike, and Joseph returned to Kirtland promising that Zion would have to be redeemed at a later date, after the completion of the Kirtland temple.

In 1833 Joseph received a revelation that, perhaps more than any other, has set its distinguishing mark upon the Mormon people, the Word of Wisdom. In it, the Lord forbade the use of tobacco, alcoholic beverages (except for home-made wine at communion), hot drinks, and excessive eating of meat. Mormon leaders of course set the example in strictly following the commandment.

Also in March of 1833 Joseph founded "The School of the Prophets," which was at first a seminary for instruction in latter-day revelation. It later included courses in Hebrew. Joseph himself became learned in many languages.

More Scriptures

In 1835 the scene was set for a fourth scripture to join the ranks of the Bible, the *Book of Mormon,* and the *Doctrine and Covenants* (or *Book of Commandments,* as it was then called). Joseph Smith purchased from a traveling lecturer four ancient mummies and some old papyri. Two of these papyri, Joseph announced, were the handwritten autobiographical works of Joseph of Egypt and of Abraham. After setting up a grammar system he later discarded, Joseph translated the Book of Abraham and copied down some of the drawings that illustrated them. In this book many lost truths were revealed, including an expanded account of the creation, and the precedent for denying Negroes the Mormon priesthood.

Another triumph in Joseph's life occurred in 1836 when the Kirtland Temple was officially dedicated. Many of the apostles prophesied and saw visions, rejoicing in ritual washings and anointings. The dedication was culminated by the appearance of Moses, Elias, and Elijah—and later the Savior Himself—to Joseph and Oliver Cowdery. This was a time of great spiritual and material prosperity in Kirtland.

The first mission to England, headed by Heber C. Kimball, Orson Hyde, and Willard Richards, was a great success. But back in Ohio, great financial and schizmatic problems began to beset the church. In early 1838 Joseph and his family went to Far West, Missouri. He was joined there by six hundred faithful Ohio Saints who wanted to escape the corruption in Kirtland.

Far West was a fine example of Joseph Smith's abilities as a town planner, and it prospered under the diligent hands of its Mormon settlers. A great new temple was begun. Not far from Far West, in Daviess County, Joseph Smith discovered and identified Adam-Ondi-Ahman, where Adam and his family lived after leaving Eden.[11]

Trouble brewing in Missouri, though, soon boiled over. Internal problems, apostasy, and friction between the Mormons and their neighbors (especially over the Mormons' right to vote in public elections) led to spiritual and physical battles that weakened the church and its material holdings in Jackson County. This resulted in a virtual civil war—involving the Mormons and the other Missourians—that terminated in the infamous "extermination order" issued by the hated Governor Boggs. This order practically gave carte blanche to all Missourians to drive the Mormons from their state, using whatever means possible. The Missouri militia slaughtered Mormons until they surrendered, and even then the murders, rapes, and pillaging continued. Joseph Smith was taken to Richmond, Missouri, where he and other Mormon leaders were imprisoned for four months in the filthy Liberty Jail before trial. Meanwhile under the leadership of Brigham Young, the Mormon exodus, a disgraceful page in the history of Missouri, was effected.

At Joseph's trial in 1839, a change of venue to another county was granted by the court, and Joseph and his friends were soon released.

The Nauvoo Period

Along with the other Saints who had escaped from Missouri, Joseph and his followers founded on the banks of the Mississippi River a beautiful city, which Joseph named Nauvoo, the Hebrew word for "beautiful plantation." The city was laid out like Far West, but was even more beautiful and orderly than Far West had been. At its height, Nauvoo boasted a hotel, two large steam-powered sawmills, a steam-powered flour mill, a foundry, and a tool factory. It had a large community farm outside the city limits, which provided employment for many, especially the hundreds of English converts who had come to America as a result of the extensive work of the missionaries. The city also had included in its charter of incorporation provisions for a university and a four-thousand-man militia for self-defense. Joseph himself was given the title of lieutenant general by the governor of Illinois. Naturally, though, this caused alarm among non-members living around Nauvoo, who remembered the problems the Mormons had had in Missouri.

Another source of friction was the beautiful, though unfinished, temple built in Nauvoo. It was a lovely building, but the secret and mysterious temple rituals performed therein caused suspicion. This, coupled with the enormous power of the Mormon voting bloc in Illinois politics, caused new trouble.

The Mormons had to fight recurrent rumors of sexual immorality, debauchery, and adultery. In addition, when an attempt was made on the life of Governor Boggs, Joseph and his followers were accused of the attempted assassination. Joseph was forced into hiding for four months to avoid being taken to Missouri on false charges. He agreed to give himself up when the legality of the extradition writ he feared was tested in Springfield, Illinois, and found to be invalid.

In 1843 the Prophet revealed the revelation that was to be the most famous of all his revelations—that on polygamy. This revelation gave the Biblical precedents for plural wives, and threatened destruction for all who did not adhere to it. Because of the delicate nature of such a doctrine, it was neither widely publicized nor practiced. But news of this doctrine, along with the efforts of an influential apostate named John Cook Bennett, resulted in Joseph's capture by Missouri law officials in 1843. He was rescued by loyal followers, and after this "close call" his dream of the sovereignty of a federal territory of Nauvoo, where the Saints would not constantly be harrassed by false charges, grew. But he realized also that the deep-seated animosities between the Mormons and their neighbors would preclude such freedom. So Joseph sent men west to Oregon and California and to what is now the southwestern United States to investigate the possibility of establishing a Mormon nation there.

Meanwhile, he became active in local politics, and even ran for president of the United States in 1844. Though he never expected actually to be elected, the power of the votes of his thousands of followers was influential. His platform included planks on freeing slaves, annexing Texas, penal reform, and abolishing the two-party system in U.S. politics and replacing it with what he called a "theodemocracy."

Enemies of Mormonism were incensed at the insolence of a spiritual leader who would so involve himself in the controversial political issues of the day. Enemies within the church, too, plotted Joseph's downfall, using as a very effective tool the apostate-operated newspaper, the *Nauvoo Expositor*. To counter the paper's slanderous charges, the press and all existing copies of the publication were destroyed.

Last Days

Joseph then assembled the Nauvoo legion, telling them of the great opposition they must face. He vowed to lose his own life, if need be, in defense of the heavenly principles and legal rights of his people. Perhaps sensing the imminence of his death, Joseph gave all the "keys" of the kingdom of God to his apostles so that the doctrine would remain pure in the event of his demise. To spare his people the pain of mass arrest at the hands of the Illinois citizens maddened by the destruction of the *Expositor* press, Joseph and some close followers crossed the flood-swollen Mississippi River to Iowa, narrowly escaping a posse sent to Nauvoo to arrest him.

Fearing he would be thought a coward, and since he was guaranteed a fair trial by the governor, Joseph returned to Nauvoo to set his legal affairs in order. He then rode into Carthage under the protection of a county militia to give himself up. All of the Mormon men arraigned on charges of riot in the *Expositor* incident were released on bond except Joseph and his brother Hyrum, who were charged with treason (in regards to the Nauvoo Legion's alleged insubordinate attitude towards the state government). They were then jailed without a hearing.

Throughout three states people were crying for the blood of Joseph Smith. When he was denied the protecting influence of the governor's presence in Carthage as had been promised, Joseph, as a last resort, sent for the Nauvoo Legion to rescue him. They never arrived.

While the Mormon leaders sat in uneasy silence in the jail, a crowd gathered stealthily outside. Members of the state militia and others who hated the prophet had painted their faces. Suddenly they stormed the little two-story jail. Hyrum Smith was killed first, shot five times. John Taylor and Willard Richards, also in the jail, somehow escaped all but minor grazing wounds.

Joseph Smith was killed by several shots; the first to his back, the others hitting him after he fell from the jail window. His last words were, "Oh my God!"

At their official funeral, only sandbags were buried in the caskets of Joseph and Hyrum, for even in death they were not safe from their enemies. Their bodies were buried and re-buried secretly to avoid possible desecration of their graves.

Schisms within the church threatened its very existence, because after Joseph's death, many members claimed the right to lead it. Chief among them were Joseph Smith III, whose rights as Joseph's son were advocated by his hot-headed uncle William Smith, brother of the prophet; and Brigham Young, whose authority to lead the church was vested in his role as president of the twelve apostles.

Eventually Joseph III and his followers split completely with the followers of Brigham Young and formed what is known as the Reorganized church of Jesus Christ of Latter Day Saints (RLDS). Since Emma denied any knowledge of a revelation on polygamy, as well as her husband's alleged participation in it, she felt her son was the only rightful heir to the Mormon leadership and regarded Brigham Young as a usurper. At last this sect centered in Independence, Missouri, where they operate to this day.

Brigham Young, meanwhile, led the Mormon people through incredible hardships across the plains of the American Midwest into the barren Salt Lake Valley, which now "blossoms as the rose" and is a mecca for the four million Mormons who live all over the world.

This, then is the story of Joseph Smith and the early church as I learned it when I was a Mormon. Most Mormons don't know all the details of this story, as I will show in the next chapter. In fact, few of them could recount any major incident in his life other than his first vision, his translation of the plates, his receiving of the revelations on polygamy, the Word of Wisdom, the Civil War, and the events surrounding his death.

I have felt it was important to tell about the major events of his life as the Mormons see it so that this can be compared to a factual account of his life. Just how much fact differs from Mormon fiction is a disgrace to the Mormon educational system, and an insult to its members.

NOTES

[1]Praise to the man who communed with Jehovah!
Jesus anointed "that Prophet and Seer"
Blessed to open the last dispensation;
Kings shall extol him, and nations revere.

Praise to his mem'ry, he died as a martyr,
Honored and blest be his ever great name!
Long shall his blood which was shed by assassins
Plead unto heav'n while the earth lauds his fame.

Great is his glory and endless his Priesthood,
Ever and ever the keys he will hold;
Faithful and true, he will enter his kingdom
Crown'd in the midst of the Prophets of old.

Sacrifice brings forth the blessings of heaven;
Earth must atone for the blood of that man;
Wake up the world for the conflict of justice,
Millions shall know "brother Joseph" again.

Hail to the Prophets, ascended to heaven!
Traitors and tyrants now fight him in vain;
Mingling with Gods, he can plan for his brethren,
Death cannot conquer the hero again.

—Wm. W. Phelps

[2]*Pearl of Great Price*, Joseph Smith 2:28.
[3]*Pearl of Great Price*; Joseph Smith 2:34.
[4]*Doctrine and Covenants*, Section 4.
[5]*Doctrine and Covenants*, 5:17.
[6]*Doctrine and Covenants*, Sections 6, 8, 9.
[7]Daniel Ludlow, *A Companion To Your Study of the Book of Mormon* (Provo, Utah: BYU Press, 1969), p. 210.
[8]*Doctrine and Covenants*, 27:13.
[9]*Doctrine and Covenants*, Section 52.
[10]*Doctrine and Covenants*, Section 103.
[11]*Doctrine and Covenants*, 107:53; see also Section 117.

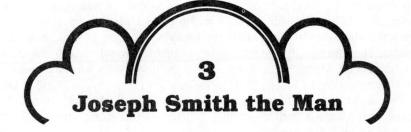

3
Joseph Smith the Man

I was left to all kinds of temptations; and, mingling with all kinds of society, I frequently fell into many foolish errors, and displayed the weakness of youth, and the foibles of human nature.

—*Pearl of Great Price*
Joseph Smith 2:28

Joseph Smith, as any Mormon convert will tell you, is the backbone of Mormonism. You cannot be baptized a Mormon while rejecting the first vision, in which Joseph Smith said he saw the Father and the Son. The high esteem in which Mormons regard Joseph Smith cannot be overestimated.

Brigham Young once stated that Joseph's consent was required for a person to be able to enter into the celestial kingdom of heaven, because Joseph was now reigning there, like God.[1] He also said that Joseph "was a god to us"[2] and that he himself was "an apostle of Joseph Smith,"[3] saying that "every spirit that does not confess that God sent Joseph Smith and revealed the everlasting gospel to and through him, is of Antichrist."[4]

It is clear, therefore, that a casual attitude about Joseph Smith is not possible for a true believer in Christ. Joseph Fielding Smith, a descendant of Hyrum Smith and who long served as historian and later as president of the Mormon Church, once stated that,

Mormonism . . . must stand or fall on the story of Joseph Smith. He was either a prophet of God, divinely called, properly appointed and commissioned, or he is one of the biggest frauds this world has ever seen. There is no middle ground. If Joseph Smith was a deceiver, who willfully attempted to mislead the people, then he should be exposed; his claims should be refuted, and his doctrines shown to be false.[5]

I take this challenge seriously. After prayer and study, I have found that the picture painted of Joseph Smith by his modern-day followers is not a good likeness of the man as he was.

Part of this is due to the overzealous efforts of Mormon historians to present only the good side of Joseph Smith to their people. Unflattering references to him and his lifestyle and role as a prophet have been removed, wherever they appeared, in today's printings of church documents. Therefore, with the information available through church channels to the average Mormon, he has no reason to doubt the Christ-like nature and divine calling of Joseph Smith. Nothing to the contrary is found in his books about the first Mormon prophet, only in anti-Mormon literature. Have anti-Mormon writers simply fabricated the stories they tell of Joseph Smith's dishonesty and carnality?

No, for the most part these stories have come directly from unexpurgated early editions of books written by faithful Mormons, or at least from firsthand witnesses to the events they describe. How do I know this? Certainly not from the texts I studied in seminary classes, for these have been ''cleaned up'' and are of little value to one who seeks the truth.

I know of these changes largely through the efforts of two other ex-Mormons who run a printing company in Salt Lake City that specializes in photographic-type copies of original Mormon documents. This couple, Jerald and Sandra Tanner, are hated by most Mormons who know of their work. Once, while I was a faithful Mormon, I came onto some of their literature that had been left at the door of my apartment, two blocks from the BYU campus. A bishop's wife told me not to read the literature; the Tanners were infamous for their sexual immorality (practicing polygamy) and the lies they propagated with forged documents that made the Mormon Church look bad (both utterly false and baseless charges). But I believed this bishop's wife and threw the pamphlet away.

My attitude was, I think, typical of the average Mormon. I didn't want to associate with such people or to further their cause by letting them plant seeds of doubt about Mormonism in my mind. Mormon history books are not unique in what they *tell* about Joseph Smith (they leave in just enough references to his humanity to make him believable), but in what they *don't* tell. And what they don't tell, dear reader, is what has shown me that Joseph Smith could not possibly have been the prophet of God that he and his followers claimed him to be.

The First Vision

Even some of the most innocuous things Joseph Smith said about his religious experiences have come back to haunt the conscientious Mormon. For instance, Joseph Smith claimed that he had been motivated in his youth to seek God's counsel on which church to join because of the religious turmoil around him. This, he said, was due to the many great religious revivals in his area in 1820.[6]

The revivals in the Palmyra area in 1820, unfortunately, existed only in the mind of Joseph Smith. Wesley P. Walters, in his pamphlet *New Light On Mormon Origins From The Palmyra (N.Y.) Revival,* shows this. Mr. Walters did extensive research in the records of the Methodist, Presbyterian, and Baptist churches of the 1820s in the Palmyra area, and discovered that the only revivals mentioned by the leaders of these churches occurred in 1817, 1824, and 1829. Since a revival is something to be proud of, it is not likely that these church leaders of the time would have had any reason to suppress information about a revival in 1820, had there been any.

Even Joseph's own accounts of the first vision must be viewed with some reservations. No mention of this first vision—which supposedly took place in 1820—was ever made in print until twenty years later when Orson Pratt, a longtime friend of Joseph Smith, published an account of the vision in a book called *Remarkable Visions.* Then in 1842 Joseph himself published an account of the two gods who appeared to him in a grove and told him not to join any existing church.

Why no hint of any kind concerning this first vision is found in any Mormon (or anti-Mormon) literature published prior to 1840, I cannot understand. Joseph Smith said in his "official" account of the first vision (found in the *Pearl of Great Price*) that when he told others immediately afterwards of what he had seen and heard in the grove, he was greatly persecuted.[7] But the evidence (or lack of it!) shows that no one even knew about it until twenty years later.

In 1831 or 1832, however, Joseph Smith did write an unpublished account of a vision, as documented in 1965 by Mormon Paul R. Cheesman, a graduate student at BYU. If this document records the first vision Mormons are familiar with, then somewhere Joseph had gotten his details mixed up. This record of a vision does not mention the revivals that reportedly caused Joseph to seek divine aid, nor the evil force he said overpowered him. It also fails to mention the appearance of God the Father—it speaks only of Christ.

Another version of the first vision has been identified by a professor of history at BYU as a previously unpublished record of how Joseph Smith told the story of his decision to join no existing church. This account, however, identifies Joseph as being fourteen at the time of the vision, and mentions "many angels" which are absent in the official 1842 version. The "pillar of light" was in this version a "pillar of fire." There were two distinct personages mentioned in this version, but they are in no way identified as God and Jesus Christ.

Even if this first vision—in whatever form it had—had really taken place, I think Joseph Smith as a prophet on whom doctrine depended should have been impressed enough with such an earth-shattering experience to remember the main details.

Could he have made the whole thing up? Mormon leaders deny it when they say he was only a teen-ager and incapable of fabricating such a thing. I'm sorry, but these Mormon leaders need only look into the many juvenile detention centers throughout our country to discover just *how* fertile a teen-ager's imagination can be in inventing excuses for erratic or anti-social behavior. Nor is a young active imagination exclusive to our century. In 1837 an illiterate youth named James Colin Brewster said that at age ten, he, like Joseph Smith, had been in direct communication with the angel Moroni. Brewster began "translating" non-existent records that he said were the lost books of Esdras, and had published numerous extracts from his work, as well as supposed translations of ancient inscriptions, all before he was twenty-one years of age. Many former Mormons, seeing similarities between Joseph Smith and this young man (who was also a visionary and money-digger), joined the church which Brewster founded in 1848.

I believe, however, that Joseph Smith did not put his story of his first vision together until he was pressed for evidence to substantiate his "many gods" theory, about 1838. He could then say, "Why, I knew that God and Jesus were separate, distinct personages with flesh and bone bodies way back in 1820, when they appeared to me." This, surely, lent credibility to his teachings on the plurality of gods and at the same time gave him a divine stamp of approval early in his life.

Translating and Treasure-Seeking

And surely he needed heavenly approval, for his younger years had many things to be ashamed of. But his followers were credulous enough to believe almost anything, it seems. An adoring public who, according to Mormon historian B. H. Roberts, believed indiscriminately in witches, warlocks, fortunetelling, and angelic visitations (all at the same time)[8] could hardly be expected to disbelieve Joseph's story of his vision.

But even their "willing suspension of disbelief" could have been easily snapped had they realized the nature and extent of the "weaknesses of youth and the foibles of human nature" in which Joseph Smith participated in the early 1820s. In 1820, the same year in which he was supposed to have received the first vision, Joseph Smith found what he called a "seer stone" in a well. According to Martin Harris, one of the witnesses to the *Book of Mormon,* this stone was used to see things like the location of the hidden gold plates and other lost or hidden objects.[9]

Joseph would place this seer stone in a hat, then close the hat tight around his face. The location of whatever he was looking for would then appear to him. He soon acquired quite a reputation for what his nineteenth-century contemporaries called a "money-digger." Mormons will vehemently deny the validity of such a statement, but the evidence from sworn witnesses is overwhelming in proving that he was heavily involved in the then-common practice of treasure hunting. Though he never was very good at it—by his own admission he never received more than about fourteen dollars a month for his efforts[10]—he was persistent, and even as long as ten years after he left the town of Palmyra the townspeople remembered his attempts at divining out buried treasure and hidden money with his peepstone.

But the most damaging evidence to prove Joseph Smith's activities with his peepstone are found in the account of a March 20, 1826, trial that was published in *Fraser's Magazine* in 1873. Joseph Smith was accused of having used his peepstone for three years to try (usually unsuccessfully) to find such things as hidden treasure, lost property, money, gold, a salt spring, and a buried trunk. He was found guilty of the charges against him and of being "disorderly and an imposter."

The record of this trial and conviction was not published until 1873, which has caused Mormon critics to cast doubt on its reliability. They have denied the authenticity of this "Bainbridge record," as it is called, saying there was no proof that the judge mentioned in it (Justice Albert Neeley) was really a judge in 1826. Nor, they contend, was there any official court record to corroborate the *Fraser's* account. Mormon scholar Hugh Nibley went so far as to say in his book *The Myth Makers* that if this court record were authentic, it would be the most damning evidence in existence against Joseph Smith.

Joseph's damnation, then, came in 1971 when researcher Wesley P. Walters found in the storage vaults of Chenango County, New York, the official appointment papers of Judge Neeley, dated November 16, 1825. Walters also located there the Judge's own records of the court costs in the 1826 trial of "Joseph Smith the Glass-Looker"—all of which corroborated perfectly with the details mentioned in the "Bainbridge record." This trial occurred about the time Joseph was supposed to have received the golden plates.

Mormon writers often mention Joseph Smith "helping to find a silver mine," or his powers of discernment in finding things "invisible to the naked eye." But they never give an inkling of the extent of his deceptions, with his stones and "powers," which he inflicted on innocent and gullible country folk. Nor do Mormon historians today deny the existence of his seer stone, for the recent President of the Mormon Church, Joseph Fielding Smith, stated in his book *Doctrines of Salvation* that "the seer stone is now in the possession of the Church."[11]

No wonder then, that the biographies of Joseph Smith currently published by the Mormon Church don't mention his activities as a treasure-hunter, charlatan, and self-avowed divine. Even Joseph Smith himself must have realized that he wasn't going to become rich or famous that way. He had to come up with something more unique than his small-change business in finding lost objects.

It is not that Joseph Smith was evil, or diabolical—I believe that he was simply possessed of a great drive for power and fame, coupled with a vivid imagination. This imagination had shown its fertility even when he was young. Joseph's mother, Lucy Mack Smith, wrote that when he was eighteen years old he used to amuse his family by describing:

> The ancient inhabitants of this continent, their dress, mode of travelling, and the animals upon which they rode; their cities, their buildings, with every particular; their mode of warfare; and also their religious worship. This he would do with ease, seemingly, as if he had spent his whole life among them.[12]

Possible Origins of the Book of Mormon *Theme*

These stories were eagerly accepted by his family, because it was the current and popular belief among even scholars of that day that the American Indians were descended from the "lost" Ten Tribes of Israel. *The Wayne Sentinel,* the local newspaper to which the Smith family subscribed, carried articles which supported this idea. A book called *View of the Hebrews; or the Ten Tribes of Israel in America* by Ethan Smith (no relation to Joseph) was published in 1823, and it mentioned the author's theories that Indians were wicked Israelites who had killed off their more civilized relatives in America and were left in their barbarous state until the coming of the white man.

The noted Mormon historian, B. H. Roberts, began late in life to ask such pointed questions as, "Did the author of the *Book of Mormon* follow too closely the course of Ethan Smith," noting that the *View of the Hebrews* was published seven to five years before the *Book of Mormon.*[13]

Other pre-Mormon books could also have furnished structural or background information used in the writing of the *Book of Mormon.* Among them were James Adair's *History of the American Indian* (London, 1775), Charles Crawford's *Essay Upon The Propagation of The Gospel, in which there are facts to prove that many of the Indians in America are descended from the Ten Tribes* (Philadelphia, 1799), Elias Boudinot's *A Star In The West; or, a Humble Attempt to Discover the Long Lost Ten Tribes of Israel* (Trenton, N.J., 1816), and Josiah Priest's *The Wonders of Nature and Providence Displayed* (Albany, 1825).

Priest's book, like the others, advanced the Hebrew-Indian theory and in addition told some new stories about the plague of darkness in

Egypt (Exod. 10:21-23)—details of which are mentioned almost verbatim in the *Book of Mormon* but are conspicuously absent in any Bible
manuscript. In fact, virtually every non-Biblical idea presented in the
Book of Mormon has its roots in one of these books, which represent only
a small portion of their kind!

Some researchers have seen the stamp of another set of personalities
on the *Book of Mormon*. In a book called *Who Really Wrote the Book of
Mormon?*, three young men, Wayne L. Cowdrey, Howard A. Davis, and
Donald R. Scales, formulated an interesting theory. Wayne Cowdrey is
an ex-Mormon and a descendant of Oliver Cowdery (some of Oliver's
descendants, including Wayne, use a variant spelling of the family
name).

Their theory, briefly stated, is this: An ex-minister, Solomon
Spaulding, wrote two historical novels in the early years of the nineteenth
century. One was entitled *Manuscript Story,* and the second one he
named *Manuscript Found.* Both purported to be written by pre-
Columbian inhabitants of America who hid the records away for future
generations.

A copy of *Manuscript Story* is still extant, and bears only slight
resemblance to the *Book of Mormon*. The second manuscript, the researchers claim, was read by many of Spaulding's acquaintances and contained references to persons named Nephi and Lehi, and told of the
Jewish origins of the American Indian, great battles between the Nephites
and the Lamanites, the latter of which finally triumphed. The three researchers of *Who Really Wrote the Book of Mormon?* claim that Rigdon
and Smith used Spaulding's *Manuscript Found* as a basis for the *Book of
Mormon*.

Translating the Inscriptions

As for producing the plates and getting people to believe in them—
Jospeh Smith kept them hidden from even his family, especially his wife
and mother, who never laid eyes on them. Once when Emma, his wife,
touched the cloth-covered bundle that Joseph said contained the plates,
she felt a metallic rustling, but she never saw the plates. Joseph, she said,
didn't even unwrap them to translate them; he just peered into the Urim
and Thummim, or his seer stone.[14]

When Martin Harris took over Emma's job as scribe, he did indeed,
as Mormons claim, take a copy of some of the characters from the plates
to Dr. Charles Anthon in New York City. But there truth and Mormon
fiction part paths. Harris claimed that Professor Anthon said that the
characters Harris brought were authentic ancient Egyptian, and were
translated correctly. The other untranslated characters, said Harris, were
declared by Anthon to be "Egyptian, Chaldaic, Assyrian, and Arabic."

However, in two separate letters he wrote later, Professor Anthon substantiated Harris' claim that he had brought the characters to Anthon, but the Professor vehemently denied that he had *ever* given the impression that the squiggles on Harris' paper were ancient Egyptian—or ancient anything, for that matter.[15] Anthon regarded the whole thing, says one truthful Mormon source, as "a trick!"[16]

But what if, as Mormons claim, Professor Anthon had indeed endorsed the translation and hieroglyphics, and then just denied it for some capricious reason of his own? Then Anthon himself would have been a fraud. In 1828, when the Anthon interview took place, the translations of Egyptian hieroglyphics were not yet published by Champollion, that great linguistics pioneer who unlocked the padlock of the ancient Egyptian language with the Rosetta Stone's key. If Anthon *had* said that the Egyptian hieroglyphics were truly translated, then he would have been whistling in the wind, for no man in America at that time (including Joseph Smith) was capable of translating ancient Egyptian—much less the "reformed Egyptian" of the *Book of Mormon*.

If the only existing copy of the inscriptions from which Joseph Smith supposedly translated can be held in such doubt, how much more the conflicting stories of the mechanics of *how* Joseph Smith performed the translations. Emma Smith, as well as David Whitmer and Martin Harris, said that Joseph translated by putting the previously-mentioned "seer stone" into his hat. He would peer into the hat, and a line of script from the plates would appear in his field of vision. Underneath it, he said, the English translation of that line would appear. Joseph would read the English to his scribe, the scribe would write it down and then repeat it to Joseph. If it was correctly written, that line of script would disappear and a new one would appear.

But other Mormons claim that the *Book of Mormon* was translated by means of the Urim and Thummim, which was a combination of a breastplate and attached spectacles that was given to Joseph by the angel, along with the plates, specifically for translation purposes. Mormons explain the conflict by saying that the seer stone was sometimes called the Urim and Thummim. Or sometimes they say that Emma said that the first 116 pages of manuscript (later lost by Martin Harris) were translated by using the Urim and Thummim, and the rest with the seer stone.

If this sounds confusing, consider the plight of the poor Mormons who are asked to believe it without ever understanding it. I remember sitting in a class at BYU where the methods of translating the *Book of Mormon* were being discussed. I didn't understand, and resolved the difficulty by returning to my prior opinions on the translation technique: I didn't know and didn't care. It was enough for me to trust that the *Book of Mormon* was true and correct. This I know to be the position of most

Mormons—they shut their eyes to what is confusing or conflicting. I'll wager that not one Mormon in a thousand can explain how the *Book of Mormon* was translated. This, indeed, is blind faith; and many will pay the price of their souls for their comfortable ignorance.

The Witnesses

Many seek solace in the thought that there were enough reliable witnesses to substantiate the *Book of Mormon*'s validity and justify their own faith in it. But just how reliable were these witnesses? Mormons often claim that none of them ever denied their testimony of the *Book of Mormon*. However, the Mormon *Journal of Discourses,* says that "some of the witnesses who handled the plates and conversed with the angels of God, were afterwards left to doubt and to disbelieve that they had ever seen an angel."[17] This must refer to Oliver Cowdery, David Whitmer, and/or Martin Harris, who alone in their written testimonies (printed in the front of each copy of the *Book of Mormon*) claimed to have both handled the plates and seen an angel. The *Journal of Discourses'* use of the plural ("some of the witnesses") indicates at least two of them doubted, though one in this passage was identified as a member of the Quorum of the Twelve Apostles who fell away.[18]

Most of the witnesses to the *Book of Mormon* did indeed fall into apostasy, and far from having the "spotless reputations" claimed for them by present-day Mormons, they were a disreputable band if we take the word of their Mormon contemporaries. Consider this:

"Such characters as McLellin, John Whitmer, David Whitmer, Oliver Cowdery, and Martin Harris are too mean to mention, and we had liked to have forgotten them."[19]

"Hiram Page (1800-1852) appears to have been somewhat fanatical. He found a stone through which he claimed to receive revelations often contrary to those received by Joseph Smith. For this he was reprimanded."[20]

Oliver Cowdery left Mormonism, became a Methodist, and "admitted error, implored forgiveness and said he was sorry and ashamed of his connection with Mormonism."[21]

David Whitmer and Oliver Cowdery were accused by Mormon associates of stealing, lying, cheating, counterfeiting money, and "scandalously disgracing" their testimonies of the *Book of Mormon.*[22]

Martin Harris was referred to twice in the *Doctrine and Covenants,* which purports to be a series of revelations from God, as "a wicked man."[23] The Mormon magazine, *The Improvement Era* of March, 1969, admitted that Martin Harris "changed his religious position eight times" including his conversion to Quakerism from Mormonism and back again during his stay in Kirtland, Ohio.

Now, does this sound like testimonies of stable, well-respected men of spotless reputations?

Perhaps we could at most give them credit for being gullible. Jerald and Sandra Tanner have explored the possibility that Joseph Smith, with the aid of Oliver Cowdery (who had been a blacksmith when young), had made some sort of metal plates which they covered up and presented to the witnesses to touch as "proof" of Joseph Smith's golden plates theory.

Not even the testimony of Joseph Smith himself is infallible. On June 15, 1828, he joined the Methodist Church. Even the esteemed Mormon writer Hyrum L. Andrus admits that Joseph became a Methodist. But he ignores the implications of this by claiming that Joseph's Methodist affiliation took place before the First Vision.

The Tanners, however, have concluded that Joseph's membership in the Methodist church "occurred eight years after he was supposed to have received his First Vision and at the very time he was translating the *Book of Mormon!*"[24]

If the testimonies of such men concerning the *Book of Mormon* were proven unreliable by their unreliable characters, then how much more can we doubt what they said about other things!

When Oliver Cowdery became Joseph's scribe, the work of translating the *Book of Mormon* progressed very rapidly. Whereas the first 116 pages had taken Joseph Smith two months to "translate" with Harris as a scribe, the rest of the 275,000 words were finished in about three months when Cowdery began helping Joseph. Part of this is no doubt due to Joseph's improvement with practice in dictation, (and the fact that when his well of inspiration ran dry he simply quoted long passages from the Bible, practically verbatim). But some of this was undoubtedly due to the influence of former schoolteacher Cowdery, who, as Fawn Brodie noted, had "a certain talent for writing." Miss Brodie continued, quoting from Oliver Cowdery himself:

> "Those days were never to be forgotten. To sit under the sound of a voice dictated by the inspiration of heaven awakened the utmost gratitude of this bosom." But he admitted on another occasion that he sometimes "had seasons of skepticism, in which I did seriously wonder whether the prophet and I were men in our sober senses when we would be translating from plates through the 'Urim and Thummim' and the plates not be in sight at all."[25]

Joseph's power over Oliver early in their relationship was apparently almost hypnotic. If Hitler could convince the German people that the Jews were a deadly threat to their personal safety and national identity, if McCarthy could frighten the ordinary American into seeing a Communist behind the actions of every liberal, then Joseph Smith could surely convince young Cowdery that he had seen an angel and the gold plates, and had received the Aaronic Priesthood from John the Baptist. At any rate, all we have is Oliver's word for it—and he, even by Joseph Smith's own admission, was "too mean to mention." So must his testimony be.

Building the Mormon Kingdom

Then, as today, the first hurdle to be crossed by a prospective Mormon was belief in the *Book of Mormon*. This must have been very difficult for those early converts. The book's first edition was filled with grammatical, punctuation, and spelling errors that necessitated almost four thousand changes to bring it to its present, slightly more readable condition. This was explained to me, as noted earlier, to be the result of having been printed by someone who hated the Mormons and wanted to make them look bad.

Even Mormon historians, though, say most of the errors couldn't be blamed on the printer or typesetter, because they weren't typographical errors.[26] But Joseph Smith boldly stated that the *Book of Mormon* was "the most correct of any book on earth."[27]

Apparently the poor quality of the book's language didn't seriously dampen its effect on the often semi-literate converts it won. Some of its first converts, who were to remain faithful for life, were Joseph's father, Joseph Smith Sr., and his brother, Hyrum. Emma, Joseph's wife, also joined the church, though she was not so tractable and believing as the others.

As a Mormon I regarded Emma with a mixture of respect and pity. I respected her because she was the Prophet's beloved wife, and was witness to a glorious age in the Restoration of the Gospel. The pity I felt for her, though, has greatly increased since I left Mormonism. She apparently was never really convinced in her heart of hearts concerning Joseph's spiritual authority, and this must have caused her great emotional turmoil. In Section 25 of the *Doctrine and Covenants,* Joseph exercised this authority in the name of God to try to shake her into being the obedient dutiful wife he needed, but he never ceased to love her for her free and independent spirit. She, indeed, is to me the true martyr of the Mormon religion—a woman torn between love for a marvelous and imaginative man and the haunting doubt that his inspiration was simply his own mind or something worse. Perhaps it was this love, and pride, that prevented her from exposing Joseph early in his career; for twenty-five years later, after his death, his legend would be one so great that even his wife could not discredit it.

For now, Joseph was busily handing out revelations directed at anyone whom he thought needed encouragement or rebuke with the authoritative clout of "thus saith the Lord" to back it up. One of the most amazing (and least-noticed) revelations he gave out is that found in *Doc-*

trine and Covenants Section 15. The heading to the revelation states: "The message is intimately and impressively personal in that the Lord tells of what was known only to John Whitmer and Himself." What is that personal matter the Lord had in mind? Starting in verse 3, we read,

> And I will tell you that which no man knoweth save me and thee alone—for many times you have desired of me to know that which would be of the most worth unto you . . . And now, behold, I say unto you, that the thing that will be of the most worth unto you will be to declare repentance unto this people.

And what is so amazing about this revelation? The fact that it is repeated *word for word* in the next section, a revelation given to Peter Whitmer. Only the names have been changed. That is how "intimately and impressively personal" the revelation to John Whitmer was!

Perhaps this was a time-saving device. Joseph was busy organizing God's kingdom on earth. On April 6, 1830, the church was organized under the name of The Church of Christ (later changed because other churches also claimed that name). Mormon history records that Joseph laid hands on Oliver, confirming him an elder in the Lord's church, and Oliver did the same to Joseph. This all makes sense to Mormons because they believe that you cannot give an office to someone without having it yourself—and the "authority" to back it. Supposedly this authority was given to Oliver and Joseph in late 1829 or early 1830. This, though, is admittedly sheer supposition on the part of Mormon theologians.

LeMar Petersen, in his book *Problems in Mormon Text,* has noted that the 1833 equivalent of what is now *Doctrine and Covenants* Section 27 (dated August, 1830) did not mention heavenly visitors and two separate ordinations of priesthood. These references were added later. "The student would expect to find all the particulars of the Restoration in this first treasured set of 65 revelations, the dates of which encompassed the bestowals of the two Priesthoods, but they are conspicuously absent. . . ."[28] notes Mr. Petersen.

I see the invention of the stories about holy ordinations as evidence that Joseph Smith often resorted to "divine revelations" to reaffirm his leadership and beat back doubters within the church. Because there were always some people who remembered the past "revelations" and ill-advised conjurings of his youth, he was always on his guard, to protect both his reputation as a prophet and holy man, and also to safeguard his creation and passport to fame, the *Book of Mormon.*

Problems in Kirtland

Things were no better in Sidney Rigdon's newly-established Mormon colony in Kirtland, Ohio. Here there were few people who had known Joseph in his treasure-hunting days, so the threat of exposure from that faction was minimized. Even more dangerous, however, were new converts who took the prophet's teachings about prophesying and spiritual gifts so seriously that instead of saying that Joseph Smith had no rights to revelation, they asked the logical question, "If Joseph can do these things, then why not us?" Here, probably, the doctrine of the necessity of authority in order to receive revelation got its start. Joseph had continually to remind his followers that he alone, as God's chosen leader, had the right to revelation concerning the whole church. Others had only the right to revelation for themselves and those under them in the church hierarchy. Thus, today, any young Mormon who would come before his bishop or stake president and announce any change in church policy because he'd received a revelation to that effect would be first counseled, then reprimanded, and finally excommunicated if he persisted in his story of such a vision. He is not entitled to any such revelation—therefore either he is lying, or the source of that revelation was not God, but Satan. Case closed.

The same was true 150 years ago, and any revelation received by church members was only considered valid if it was approved by Joseph Smith, because any revelation that contradicted Joseph's just couldn't be true. It pains me to think how the Spirit of God was stifled in the hearts of those who thought they had found truth in Mormonism, and were taught to reject all feelings of doubt and disbelief because those feelings must be from the devil.

There were other problems in Kirtland, too. The idea of communal living, having all things in common, was not a new one to the American scene of Joseph Smith's time. It was Sidney Rigdon who, after seeing the success of colonies like Robert Owen's New Harmony, persuaded Joseph to start one like it. Dubbed "The United Order of Enoch," it was patterned loosely like other communistic ventures, and, like them, it was a good idea at heart. A church member would deed all his personal property and belongings to the church permanently, and would in turn be given "stewardship" over enough to make a living for his family, as well as enough to purchase necessary clothing and modest personal belongings. Any profit made from a man's stewardship went back to the church as a whole under the direction of Bishop Edward Partridge, who distributed surplus as he saw fit.

I saw a play presented at BYU that depicted life in a colony practicing the United Order. I was impressed, as would be any idealist, with the idea of a church-centered life where all things are shared. I never understood why such a good idea could fail when its leadership was divine. But the Mormon system failed for the same reasons that all the other communistic ventures of its time failed—reasons even the most faithful Mormon will acknowledge to be true ones. Communism works on a group of people only if they have no alternative. Mormons in the early 1830s were in the middle of industrial and cultural changes sparked by and sustained by the free enterprise-capitalist ideal. In other words, the spirit was willing, but the flesh was weak.

While at Kirtland, Joseph made a prophecy that is unfamiliar to most Mormons. Just before the first general church conference, he predicted that "not three days should pass away before some should see the Savior face to face."[29]

At this conference a man seemed to have been suddenly stricken deaf and dumb, so Joseph exorcised the devil from him. Then Joseph tried unsuccessfully to heal a crippled man's hand, and another's lame leg, and finally to raise a lifeless child from the dead. This spiritual debacle, along with news that the Mormons were soon to be legally ejected from Ohio, spurred Joseph to leave quickly with thirty other men and go to Jackson County, Missouri. Cheered by the glorious visions of a perfect place where they could worship unmolested, the Mormon people began to blame the unspiritual atmosphere in Ohio for Joseph's failures, and they were soon forgotten by most.

Joseph Smith electrified his followers when he announced a revelation that identified Missouri as the promised land. When he and a number of others traveled to the area near Independence, Missouri, they chose a site for a new temple to be built there. This was to be a special place, this "New Jerusalem," as Joseph called it—he even prophesied that its inhabitants would be "the only people that shall not be at war with one another."[30]

The hopeful tone of his prophecy, however, was soon marred by the tragedy and bloodshed that would eventually mark the end of Mormon life there. But for the time being, Joseph had planned his choice of the Zion of America well.

Continuing Revelations

Joseph Smith returned to Ohio after Mormon settlers from New York were established in the area that is now Kansas City. These settlers began to live the United Order, though in extreme proverty. Back in Ohio, Joseph started what is known as the "Inspired Revision" of the Bible. The idea that the King James Version (though better than all other non-Mormon versions) is in some places erroneous and incomplete is essential to Mormon doctrine. Why else would there be a need for additional revelation such as the *Book of Mormon?* Thus it was only logical that Joseph Smith should put the Bible back into its original divinely correct form. This included inserting in his version of Genesis a prophecy concerning his own coming as a great prophet. While in Ohio, also, he developed the doctrine of the three degrees of heaven—the celestial, the terrestrial, and the telestial—where all people on earth would eventually dwell after death. All, that is, except for a very few "sons of perdition" who would end up in hell.

In 1832 Joseph issued one of his most famous prophecies—that which predicted the outbreak of the Civil War. Though his revelations were often personal in tone and aimed at particular individuals and their problems, rarely did he seek inspiration for problems as sweeping as the Civil War. Mormons today regard this prophecy as sure proof to us Gentiles of Joseph Smith's divine powers of prophecy, that he could foretell events which did not happen until much later. Most Mormons don't realize that in 1832, when Joseph issued this "revelation," secular periodicals in his area were predicting the same thing—imminent civil war because of South Carolina's threats to secede. But the newspapers and magazines were as wrong as Joseph Smith: the Civil War didn't occur until many years later. Mormons assume, too, that Joseph Smith prophesied the 1832 rebellion of South Carolina when in fact *it had already occurred* at the time Joseph announced his predictions.

Part of the revelation reads,

> Behold, the Southern States shall be divided against the Northern States, and the Southern States will call on other nations, even the nation of Great Britain, as it is called, and they shall call upon other nations, in order to defend themselves against other nations; and then war shall be poured out upon all nations.[31]

This certainly gives the impression that the American Civil War would involve the whole world; which of course it did not. But that is what the contemporaries of Joseph Smith expected. Orson Pratt prophesied in all seriousness in 1861 that some in his listening audience would see New York City and other great cities completely ruined and "desolate of inhabitants," saying of the Civil War, "This great war is only a small degree of chastisement, just the beginning."[32]

Unless some of his listeners are still alive at the age of 118-plus, both Pratt and Joseph Smith were dead wrong about the results of the Civil War.

This is easy to see in hindsight, but the Mormons of 1832 were full of rejoicing over a prophet who could produce such important predictions. Caught up in all this excitement was burly youthful Brigham Young, who eagerly joined the inhabitants of Kirtland in beginning one of Joseph's greatest projects—the building of the first latter-day temple.

The next year some of this enthusiasm was channeled into helping out the Missouri Mormons, who, in one of the blackest pages of anti-Mormon history, were savagely treated and turned out of their homes in the dead of winter. I agree with the non-Mormon Missourians of that time that the Mormon Church was (and is) built on false revelation, but the

39

treatment the Mormons received cannot ever be justified. Of course the Ohio Mormons were enraged at the insensitivity of Missouri law officials, but Joseph Smith made one of the greatest mistakes of his life when he announced that the Lord had said that Zion (Jackson County, Missouri) could be regained by force.[33]

When he and his pitiful two-hundred-man force returned from Missouri, ravaged by cholera and discouraged, the best he could do was promise that Zion's redemption lay still in the future. This Mormons sincerely believe today, confident that Jackson County, Missiouri, will be the site of the New Jerusalem where all the lost tribes of Israel will gather at some future date.

In 1833 the famous health-law revelation, called the Word of Wisdom, was announced by Joseph Smith. Undoubtedly this revelation was a natural outgrowth of the nineteenth-century temperance movement. Since, though, this was supposedly a divine commandment, one could expect complete obedience to it from men like Joseph Smith. Such, unfortunately, was not the case.

Mormons are taught that abstinence from tea, coffee, alcohol, and tobacco are essential for entrance into the celestial kingdom. If this is true, Joseph Smith must be a candidate for the terrestrial or telestial kingdoms because he repeatedly violated the Word of Wisdom. An examination of early church sources in the original editions compared to the corresponding modern-day versions shows that the references to the drinking habits of early Mormon leaders have been purged from the original records. In other words, a great cover-up has been effected.

This is hard to prove to Mormons unless they see with their own eyes the original documents, or microfilms of them, which of course aren't usually available. In Jerald and Sandra Tanner's book, *Mormonism— Shadow or Reality?,* they say,

> The Mormon leaders have made three important changes concerning the Word of Wisdom in Joseph Smith's *History of the Church* . . . In one instance, Joseph Smith asked 'Brother Markam' to get 'a pipe and some tobacco' for the Apostle Willard Richards. These words have been replaced with the word 'medicine' in recent editions of the *History of the Church*. At another time Joseph Smith related that he gave some of the 'brethren' a 'couple of dollars with directions to replenish' their supply of 'whiskey.' In modern editions of the *History of the Church*, 23 words have been deleted from this reference to cover up the fact that Joseph Smith encouraged the 'brethren' to disobey the Word of Wisdom. In the third instance, Joseph Smith frankly admitted that he had 'drank a glass of beer at Moessers.' These words have been omitted in recent editions of *History of the Church*.[34]

Now, this is not to say that Joseph Smith was a drunkard. I don't think anyone believes that. But the fact that he compromised on one of his own rules compromises him. Add to this evidence that for a short while he kept a well-stocked bar in his own home in Nauvoo (ostensibly for entertaining visitors from out of town) that he removed only when his wife threatened to move out of the house—does this look like a defender of truth and temperance?

Any Mormon who might "lose his testimony" of Joseph Smith after hearing of these things can find comfort in knowing that he is not the first to be so bitterly disappointed. A whole family once apostatized when Joseph Smith's wife offered them tea and coffee while entertaining them at the Smith's home.[35]

Joseph the Translator, Temple Builder, Financeer

Probably Joseph's intemperate use of alcohol and tobacco (he smoked cigars while in Nauvoo) are not as embarrassing to modern Mormons as his boasts of knowing many languages. On one occasion he quoted from seventeen different languages (not always accurately). At another time he claimed, "I know more than all the world put together" and went on to discuss the meaning of various Hebrew, Latin, German, and Greek versions of the Bible.[36]

Joseph Smith's self-avowed abilities as a great linguist have been shown to be doubtful by scholars studying the Mormon scripture called the *Pearl of Great Price*. Joseph Smith supposedly "translated" this book from some ancient Egyptian papyri. Until a few years ago, his translations could not be challenged because the papyri were thought to have been destroyed in the great 1871 Chicago fire.

But a few years ago the original papyri were rediscovered in a research room of the Metropolitan Museum of Art in New York City. They had been stored away and forgotten for years.

The science of Egyptology has been greatly refined since 1835, and modern archaeological linguists (even the braver Mormon ones) agree that the writing on the scrolls has *nothing* whatsoever to do with Abraham, Moses, Joseph, or anything else even remotely Judaic or Christian. The fact that this book contains the basis for the Mormons' anti-Negro policies is another source of friction. But the Mormons of 1835 rejoiced, happy that another new scripture had been given to them.

In 1836 the first Mormon temple was officially dedicated. In an all-male gathering inside the temple, the ordinances of footwashing and anointing with oil were instituted. Joseph encouraged the many men present to prophesy, promising that the first one who would do so would be endued with the spirit of prophecy. Anxious to outdo each other, the men began to predict marvelous events of the future. This, it must be noted, occurred after a twenty-four-hour fast had been broken by drinking wine and eating bread. This could explain the "visions" some of the men saw, and their boldness in prophesying and cursing their enemies.

Part of the prosperity in Kirtland was due to Joseph's ingenuous issuing of bank bills which paid everyone's debts off, until it was realized that they weren't backed by gold, silver, or anything of value. When local merchants refused to trade with the Mormon currency, the Mormons were incredulous. Many apostatized, including Warren Parrish, an apostle and bank officer, because they had been taught that this divinely-inspired banking institution was incapable of financial failure. Joseph Smith resigned from the bank, claiming that the debacle of the "Kirtland Anti-Banking Society," as the bank was called, was due not to its own faults, but to the "age of darkness, speculation, and wickedness"[37] in which it was operating.

The blame was largely put on the apostates such as Warren Parrish, who was accused of stealing $25,000—to which Fawn Brodie has pointed out, "If he took the sum it must have been in worthless bank notes, since that amount of specie in the vaults would have saved the bank, at least during Joseph's term as cashier."[38]

Joseph's resignation from the bank didn't keep his angered creditors from besieging him with warrants for his arrest. Even Parley P. Pratt, an apostle, threatened to sue him. But as other banks around the country began to fail during this time of general financial instability, the Mormons regained faith in their leader. He sent many on missions to England where they could forget their financial woes in the fervor of proselyting. Joseph himself went on a short missionary journey to Canada, but was aghast when he returned to find the church split.

The three witnesses to the *Book of Mormon*—David Whitmer, Martin Harris, and Oliver Cowdery—along with many others had fallen in behind the leadership of a Shaker-like dancing prophetess, a young girl who used a seer stone to foretell the future. All three witnesses were severely rebuked, but Martin Harris was finally excommunicated when he refused to repent to Joseph's satisfaction.

Missouri

Dissension continued, and finally Joseph Smith himself left Kirtland in the dead of night to escape two things: a warrant for his arrest for banking fraud, and the scores of men who took over the temple, Joseph's pride and joy, and cursed his influence in Kirtland.

By the time Joseph reached Far West, Missouri, he had turned the financial and spiritual ruin in Kirtland into a sign of God's providence in sending the cream of Mormonism to the promised land. If Joseph Smith thought he could leave all his problems behind in Ohio he must have been sorely disappointed. Here in Missouri his woes were not only financial but political. Since most of his converts were Northerners opposed to slavery, Missouri was a tinderbox and they the insuppressible sparks.

Soon the Mormons' basically neutral position was undermined by the organization of the church-sanctioned group called the Danites. Though Joseph Smith alternately denied and affirmed the existence of such a group, numerous testimonies as to the operations and purposes of this murderous clandestine organization exist. Though the names of this group changed, it had several distinguishing characteristics: the use of secret signs and passwords among members (both of which are strictly forbidden by the *Book of Mormon*), oaths to preserve the secret nature of the group, instructions to members to lie to protect and defend each other and to ''waste away the Gentiles by robbing and plundering them of their property,''[39] and the commitment to carrying out the aims of the Danite band *without regard to personal feelings of conscience.*

If this sounds like something the present-day Mormons should be ashamed of, it is! Most modern Mormons have never heard of the Danites, because most Mormon writers deny they existed. But some, such as William E. Berrett, have the courage to admit that the Danite organization did exist, and that ''the organization had been for the purpose of plundering and murdering enemies of the Saints.''[40]

The most embarrassing fact about the Danite persecution was not their treatment (though deplorable) of non-Mormons, but their sacking of the homes of dissident *church members.*

Perhaps in an attempt to divert attention from the underground activities of the Danites, Joseph Smith tried unsuccessfully to reinstate the United Order among church members. But they were suspicious after the recent financial problems in Kirtland, and the plan was modified into work-produce cooperatives. This, and the fervor exhibited by the cornerstone-laying ceremonies for the (never-completed) Far West temple frightened the Missouri natives, for Sidney Rigdon whipped a listening crowd into a frenzy with a speech that advocated ''a war of extermination'' between the Mormons and the Gentiles.

Just over a month later a fracas between a small group of Mormons and some Missourians over voting privileges on Election Day was amplified by word of mouth until half the county believed that there had been a full-scale battle. A warrant was issued for Joseph's arrest, and though he was bound over on bond to avoid a showdown, it was the average Mormon who suffered. Non-Mormon businessmen, especially millers, refused to trade with them, and when flour ran out in Far West, there was no more to be had. Mobs of Missourians plundered Mormon property throughout the state, and the Danite band grew to include all healthy Mormon men. Now it was called ''The Army of Israel.''

The Mormon Mohammed

Joseph Smith likened himself to a Mohammed for that army, saying,

> If the people will let us alone, we will preach the gospel in peace.
> But if they come upon us to molest us, we will establish our religion
> by the sword. We will trample down our enemies and make it one
> gore of blood from the Rocky Mountains to the Atlantic Ocean. I will
> be to this generation a second Mohammed, whose motto in treating
> for peace was, 'the Alcoran or the Sword.' So shall it eventually be
> with us—'Joseph Smith or the Sword!'[41]

For all the sanguinity of this speech, it still reflects the basic feelings
of Joseph and his followers at this time. They wanted peace badly—but
not at the expense of their homes, their personal safety, and their human
dignity. And these things were exactly what the Missourians most wanted
to take from them.

This, and prophecies made by the Mormon leaders regarding the
invincibility of the Army of Israel, spurred the Mormons to the offensive.
When they began to return like for like, many Mormons, including two
apostles, left Far West.

The Missourians stepped up their plundering activities. News of
actual and imaginary Mormon raids so alarmed the governor, Liliburn
Boggs, that he issued his "extermination order." One of the results of
this order was the massacre of many Mormons at an outlying settlement
called Haun's Mill. Secretly Joseph Smith sent word to the military
leaders of Missouri that the Mormons wanted peace—at any cost. The
price General Lucas demanded was high: a complete exodus from
Missouri by all Mormons, after surrender of their arms and confiscation
and sale of their property to pay "damages," punitive and actual. The
only ones excepted were the church leaders who were to stay in Missouri
to stand trial for treason.

Far West was the scene of rapes, pillaging, starvation, and humiliation for the Mormons, who were forced to stay there under Missouri
militia rule. Joseph Smith and others were imprisoned in the jail at
Richmond. When they were arraigned, one of the star witnesses for the
prosecution was an apostate who spilled the beans about his own involvement in the Danite activities.

Joseph and five others were indicted without bail and spent the next
four months in Liberty Jail. While here, Joseph began formulating the
doctrine he then called "the patriarchal order of marriage," or polygamy.
Meanwhile the belongings of his people were auctioned off. Brigham
Young, who had somehow escaped indictment, was the leader to whom
the homeless Mormons turned for guidance. They left Missouri, crossing
the Mississippi River into Illinois, where they were treated kindly by most

people but exploited by the land speculators. Joseph was returned meanwhile to Daviess County, where, since no impartial jurymen could be found, he argued and won a change of venue into another, less prejudiced, county.

On the way, however, he bribed his guard and escaped with his fellow prisoners to the Mississippi River that marked his freedom. In Illinois, Joseph founded a city which he called Nauvoo. He said this name meant "beautiful plantation" in Hebrew, but the word never existed except in his mind. From his mind, too, sprang this lovely, well-ordered city; and it took shape through the hard work of his followers. What Mormon history does not record, in recounting the virtues of Nauvoo, though, is the brewery authorized by Joseph Smith, nor the bar he had in his own house, nor the short-lived Nauvoo whorehouse, nor the Masonic temple where Joseph himself "became a first-degree Mason on the night of installation, and the next night rose to the sublime degree."[42] You won't hear these things from a Mormon—most don't know of it and would deny it anyway, because Joseph Smith taught against all these things.

It is impossible to overestimate the power and influence of Joseph Smith in Nauvoo. What he wanted, he got—either by exercising his civic powers (he was mayor) or by revealing a "revelation," as in the case of the "Lord" awarding Joseph's family and posterity five rooms and free board in the town hotel.[43]

It is impossible, too, to overestimate the size of this man's ego. A visitor to Nauvoo in 1843 characterized him as "the greatest egotist I ever met." Supposedly to test his people's faith, Joseph once preached a sermon and then rode through the streets of the city smoking a big cigar.[44]

Joseph boasted to visitors of his intelligence and good looks. He persuaded many church leaders, among them Brigham Young, to leave their families practically destitute and go on missions to England. Success there was phenomenal, and many converts came to Nauvoo. Meanwhile Joseph reigned supreme and unrivaled in his beautiful city.

If "reigned" seems too presumptuous a word, it is substantiated by evidence that Joseph Smith actually had himself ordained a king. In the words of Mormon writer Klaus J. Hansen,

> The scriptures indicated that Christ would rule as king over the kingdom of God. Smith took this idea quite literally and thought it only logical, that he, as predecessor of the Savior, should enjoy certain prerogatives of royalty. Consequently, shortly before his death, the prophet apparently had himself ordained as "king on earth."[45]

Because this was kept very secret, even from most Mormons of that time, the non-Mormons who lived around Nauvoo were not alarmed by

Joseph's aspirations to royalty denied him by blood. Illinoisians did, however, resent the pious attitude reflected by town regulations forbidding swearing and vagrancy inside the Nauvoo town limits. The new Mormon temple there became a symbol of the "clannishness" and secretiveness they claimed was characteristic of the Mormons. In this temple, unspeakable (or at least unmentionable) rites were performed, strange garments worn, and terrible oaths of vengeance sworn.

Non-Mormons also chafed when the "Nauvoo Legion" of four thousand men was hastily chartered by an Illinois legislature anxious to corner the numerous Mormon votes before the coming election. What this charter gave the Mormons, as they saw it, was independence from Illinois law and great military power in its own right. Joseph Smith embraced the role of military leader with as much gusto as he wore his role of spiritual leader, and preferred the title of Lieutenant General (given to him by Illinois Governor Carlin) above even the title of president of the church. He was proud of his snappy uniform and his troops, which represented to him a defense against his constant fear of extradition to Missouri. He even had a personal bodyguard of twelve devoted and physically powerful men, most former Danites.

All of these things brought to the minds of the people of Illinois the troubles their neighbors in Missouri had experienced with the Mormons, and they waited uneasily as the Mormons grew in numbers, prosperity, and visible military strength. This feeling of uneasiness grew greater when it became common knowledge that Orin Porter Rockwell, Joseph's blindly faithful and immensely strong bodyguard companion, had been in Missouri at about the same time the hated Missouri official Boggs had been shot three times in the head. When Rockwell returned from what he admitted was a trip to Missouri, his pockets full of much more money than he'd had when he left Illinois, people began to remember a prophecy made by Joseph the year before. This prophecy stated that Boggs would die violently. Most assumed that Rockwell had merely expedited the prophecy, and he and Joseph Smith were served a writ of extradition from the governor of Missouri. Stalling for time, both Joseph and Rockwell escaped into hiding after they were released on a writ of habeas corpus.

Joseph feared the improbable conviction on charges of accessory to the attempted murder of Boggs (who miraculously recovered) not so much as he feared the atmosphere of rekindled hatred toward Mormons that he was sure he would find in Missouri after the Boggs shooting. Missouri wanted blood—and Joseph wanted to make sure they got none of his.

He was in hiding in and around Nauvoo for almost four months. During this time more and more stories and gossip surfaced about polygamy. For a long time Joseph had been angrily denying the recurrent rumors that Emma was not the only woman with whom he shared matrimonial vows and privileges.

Joseph Smith once said publicly that he had to "pray for grace" whenever he saw a pretty woman. But he had a reputation to protect, and he resolved the conflict between his rakish tendencies and the teachings of the Bible and the *Book of Mormon* on monogamy in the same way that had always worked before. He got a "revelation" permitting him and other faithful Mormon men to have as many wives as they pleased.

Many Mormons believe that though Joseph Smith believed in polygamy, he never practiced it. This attitude is the result of two things: first, their own ignorance of their history; and second, the Mormon Church's practice of just "not talking" about issues that would tend to confuse the average member—or cause him to think deeply.

After all, the Church has had to reconcile Joseph's statements about the vital necessity of polygamy with the Church's modern abhorrence of the practice.

Joseph Smith had formulated the concept of a man's privilege of having more than one wife here on earth, as well as in heaven, but it was a theory that had to be advanced slowly. He first tried it out on men he most trusted. Joseph of course led the way. By the time he died, he had at least twenty-seven wives (as documented by Mormon Church Historian Andrew Jenson) and perhaps as many as forty-eight (the number documented by Fawn Brodie)—not counting Emma.

Surely Emma Smith was one of the most patient women alive. When I was a Mormon I used to wonder what I would do if polygamy was reinstated as a commandment and I was asked to give my permission to my husband to take another wife. I was taught that a first wife's permission was necessary, but history shows that Emma never knew about many of her husband's other wives. The humiliation of giving permission for another wife (surely a symbol to her of Joseph's view of her own inadequacy) was enough to encourage Joseph to keep many of his newer wives under cover.

No pun was intended there—but it is a fact that some of Joseph's plural wives claimed privately to have conceived by him. One plural wife, Eliza R. Snow, who wrote the lyrics to some of Mormonism's most famous hymns, miscarried Joseph's child when she fell down a flight of stairs after having been beaten violently with a broom by Emma. Emma, it seems, had come upon Eliza and Joseph embracing in the hallway of the Smith home, and for once could not contain her rage.

This vignette alone should be enough to dispel the popular Mormon myth that plural wives lived together amicably as sisters. Perhaps some did, but those who were human had jealousies and rivalries. Perhaps the striving to please a husband in every way is responsible for the overwhelming majority of Mormon women who even today excel in cooking, sewing, canning, and living on a budget.

Be that as it may, polygamy wasn't very popular at all in its early years. Church leaders fought it, but soon succumbed to "reason" when they saw a new wife could be justified—even commanded—by God's laws. One thing Gentiles found particularly repugnant was the fact that Joseph Smith had married at least twelve women whose husbands were still living. This special marriage contract was for "time" only—for earth life only. He would allow their first husbands, with whom most of them continued to share dwelling places, the privilege of reclaiming their wives in eternity. Meanwhile, it was share and share alike.

Joseph's many wives ranged in age from 15 to 59. He married five pairs of sisters, and one mother and daughter.[46] After his death, many of his wives were sealed to Brigham Young or others. Many of the marriages were performed before the release of the official "revelation" on polygamy, dated August 12, 1843. This revelation contained a threat that Emma (poor Emma) would be "destroyed" if she didn't submit to the results of polygamy. In addition, Joseph excommunicated anyone who taught or practiced polygamy without his express permission and approval.

In 1843 there occurred another incident most Mormons would rather forget. Joseph had been released in January of that year when, after the four months of hiding, he had given himself up to Illinois officials. The Missouri writ of extradition (as to involvement in the Boggs shooting) he had so feared was declared in court to be invalid. Rockwell, too, was cleared after some months, though in later years he boasted of having shot Boggs. It was with an air of renewed confidence, then, that Joseph Smith faced the world in the spring of 1843. He was so confident of himself and his powers that when six inscribed metal plates were brought to him by men who had dug them out of the ground, he wrote in his journal—

> Monday, May 1. I insert fac-similes of the six brass plates found near Kinderhook . . . I have translated a portion of them, and find they contain the history of the person with which they were found. He was a descendant of Ham, through the loins of Pharaoh, king of Egypt, and that he received his kingdom from the Ruler of heaven and earth.[47]

Unfortunately for Joseph's future reputation as a translator, one of the men who claimed to have "found" the plates also confessed to having helped "engrave" them with acid, using as a model for the hieroglyphics the characters on the lid of a Chinese tea box. He and some friends then "aged" the plates with rust, concocted the story of a dream revealing their whereabouts, and pretended to discover them in the presence of a Mormon elder.

The Mormon community was overjoyed in the prospects of a sequel to the *Book of Mormon* that would verify Apostle Pratt's prophecy that more revelation would come from the ground as did the golden plates. When Joseph let it be published that he was working on a translation, the conspirators, too, were overjoyed at the prospects of a new "scripture" from their forged plates. But Joseph died before the translation apparently was finished, and the forgers spent a long 40 years waiting for the Mormon Church to publish the part that Joseph translated. Some Mormons have interpreted this waiting as a sign that the plates were genuine; the only hoax being the story that they claim the forgers made up.

Since one of the plates is still in existence, though, modern scientists have inspected it and agreed that its composition and construction are compatible with the theory that they were forged in a blacksmith's shop of the Midwest in the 1840s, and that the inscriptions could indeed have been made with acid, and finally that the inscription is in the Lo language of China—all of which fits the men's story of forging, aging, and inscribing the plates with symbols copied from a Chinese box.

So what do the "Kinderhook Plates" (which I never heard of while a Mormon) prove about Joseph Smith? No one said it better than Charles Shook, who put it succinctly: "Only a bogus prophet translates bogus plates."

More Legal Problems

John Cook Bennett, who in his apostasy had developed a hatred for Joseph Smith that bordered on rabidness, pressured Missouri Governor Reynolds in June of 1843 to try once more to extradite Joseph to Missouri where he could be tried on the old treason charge. Joseph was ambushed and kidnapped by a Missouri posse, and taken to Dixon, Illinois. On the way to Quincy from there they were joined by a one-hundred-forty-man armed escort from the Nauvoo Legion, who feared a second kidnapping. Instead of going to Quincy, they rode on in to Nauvoo, where Joseph won his freedom by claiming that he was not the Joseph Smith Jr. named in the Missouri writ, but Joseph Smith Sr. This was at best a half-truth, as both his son and his father were named Joseph Smith, therefore he was *both* Sr. and Jr. He also denied having committed treason, or ever having been a fugitive from justice (both of which denials depend for their truthfulness on how he defined "treason" and "justice") and claimed that his Nauvoo court had the right to issue a writ of habeas corpus (a legally untenable provision of the city's special charter).

He was aided in his legal battle for his life by Cyrus Walker, the influential head of the Illinois Whig Party, to whom he pledged his vote and that of his people in the upcoming election. Joseph won his case, but infuriated the Whigs by indirectly endorsing Walker's Democratic opponent a few days before the election. Hyrum Smith, Joseph's brother (who had been promised a seat in the state legislature if the Mormons voted Democrat), conveniently received a "revelation" telling the Mormons to vote Democratic. He publicized his revelation widely. Thus torn between conflicting loyalties, Joseph proved the old adage about the thickness of blood over water. And after the election, the defeated Whigs thirsted for Joseph's traitorous blood.

Joseph saw as a solution to this dilemma the endowment of Nauvoo with legal rights that ignored the laws of the state and county in which it lay. Thus he could make and enforce laws without interference from civic officials. He wanted Nauvoo to be declared an independent federal territory whose mayor (himself) could call out troops (the Nauvoo Legion) whenever he saw fit (such as when he thought a writ of extradition was about to be served on him). The most flagrant of his proposed laws called for life imprisonment in the Nauvoo jail for anyone who entered the town bearing a writ for the old treason charge. The criminal's only recourse for mercy? A pardon from Joseph himself.

For Joseph, being commander-in-chief of the powerful Nauvoo Legion was not enough. Being mayor of a city or the governor of the federal territory of Nauvoo was not enough. Being prophet, seer, and revelator was not enough. Being "king of God's kingdom on earth" was not enough. Joseph Smith wanted to be president of the United States of America.

In truth, I don't think he ever really expected to win the 1844 national election. But like many one-cause-oriented candidates of today's politics, he knew that the publicity he would receive from just entering the race would focus national attention on his cause. And he knew well from his experience in state politics (however unwisely he had gained that experience) that a bloc of voters as large as the Mormons' could well decide an election and make their good graces a commodity to be desired by other candidates.

The "theodemocracy" he advocated was not really that, for in its ultimate state it would have been a one-party system. As the Mormons would say, "the right party," meaning the Mormon party. Joseph also advocated abolition of slavery, annexation of Texas, and drastic penal reform.

While Joseph was riding the crest of a wave of confidence that seemed would never break on the shores of reality, some of his closest counselors and friends stood on the sand watching bitterly. Some he had alienated by approaching their wives, trying to fatten his polygamous harem. Others he had denounced publicly for crimes of which they felt themselves innocent. Still others were disgusted by Joseph's use of church money to buy property which he sold at a profit to new converts, while the workers on the Nauvoo temple were ill-fed and lived in shacks. Some still believed in the doctrines of early Mormonism, but felt that Joseph had fallen from the favor of God by abusing his authority.

Some of these men brought suit against Joseph for slander, false swearing, and adultery and polygamy. Their charges were countered by claims in the Nauvoo Mormon newspapers that the accusers were sexual profligates who had seduced many innocent women. In May Joseph himself denied publicly that he had ever had more than one wife. This may have satisfied those who were ignorant of his scores of wives, but what soul-searching it must have caused those who knew the truth, and heard such a monstrous lie coming from the lips of God's mouthpiece!

But the press run by the Mormon dissidents, *The Expositor,* gave out details of the involvement of high church officials with polygamy. To spare humiliation to the "spiritual wives," many of whom had been bullied, seduced, or tricked into accepting their polygamous unions, *The Expositor* mentioned no names. But the readers of the newspaper recognized in its stories the situations of many friends and loved ones, and more and more began to mistrust the prophet's vehement denials of the existence of polygamy and the extent to which it was practiced.

Joseph's solution to this challenge to his authority was simple. The staff members of *The Expositor* were "tried" without judge, jury, or witness for their own defense, accused by members of the city council and declared to be operating a public nuisance. Part of the Nauvoo Legion was dispatched to destroy the presses and all existing copies of the publication; and in its smoking ruins Joseph thought he saw a return to peace in Nauvoo. When news reached the shocked outside world, though, the flame of Joseph's life flickered on a shrinking wick.

Perhaps Joseph realized it, for some Latter-day Saints claim that not long before this he had given to his son, Joseph, a "father's blessing," which concluded with the promise that young Joseph would be his father's successor as leader of the church.[48] In addition, more and more of Joseph's public statements and prophecies referred to his imminent death.

The people of Illinois were aghast to learn of the destruction of the *Expositor* press. Some local militia from surrounding towns were ready to attack Nauvoo at a moment's notice, but to prevent mob invasion Governor Ford ordered Joseph and his co-conspirators to appear in Carthage, Illinois, for trial. Joseph and his brother Hyrum, along with Willard Richards and Orin Porter Rockwell, escaped into Iowa Territory across the flood-swollen Mississippi River.

The leaderless Mormon people, under imminent attack from all sides, felt betrayed by Joseph's flight. Word was sent to the fugitives, imploring them to return. Joseph, upon hearing the urgent message, reflected, "If my life is of no value to my friends, it is of no value to myself." He and the others returned to Nauvoo, where Joseph prepared his legal defense, and then rode on into Carthage.

There they faced charges of rioting. Though most of the men were released on bail, Joseph and Hyrum were put into the two-story stone Carthage jail, even before the preliminary hearing. Joseph's friends brought news to him that some of the militia troops were planning to storm the jail. When the word was conveyed to Governor Ford, he dismissed the possibility, and, confident of Joseph's safety, returned to Nauvoo. In desperation, Joseph sent for the Nauvoo Legion with a message that entreated them to break him out of the jail, for he feared for his life.

The message never reached Nauvoo. As Joseph and Hyrum and their two visitors, Willard Richards and John Taylor, sat sipping wine, a commotion outside made them jump for their two smuggled guns.

When the smoke cleared, Taylor was slightly wounded, and Richards untouched. But the blood-crazed mob was sated. Joseph and Hyrum were dead.

Those who hoped Mormonism would die with Joseph were disappointed. Had his desire that his son succeed him been realized, perhaps Mormonism would not be so powerful today. Those who thought that was what was needed followed Joseph Smith III and his mother Emma, renouncing the doctrines of plural marriage, the teachings on the Negro, and other doctrines, saying that these were perversions of truth, and that Joseph Smith had "fallen" in his later years.

What Mormonism did need, and got, was the strong leadership of a man like Brigham Young. Mormons are taught that he was a gruff, plainspoken man. What they fail to appreciate is how power affected that man. The triumph of leading his people in the trek across the American Plains never wore off. When he arrived in Utah, he became a despot who controlled with a grasping hand the economy, religion, and morals of the people of the Salt Lake Valley. His legendary scores of wives, his excesses of rage, his amazing (and now-suppressed) teachings on blood atonement, all are unknown or unnoticed by Mormons of today who admire in him the ideal of work and fortitude.

Perhaps the Mormon people, for survival *as* a people, needed a prophet like that. Perhaps they needed a Joseph Smith.

But a Christian needs only Christ.

NOTES

[1]*Journal of Discourses,* VII, 289.
[2]*Journal of Discourses,* VIII, 321.
[3]*Journal of Discourses,* III, 212.

[4]*Journal of Discourses,* VIII, 176.

[5]Joseph Fielding Smith, *Doctrines of Salvation* (Salt Lake City: Bookcraft, 1954-56), I, 188.

[6]*Pearl of Great Price,* Joseph Smith 2:5-10.

[7]*Pearl of Great Price,* Joseph Smith 2:21-25.

[8]B. H. Roberts, *A Comprehensive History of the Church of Jesus Christ of Latter-day Saints* (Salt Lake City: Deseret Press, 1930), I, 26.

[9]Interview with Martin Harris, *Tiffany's Monthly,* 1859, pp. 163-169.

[10]As quoted in Jerald and Sandra Tanner, *Mormonism—Shadow or Reality?* (Salt Lake City: Modern Microfilm Co., 1972), p. 41.

[11]Joseph Fielding Smith, *Doctrines of Salvation* (Salt Lake City: Bookcraft, 1954-56), III, 225.

[12]Lucy Mack Smith, *Biographical Sketches of Joseph Smith the Prophet and His Progenitors for Many Generations* (Liverpool: 1853), p. 87.

[13]Hal Hougey, *"A Parallel---The Basis of the Book of Mormon* (Concord, California: Pacific Publishing Company, 1963), p. 15.

[14]Fawn McKay Brodie, *No Man Knows My History* (New York: Alfred A. Knopf, 1946), p. 43.

[15]In 1980 the LDS Church magazine, *The Ensign,* featured the "discovery" of a document known as the "Anthon transcript," which it said was authentic, showing characters copied directly from the gold plates. Unfortunately for both Mormons and non-Mormons, the document was a modern forgery.

[16]B. H. Roberts, *A Comprehensive History,* p. 103.

[17]*Journal of Discourses,* VII, 164.

[18]Another reference to the apostasy of the *Book of Mormon* witnesses is found in the *Journal of Discourses,* VII, 114-115.

[19]Statement by Joseph Smith, *Documentary History of the Church,* Vol. III, p. 232. All but McLellin were witnesses to the *Book of Mormon.*

[20]John A. Widtsoe, *Joseph Smith—Seeker After Truth* (Salt Lake City: Bookcraft, 1951), p. 58. See also *Doctrine and Covenants,* 28:11.

[21]From a sworn affidavit by Frank L. Emich, Notary Public in Seneca, Ohio, quoted by Jerald and Sandra Tanner, *Mormonism—Shadow or Reality?* (Salt Lake City: Modern Microfilm Co., 1972), pp. 54-55.

[22]From a letter quoted in *Senate Document 189,* February 15, 1841, pp. 6-9.

[23]*Doctrine and Covenants,* 3:12; 10:7.

[24]Jerald and Sandra Tanner, *Mormonism—Shadow or Reality?* p. 162.

[25]Brodie, *No Man Knows My History,* pp. 60-61.

[26]Francis J. Kirkham, *A New Witness For Christ In America: the Book of Mormon* (Independence, Missouri: Zion's Printing and Publishing Company, 1951), I, 200-201.

[27]Joseph Smith Jr., *Documentary History of the Church,* IV, p. 461.

[28]Lamar Petersen, *Problems in Mormon Text* (Salt Lake City: privately printed, 1957), p. 7.

[29]As quoted from Ezra Booth by Fawn Brodie, *No Man Knows My History,* p. 111ff.

[30]*Doctrine and Covenants,* 45:69.

[31]*Doctrine and Covenants,* 87:3.

[32]*Journal of Discourses,* XII, 344.

[33]*Doctrine and Covenants,* Section 103.

[34]Tanner, *Mormonism—Shadow or Reality?* p. 407.

[35]*Journal of Discourses,* II, 214.

[36]*Times and Seasons,* Vol. V, pp. 614-617.

[37]Joseph Smith Jr., *Documentary History of the Church,* II, p. 497.

[38]Brodie, *No Man Knows My History,* p. 198.

[39]Joseph Smith Jr., *Documentary History of the Church,* III, pp. 180-181.

[40]William E. Berrett, *The Restored Church* (Salt Lake City, Utah: 1956), p. 198.

[41]George Hinkle, James B. Turner, and John D. Lee quoted by Fawn Brodie, *No Man Knows My History,* 230-231.

[42]Ibid., p. 280.

[43]*Doctrine and Covenants,* 124:56.

[44]Gary Dean Guthrie, "Joseph Smith as an Administrator" (unpublished Master's Thesis, BYU, May 1969), p. 161.

[45]Klaus J. Hansen, quoted in Tanner, *Mormonisn—Shadow or Reality?* p. 415.

[46]Brodie, *No Man Knows My History,* p. 336.

[47]Joseph Smith, Jr., *Documentary History of the Church,* V, p. 372.

[48]Mormon Apostle Gordon B. Hinckley announced at the church's April 1981 conference that an actual transcript of this blessing had been authenticated by the LDS church. He claimed, however, that its contents weren't binding *as prophecy,* stating that it was the transcript of a blessing, "not a record of ordination."

4
The Book of Mormon:
"The Most Correct of Any Book"?

I told the brethren that the *Book of Mormon* was the most correct of any book on earth, and the keystone of our religion, and a man would get nearer to God by abiding by its precepts, than by any other book.
—Joseph Smith in
Documentary History of the Church
Vol. IV, p. 461.

Advertising executives of today know that the most effective way to sell a new product is to convince the consumer that he has a need for this product. If such a need does not exist, it is up to the wise advertiser to create the need, or make the consumer *believe* the need exists in his life. In a way, that is how Mormonism as a whole is sold to proselytes and members alike. The biggest obstacle to the Mormon way of life, though, is the *Book of Mormon,* (subtitled: *Another Testament of Jesus Christ*). Its teachings and the claims for it have made many a prospective member hesitate before taking the watery step into the church. Once you accept the *Book of Mormon,* you can swallow anything Mormonism gives you. But like a gossiper who tears down the reputations of others to exalt himself, Mormonism must denigrate the Bible in order to create a "need" for a scripture such as the *Book of Mormon.*

The "Lost Books"

This devaluation of Holy Writ is accomplished in two ways. First, Mormons point to works by Hebrew writers, such as the "Book of the Wars of Israel" and the "Book of the Covenant" mentioned by Moses, the "Book of Jasher" mentioned by Joshua, the "Book of the Acts of Solomon" mentioned in First Kings, the "Book of Jehu" and "Acts of Uzziah" by Isaiah, the "Sayings of the Seers," as well as "lost" books we might title "Third Corinthians," "Second Ephesians," and the

"Epistle to the Laodiceans" referred to in the New Testament. Mormons say, "See—these books are missing from the Bible. It is incomplete and thus unreliable."

James D. Bales in his book *The Book of Mormon?* makes the very valid point that, "A book is not inspired just because it is mentioned in the Bible. A citation to a book does not in itself prove the inspiration of that book."[1] Bales then gives New Testament examples of where the apostle Paul quoted from pagan Greek writers (Acts 17:28; Titus 1:12) and asks if the complete works from which *they* were taken should be regarded by us as Scripture.

An argument citing the "incompleteness" of the Bible is indeed a weak crutch upon which to lean the plea for the necessity of more Scripture. If these "missing" books of the Bible were necessary for our salvation, why didn't Mormonism just *restore* them?

This same argument equating "incompleteness" with invalidity must hold true also for the Mormon when he considers that the writings of Zenos, Zenock, Neum, and Ezias are all mentioned in the *Book of Mormon*.[2] What must he assume, knowing that these works don't appear there (or anywhere else), except in partial form or passing reference?

Of course, we know that the works mentioned in the Bible that do not appear there in their completeness are not necessary for our salvation. John 20:30-31 clearly tells the believer that not every detail regarding the life of Christ was written down by His gospel biographers. (Perhaps an important part of divine inspiration was selectivity!) At any rate, this Scripture passage teaches us that what *was* written was for the express purpose of saving our souls. Dare we ask more of a generous God?

The Mormons do so dare. They claim that not only are there parts of the Bible missing which are mentioned in Holy Scripture, but that many "plain and precious parts" were edited out of the Bible we have. In a notebook given to me for use in a seminary class, there was a page that was intended to teach the young Mormon student exactly how these "plain and precious parts" found their way out of the Bible. On this page was a drawing of a medieval-type priest, brows knit together and smirking wickedly, who was furtively scratching out lines written on a scroll. This was intended to show how wicked priests just blotted out the parts of the Bible with which they did not agree.

Now, anyone who has ever studied about Bible manuscripts knows that those manuscripts which are now in existence, from the earliest to the later ones, are a striking testimony to the divine protection of God over His holy records. It has been truly said by R. A. Torrey,

> We now possess so many good copies [of the Bible] that by comparing one with another we can tell with great precision just what the original text was. Indeed, for all practical purposes the original text

is now settled. There is not one important doctrine that hangs upon any doubtful reading of the text.[3]

It is interesting to note that Torrey penned these words almost fifty years before the discovery of the Dead Sea Scrolls, which substantiated everything Christians had been saying all along about the reliability of the Scriptures.

The discovery of Bible manuscripts is going on all the time. We have some manuscripts that are only removed in time a few years from their inspired authors. The older the manuscripts discovered, the narrower the time period in which such falsification claimed by Mormons would have to have happened. Perhaps someday Christians will be blessed with the discovery of part of a Bible manuscript contemporaneous with its author, and faith tells us that it will not differ substantially, if indeed at all, from the Bible versions we read today.

The Restoration of the "Plain and Precious" Gospel

A claim made proudly by Mormons is that they practice Christianity in its pure first-century form. However, if we look at Mormonism today and compare it with what we know of earliest Christianity, we can see some major differences.

Mormon doctrine of the past and present teaches polygamy, temple rites, Negro discrimination, and other strange doctrines. Since they are the "extras" we don't find in traditional Christianity, we can only assume that these are included in the "plain and precious parts" the *Book of Mormon* needed to restore. But why is there no mention of such things being practiced by early Christians, even in the writings of secular historians who surely would have noted such deviations from the Jewish norm? Does the *Book of Mormon* itself restore—or even mention—any of these doctrines? I challenge any reader, Mormon or Christian, to find any endorsement of such things as secret temple worship, divinely-approved plural marriage, or refusal of priesthood privileges to blacks inside the covers of any edition of the *Book of Mormon*. They simply aren't there.

This matter of "plain and precious parts" has puzzled Christians since 1830. Precious—yes, it would be wonderful to have additional teachings on the gospel by inspired writers, as the mythical *Book of Mormon* writers such as Nephi and Moroni claimed to be. But is the *Book of Mormon* plain?

A kind way to put it is to say that it is certainly no easier to understand than the Bible. Nor does it explain in any greater detail any Biblical tenet. Though the *Book of Mormon* does go off on tangents like Christ's visit to the Americas, and Lehi's vision of the world, these and other stories don't explain, or make plainer, any ideas found in the Bible. In fact, in many cases they are barefaced contradictions of the Bible.

The Bible-believing Christian does not have to search the Scriptures for long to effectively refute the claim that our Bible is incomplete. First Peter 1:25 says that the word of the Lord—the gospel—will abide forever. Second Timothy 3:16-17 says that the Bible ("all Scripture") will completely equip the man of God.

Contrast this to Second Nephi 29:3-6 which bluntly asserts that only a fool would accept the Bible as God's only scripture. So the supplement offered by Mormonism is their *Book of Mormon*.

Joseph Fielding Smith, former president of the Mormon Church and perhaps its most prolific modern-day theologian, explained that there are many as-yet unexplained principles relating to the celestial kingdom and to exaltation, but that "the Lord has revealed in the *Book of Mormon* all that is needful to direct people who are willing to hearken to its precepts to a fulness of the blessings of the Kingdom of God."[4] If this be true, that the *Book of Mormon* can guide men to salvation where no other book could, then we could certainly expect its predecessor, the Bible—though incomplete—to point us toward such an essential scripture. In support of this theory we are offered many Scripture passages from the Bible that supposedly herald the advent of Mormonism.

It must be noted parenthetically here that those Scripture references which will follow are taken from the King James Version of the Bible, which Mormons claim is the most correct one (aside from the standard German translation which Joseph Smith lauded as a nearly perfect rendering of God's Word). Anyone who reads the *Book of Mormon*'s often bumbling attempts at imitating seventheenth century English, however, would be hard pressed to understand why Mormons are so anxious to constantly invite a comparison between the sublime and the ridiculous.

Wresting of Bible Scriptures

At any rate, the only authorized version used by Mormons, missionary and layman alike, is King James; and one of the first Bible Scriptures with which every LDS student becomes familiar is found in Ezekiel 37:15-20.

> The word of the Lord came again unto me, saying, Moreover, thou son of man, take thee one stick, and write upon it, For Judah, and for the children of Israel his companions: then take another stick, and write upon it, For Joseph, the stick of Ephriam, and for all the house of Israel his companions: And join them one to another into one stick; and they shall become one in thine hand. And when the children of thy people shall speak unto thee, saying, Wilt thou not shew us what thou meanest by these? Say unto them, Thus saith the Lord GOD; Behold, I will take the stick of Joseph, which is in the hand of Ephraim, and the tribes of Israel his fellows, and will put them with

him, even with the stick of Judah, and make them one stick, and they shall be one in mine hand. And the sticks whereon thou writest shall be in thine hand before their eyes.

The Mormon writer Hugh Nibley puts forth the standard Mormon explanation that the "stick of Judah" here mentioned is the Bible, because it was written by Judah's descendants, the Jews; and that the "stick of Ephriam" is the *Book of Mormon,* written by the Nephites who were descended from Ephriam. Everyone knows, say the Mormons, that oldtime scrolls were rolled up on sticks and from this the conclusion is drawn that the Ezekiel passage refers to two books of scripture that would be of equal importance and united in purpose in the hand of the Lord.[5]

There are several serious flaws in this interpretation of this section of Ezekiel's writings. First of all, the Hebrew word for "stick" used here is found in other places in the Bible (Num. 15:32; 1 Kings 17:10; 2 Kings 6:6), but in every instance it is used, it means a piece of wood. Another, different word is used in the Bible for the word scroll. I think that if God had meant scroll in Ezekiel 37, He would have said it.

Even if the word "stick" were meant to signify a scroll, we are left with a dilemma: it is true that the Bible was recorded on scrolls, but what about the *Book of Mormon*'s golden plates?

Finally, James D. Bales points out that Ezekiel himself ("thou son of man") was told to inscribe the two sticks. Always in Ezekiel's prophecy the phrase "thou son of man" (used 91 times) refers specifically to the man Ezekiel. Thus if the prophet Ezekiel was to *write* on these two sticks we can either accept the fact that he was told to inscribe a few words on two pieces of wood, or follow the Mormon argument to its logical conclusion: Ezekiel must have written both the Bible and the *Book of Mormon.*[6]

The second Scripture used by Mormons to show a Biblical foreshadowing of the coming of the *Book of Mormon* is found in Isaiah 29:1-4.

> Woe to Ariel, to Ariel, the city where David dwelt! add ye year to year; let them kill sacrifices. Yet I will distress Ariel, and there shall be heaviness and sorrow: and it shall be unto me as Ariel. And I will camp against thee round about, and will lay siege against thee with a mount, and I will raise forts against thee. And thou shalt be brought down, and shalt speak out of the ground, and thy speech shall be low out of the dust, and thy voice shall be, as of one that hath a familiar spirit, out of the ground, and thy speech shall whisper out of the dust.

Mormons say that the voice from the dust with a familiar spirit is the *Book of Mormon* which was buried in the ground and which contained some of the teachings of the old Jewish prophets such as Isaiah.[7] With this interpretation Mormons have violated one of the most valuable principles of Scriptural exposition. They have taken the idea of "voices from the dust with a familiar spirit" entirely out of context.

The careful reader will note that Ariel, or Jerusalem, is in this passage *rebuked* for its spiritual debauchery which is exemplified by her intimacy with "familiar spirits"—or the practice of the black arts. The Hebrew word used here for "familiar spirit"—*ob*—means demon. In other words, the Jews were practicing witchcraft. Do the Mormons really want to use these verses to support their own scriptures?

A third favorite Bible Scripture used by the Mormons is Isaiah 29:10-11.

> For the LORD hath poured out upon you the spirit of deep sleep, and hath closed your eyes: the prophets and your rulers, the seers hath he covered. And the vision of all is become unto you as the words of a book that is sealed, which men deliver to one that is learned, saying, Read this, I pray thee: and he saith, I cannot; for it is sealed.

This Scripture passage was supposedly fulfilled when Martin Harris took the papers containing characters copied from the golden plates to Dr. Anthon. When Anthon asked for additional documentation to ascertain the authenticity of the plates, he was told that the plates were sealed. He replied, "I cannot read a sealed book," and thus unwittingly fulfilled Isaiah's prophecy. However, after reading Dr. Anthon's scathing denunciation of the inscriptions, Martin Harris and Joseph Smith, and the lies they told about him, and Mormonism as a whole, one would think the Mormons would just as soon forget connecting Isaiah 29:11 with this Dr. Anthon.

Mormons also use Second Corinthians 13:1 to show the necessity for scripture such as the *Book of Mormon*. The latter part of this verse states, "In the mouth of two or three witnesses shall every word be established." The Bible, say the Mormons, is only one witness and alone it is unsubstantiated without the corroboration of another book. However, if I regarded the Bible as fallible and thus imperfect, I wouldn't think that it could be corroborated by another scripture—you can't build successfully upon a faulty foundation! We cannot ignore the fact that a gracious and generous God has already given us two witnesses, the Old and the New Testaments, and added to these the confirming witness of the Holy Ghost (Heb. 10:15).

Mormon missionaries often combine two Scriptures from the Books of John and Matthew to raise questions in the mind of a Christian.

> And other sheep I have, which are not of this fold: them also I must bring, and they shall hear my voice; and there shall be one fold, and one shepherd.　　　　　　　　　　　　　　　—John 10:16

> But he answered and said, I am not sent but unto the lost sheep of the house of Israel.　　　　　　　　　　　　　　　—Matt. 15:24

If, Mormons say, Jesus was to go to other sheep, and if the other sheep were only of the house of Israel, then the other sheep must be displaced Jews—displaced in, say, America. They assert that the other sheep could not possibly be Gentiles because of what Matthew 15:24 says. Again, this is a problem caused by taking Scripture out of context. When we read the entire "lost sheep" passage in Matthew 15:21-28, we find that at least one time Jesus did indeed minister to a non-Jew who heard his voice. But this is only a peripheral issue. What is important is that Christians of today are certainly Christ's sheep, though many have no traceable Jewish heritage. Christ promised to *bring* us, which (praise His name) He has done; not visit us as the Mormons claim He did to the Nephites; not watch us receive the Holy Spirit in His presence (compare John 16:7 to 3 Nephi 19:20-22); and certainly not to endorse a gospel so foreign to His own!

The Author of the Book of Mormon

When Joseph Smith went to register the first edition of the book with the New York state authorities, he listed himself as "author and proprietor" of it. Mormon apologists say that this is because the New York copyright laws required such a statement from any prospective publishing author to protect others from plagiarism. But in this the Mormons are mistaken. The law required that one list himself as *either* author *or* proprietor.[8] Why did he claim to be both if he were in truth only a proprietor?

Even if these laws had required Joseph to claim to be both author and proprietor, the laws didn't apply to the printed testimony of the witnesses which in the early edition of the *Book of Mormon* also claimed that Joseph was both author and proprietor. These testimonies, as well as the title page in the present-day edition, now have the words "author and proprietor" deleted altogether and substituted by the word "translator." But when you change a person's sworn testimony, do you not therefore invalidate it? (And when you later make almost four thousand changes in the work about which they testified, you really have a mess.) As a parallel, what would happen if I had a notary public witness a will for me, and then I altered the notary's seal (his "testimony") and then changed the wording, punctuation, and spelling of the will in numerous places? Of course the will would be worthless and the notary's witnessing of it meaningless.

If Joseph Smith was the author, then the *Book of Mormon* is obviously not divine. If he weren't the author, then why did he and eleven witnesses say otherwise? And why should we trust the word of any of them in any other matter?

One such matter that is very hard for the non-Mormon to understand is the process of translation used in the production of the *Book of Mormon*. Accounts from eyewitnesses vary greatly, but according to Joseph Smith (who, if anyone, should know), much of the translation was accomplished with the aid of the Urim and Thummim. Just what these were is a mystery to Mormon and non-Mormon alike. They were mentioned in Exodus 28:30, Leviticus 8:8, Numbers 27:21, Deuteronomy 33:8, and First Samuel 28:6, and from these references we infer that they were treasured objects used by the High Priest to inquire of the Lord. According to Joseph Smith they were prepared by God for the express purpose of translating the gold plates and were used also by the Nephite prophet Mosiah[9] and subsequently buried with the gold plates. (One might wonder how they got from the possession of the Jewish High Priest into the hands of the Nephites. God gave them to the Jaredite party before they left the Old World at the time of the building of the Tower of Babel, and they brought them to the Americas, according to Mormon writers Reynold and Sjodahl.[10] This explanation, though, leaves one wondering about how the Bible was still talking about the Urim at least in First Samuel, in the time of Saul.)

As described by Joseph, the Urim and Thummim were two stones fastened in silver bows and attached to a breastplate.[11] One early Mormon drawing of them suggests that they were mounted on the breastplate in such a way that when the breastplate was worn, they formed spectacles through which the wearer could look and so translate.

In spite of such a marvelous tool for translation, even modern editions of the *Book of Mormon* show evidence of where Joseph "slipped" in dictating and had to backtrack. Consider the following:

> Now behold, the people who were in the land Bountiful, *or rather Moroni,* feared that they would hearken to the words of Morianton and unite with his people, and thus he would obtain possession of those parts of the land, which would lay a foundation for serious consequences among the people of Nephi, yea, which consequences would lead to the overthrow of their liberty (italics mine).
> —Alma 50:32

(See also Alma 24:19; Mosiah 7:8; Helaman 3:33.)

Mormons explain that such errors existed before the translation— they were on the plates themselves when the Nephite writers etched them into the metal; and because of the time and trouble involved in scratching out mistakes, the Nephite prophets just corrected their mistakes as they went along. But behind this careful backtracking to correct obvious mistakes, I see not the efforts of a prophet to preserve a record from error, but the efforts of a deceiver to protect himself from exposure.

This point of criticism is mild compared to the self-evident grammatical errors of the *Book of Mormon*'s first edition. Jerald and

Sandra Tanner have in *Mormonisn—Shadow or Reality?* compiled a list of grammatical errors of early editions of the *Book of Mormon* that are guaranteed to make an English teacher swoon. Some examples of the later-corrected grammar of the 1830 edition include its use of "wrecked" for racked (as with pain), "was" for were, "is" for are, "much" for many, "had not" for ought not, "arrest" for wrest, "arriven" for arrived, "wrote" for written, "done" for did, "exceeding fraid" for exceedingly afraid, "began" for begun, "took" for taken, "gave" for given, "no" for any, and many other errors involving double negatives. Mormons try to brush off criticisms of the first edition by saying the translation was not as automatic as some early church leaders described it (*i.e.*, the mechanical writing). At least this new explanation absolves God of having the bad grammar! But saying that Joseph Smith just used his own manner of speaking leads one to the logical conclusion that Joseph Smith spoke in a kind of Elizabethan English—surely a strange dialect for a nineteenth-century New Englander!

Then, too, the *Book of Mormon* (and any reader of it) is cursed with the clumsy, repetitive phrase "and it came to pass" that appears hundreds of times in the book, on almost every page. When the *Book of Mormon* was translated into German, those lucky people were spared having to read and reread that phrase, because it is not translatable into their tongue. Therefore, in every German edition of the *Book of Mormon,* this phrase was replaced by closed brackets, [ ], and an explanatory note on the first page of the text; all of which makes the reading of the book in German a whole lot smoother.

Reformed Egyptian

No more clumsy than this phrase, though, was the form of Egyptian the Mormons say was utilized on the gold plates. Even Mormon writer Hugh Nibley admits that demotic (the form of ancient Egyptian he theorizes was used by Nephi) was the most unwieldy and impractical system of writing that Nephi could have chosen, or indeed, that has ever been invented. If we look at the America of Joseph Smith's day, however, it is easier to understand why he claimed that the plates were inscribed in a type of Egyptian. In the early nineteenth century, the entire United States was caught up in an antiquities craze. Joseph Smith merely cashed in on this and at the same time gambled on the likelihood that Egyptian would never be deciphered. Indeed, were it not for the lucky survival of the Rosetta Stone (which, before its importance was realized, was even used as a grindstone by ignorant peasants), Joseph Smith might have to this day gotten away with more of his claims for the *Book of Mormon* and the *Pearl of Great Price*.

Some Mormon experts say that the original plates written by Nephi (the earliest *Book of Mormon* writer), as well as the brass plates of Old Testament Scripture brought from Jerusalem, were in pure Egyptian, but by the time that Moroni, the compiler of the book wrote, one thousand years later, the language had been altered to "reformed Egyptian."[12] One Mormon apologist, Sidney P. Sperry, claims that Nephi wrote Hebrew characters ("learning of the Jews and the language of the Egyptians" as described in 1 Nephi 1:2) which he compares to writing English in Gregg shorthand.[13]

Aside from the obvious flaw in this comparison that ignores the fact that Gregg shorthand was invented specifically for writing English, a devout Jew such as Nephi should have been horrified at writing scripture in a foreign tongue. To the Jew, the Hebrew language is sacred, and recording it in the pagan Egyptian language would be an unthinkable sacrilege.

Nor could it be argued that Egyptian would be a more compact way of writing on the plates, for it is a very bulky language to laboriously inscribe upon metal plates. Mormon 9:33 explains, "If our plates had been sufficiently large, we should have written in Hebrew." If, as the *Book of Mormon* claims, there was such an abundance of gold that it was used to make weapons, jewelry, and currency, why didn't the keepers of the Nephite records merely make more plates, or larger ones?

The *Book of Mormon* is silent on this logical solution to their problem. It does, however, say that only the Nephites knew the reformed Egyptian language, because they had changed the original Egyptian in such a way as to fit their own purposes. Again, the claim of Joseph Smith that Professor Anthon had endorsed Smith's translation of the reformed Egyptian is shown to be a false one. If only the Nephites (and Joseph Smith) could read this special form of Egyptian, that leaves out Anthon as an authority either way.

Middle America was where most of the events of the *Book of Mormon* were supposed to have taken place. It is not surprising, though, that the surviving Indian tongues of this area—Maya, Quechua, Nahuatl—bear no resemblance to Hebrew or any form of Egyptian.[14] However, some of the names of characters in the *Book of Mormon,* such as Jacob, Joseph, Ishmael, Laban, and Nimrod, to name a few, are definitely Hebrew—they appear in the Bible.

Whatever the languages of the ancient Americans, it can be safely assumed that they knew no Greek. But Greek words are used in the *Book of Mormon:* "Alpha and Omega,"[15] the Greek name Timothy,[16] and the New Testament version of the name Jonah which is the Greek Jonas.[17] This is despite the blanket statement of the LDS Church that no Greek words appear in the *Book of Mormon.*

Although some names are thus of Greek origin, others are lifted from the King James Version with spelling idiosyncrasies intact, some are a hodgepodge of miscellaneous Hebrew syllables, and many others have solely Indo-Aryan roots that cannot be justified as coming from an ancient Jewish culture. One interesting example of a strangely constructed word is the "Liahona," the name given to the compass or director used in 600 B.C. by Lehi in the wilderness (despite the fact that compasses weren't used in the western world until the twelfth century A.D. according to history books). This word is supposedly a Hebrew name with an Egyptian ending translating to "Of God Is Light." That is something like an American interested in Spanish culture calling such an instrument Godsluz (which transliterates to approximately the same thing).

Many other names unfamiliar to us which are found in the *Book of Mormon* can be formed by combining parts of Bible or Apocrypha names (for example, Sariah is a combination of Sarah and Saria, both Bible names), or by altering such names slightly by simple means such as the transposition of letters.

Was Joseph Smith capable of manufacturing words in such a manner? He was never accused of lack of imagination or ingenuity, and he certainly had the resources—his personal Bible contained an Apocrypha and a list of all the names of the Bible alphabetically arranged.[18] Give me the same materials, and I guarantee you that I or anyone else could come up with 180 "new" names like those found in the *Book of Mormon*.

The History of the Ancient Americas

Surely just thinking up a few names was not the greatest challenge that Joseph faced in writing his epic of the Nephite people. Coming up with a plot line as tangled and intricate as is found there surely must have involved a great deal of time. Perhaps, as Cowdrey, Scales, and Davis have suggested, Solomon Spaulding's work did indeed suggest a great deal of the plot of the *Book of Mormon* to the mind of Joseph Smith, because Spaulding had so much idle time on his hands, being retired. But since Joseph Smith was not known by his contemporaries for his ability to hold a job for very long, he himself must have had a lot of time, too.

Dr. Ross T. Christianson of Brigham Young University in speaking of the *Book of Mormon* once made the statement that "if the book's history is fallacious, its doctrine cannot be genuine."[19] Just what *is* the story told by the Mormon scripture?

It ambitiously covers a time period of some 2600 years—from about 2200 B.C. to A.D. 421. Much time is spent in recounting events in the lives of the heroes of the book, perhaps to keep the reader from noticing the introduction of strange doctrinal material along the way. For instance, the detailed accounts of Lehi and Nephi sugar-coat the idea of Adam's "fall upward"; and the story of the great faith of the brother of Jared is to prepare us for the idea that he could see and talk to God, literally face to face.

The *Book of Mormon* skims over vast years of history in little books like those of Jarom and Omni, using the "smallness of the plates"[20] and the wickedness of the record-keepers as an excuse, but quotes proliferously from Isaiah, seemingly only to fill up space. It drags the reader through rivers of blood recounting battles and wars, recording details that interest no one but Mormonism's critics, then plays catch-up in the final book of Moroni—filling in the reader on the divine truth about infant baptism, the sacrament, and other doctrinal matters all squeezed compactly into a few short chapters.

Basically the book follows the histories of three groups of people who migrated from the Holy Land to the Americas. The first group to migrate were the Jaredites, who were named after their leader, Jared. As recorded in the *Book of Mormon* in the book of Ether, they left the Old World about the time of the Tower of Babel, escaping the confusion of tongues and thus, according to Joseph Fielding Smith, they spoke and wrote the pure Adamic language of God.[21] Jared's brother, who was identified in later revelation as having the name Mahonri Moriancumer (no wonder Joseph Smith neglected to mention it in the *Book of Mormon*), was a man so full of faith that the Lord was unable to prevent him from seeing His body in its entirety.[22] God instructed the Jaredites in how to build eight small, light, airtight, seaworthy vessels in which to cross the Atlantic to the New World. The Lord also touched with His finger some molten rocks supplied by the brother of Jared, and caused them to glow, thus providing a source of light for the ships. About fifty Jaredites crossed the ocean in the eight boats. Also on board these boats were a food supply for them, flocks, herds, fowl, fish (and, we would assume, a food supply for all), bees, seeds, tools, and personal possessions.[23] All eight boats landed miraculously in the New World at the same time after a journey that lasted 344 days.

Then they established themselves and anointed a king who reigned righteously, but soon wars and contentions broke out among the people. As in the Bible, the people went through cycles of righteousness and peace, then apostasy and "secret combinations."[24] A great prophet named Ether arose in the Jaredite nation's blackest period, predicting the coming of Christ and the fall of the Jaredite people if they did not repent. He, like all the great men of his time, was persecuted. A great battle between the righteous and unrighteous factions ensued at the Hill Cumorah, and all of the more than two million people of the Jaredite nation were destroyed except Ether (whose fate is unknown) and a warrior named Coriantumr, of whom we shall hear more later.

The second and least significant migration to the Americas occurred much later in 589 B.C. when Mulek, the son of Zedekiah King of Judah, came over with a party about the time of the Babylonian captivity. They brought with them none of the sacred Scriptures of the Jewish faith, and thus their descendants soon fell into apostasy and moral decay, with even their language becoming corrupted. In about 189 B.C. they discovered our friend Coriantumr who lived with them about nine months and left with them a written account of the history of his now-extinct people, the Jaredites. We shall hear more of the fate of the Mulekites, or the people of Zarahemla as they were sometimes called, later on.

The third and by far the most important migration to America recorded by the *Book of Mormon* occurred in about 600 B.C. when a holy man of Jerusalem, Lehi by name, took his wife (Sariah—one of the three women mentioned by name in the *Book of Mormon*), his daughters, and his sons (Laman, Lemuel, Nephi, and Sam) out of the land of his forebears where his life had been threatened by those who ignored his urgings to repent. Lehi's family was joined in the wilderness by a man named Zoram. The Lehite party was completed by a man named Ishmael, his wife, five daughters (who married the sons of Lehi and Zoram), two sons, two daughters-in-law, and their children.

The combined party then traveled down the western edge of the Arabian Peninsula with the aid of the Liahona, that divine "director" ball that guided them. Contentions soon developed between the wicked young men: Laman, Lemuel, and the sons of Ishmael; and the righteous ones: Nephi, Sam, and Zoram. After much difficulty, they built a ship and in about 589 B.C. the group, along with two new sons born to Lehi in the wilderness (making a party of at least twenty-four persons), arrived in the promised land of America.

There they settled and began to till the ground, but the rift between the righteous and the unrighteous ones began to widen. They soon separated into two distinct groups, the wicked Lamanites and the good Nephites; and the bulk of the *Book of Mormon* is taken up with the struggles between these two factions.

The Lamanites, though, were always the aggressors in warfare, for the Nephites believed in fighting only to protect themselves. The wicked Lamanites were punished for their rebellion when God turned their skins dark, and they continued in their savage and warlike ways. Meanwhile, the Nephites lived upright lives, keeping records of their history and theology on plates of gold, and built temples, like those of Solomon, to their God.

In about 200 B.C. the Nephites anointed their first king, Mosiah, who discovered the people of Zarahemla (our friends the Mulekites) who then united themselves with the Nephites from that day forward. Many other kings followed, both good and wicked—Benjamin, Mosiah II, Zeniff,

Noah, and Limhi. Then from about 91 B.C. to the coming of Christ the Nephites were governed by at least thirteen judges, among them Alma the Younger, Nephihah, Pahoran I, Pahoran II, Pacumeni, Helaman II, Nephi, Cezoram, the son of Cezoram, Seezoram, Lachoneus I, and Lachoneus II.

During this time many of the Nephites had become wicked, while many Lamanites were converted and lived righteous lives. After being smitten with a pestilence, the Nephites returned to God. Great prophecies of the coming of Christ were relayed by prophets to the people, and the day Christ was born great signs appeared in the New World. However, many hardened their hearts and were led to disbelieve, but those Lamanites who remained faithful became "white and delightsome" again, and were from then on numbered as Nephites. However, the church itself was rent by dissension between the times of Christ's birth and death.

In America, great signs accompanied the crucifixion of Christ. There were tempests, earthquakes, whirlwinds, fires, three days of total darkness, a great voice from heaven, and the complete destruction of every wicked person in the land. The people who remained alive gathered at the temple where Jesus Christ appeared to them, teaching and healing and blessing them. The Holy Ghost was bestowed and twelve Nephite disciples chosen—all of whom were granted their hearts' desires. Three of them desired never to die and were granted the privilege of staying on earth until the second coming of Christ.

For almost two centuries after Christ's return to heaven, the American church flourished in righteousness. But soon many dissented and began to call themselves by the name of Lamanites and to practice the unregenerate ways of their namesakes. They began to outnumber the righteous people and went to war with them. The final battle at the Hill Cumorah (where you will remember the Jaredites exterminated themselves) saw 230,000 men die in battle. The holy records on the golden plates were completed by Mormon and Moroni, who like their brethren also perished, and the history of the *Book of Mormon* came to an end.

The Curse of the Dark Skin

The Lamanites of course continued in their lawless and wicked state, and so have remained. In 1 Nephi 12:23, they were described as "dark and loathsome and a filthy people, full of idleness and all manner of abominations." This dark skin, according to 2 Nephi 5:21-23 had four characteristics. *First,* it was "black"; *second,* it marked the curse indelibly upon them; *third,* it made them loathsome to righteous people, so that *fourth,* it would prevent the Nephites from intermarrying with them, thus mixing their blood and marking their children to share in the curse. Much confusion is due to the fact that the *Book of Mormon* identifies the

Lamanites' skin as being black. Mormons say this is because the words "dark" and "black" are interchangeable in the Hebrew language. This argument hinges on the assumption that the golden plates were written in Hebrew, which is a point of contention even among Mormons.

Milton Hunter, a Mormon writer, has further muddied the waters by publishing a book which shows pictures of light-skinned Lacandone Indians. They are obviously albinos—and Mongoloid albinos, at that.[25] Hunter thought he could prove the theory about the light-skinned Indians this way, but unfortunately these Lacandone Indians are *not* Mormons, which shoots all kinds of holes in the light-skinned good guys versus the dark-skinned bad guys theory of the *Book of Mormon*.

It is now an accepted fact of anthropology that the American Indian has the prominent features of the typical Mongoloid: sparse facial and body hair; head hair that is coarse in texture and is black and straight; a reddish skin; a wide-shaped head with prominent cheekbones; and having two distinctive features that are characteristic of the Mongoloid only; the epicanthic eyefold and the "mongolian spot" that appears on the backs of their newborn children.

This spot is absent in the typical Semite. Their eyes are deepset and their cheekbones hardly prominent, their heads much narrower than those of the Mongoloids. Their skin, far from having the auburn cast of the Mongoloid, is olive-gray; their hair is fine in texture, usually brown, and their bodies and faces usually covered with hair.[26]

Reputable archaeologists admit the possibility of the American Indian being the descendant of any or all of the following peoples: Mongoloids, Asian Negroids, Australoids, Phoenicians, Scandanavians, and/or Irish. The Mormon asks: why not Israelites? First of all, their doctrine teaches that the American Indian is of purely Israelite origin, at least before A.D. 400. Since the *Book of Mormon* mentions no non-Hebrew migrations, if any occurred, they must have been after the close of the *Book of Mormon*. Even the parties of the earliest secularly recorded visitors to the New World (Eric the Red in A.D. 950, Leif Ericson in A.D. 1000, Columbus in A.D. 1500) did not have the Mongoloid characteristics seen in the American Indian, so we can't blame them for breeding in these characteristics to the Lamanite race. Columbus and earlier visitors, in fact, give us no reason to believe that the Indians they found here were any different, as far as physical and racial characteristics, from the Indian of today.

If the *Book of Mormon* were right about the pure Hebrew origins of its people, then there would be only one way to explain how the American Indian became predominately Mongoloid in his physical characteristics. Mongoloids would have had to have come from some other place and intermarried with the Jewish Lamanites. Any such intermarrying would have had to have taken place between A.D. 400 (the close of the *Book of Mormon*) and A.D. 1000 (when the first recorded western explorers came to the Americas), and would have had to have been by such an overwhelmingly large number of Mongoloids that the Semite characteristics of the Lamanites would have had to have been *completely bred out* in just 600 years!

Even if there *were* Semite blood running in the veins of every American Indian, as the Mormons claim, this still would not prove that it came about via the improbable Lehite-Mulekite-Jaredite saga of the *Book of Mormon*. In view of the overwhelming evidence that American Indians are of Mongoloid origin, the LDS Church has had to backtrack on previous statements. While they still assure their Indian converts that they are descendants of the noble race of Lehi, they nonetheless have had to caution missionaries who might make wild statements about the Hebrew origins of all Indians. They say now that it is true that many of the American Indians are descended from Mongoloid types who immigrated, probably via the Bering Strait, from Asia. This theory gets the Mormons out of one pickle and into another, since it offers no explanation of where these Mongoloid types were during the 2600 years of *Book of Mormon* history, for their presence is not even hinted at.

I have heard it said by Mormons that these Mongoloids could have mixed with the Jaredites and Lehites from the beginning. This is not likely considering that Hebrews (such as the Jaredites and Nephites claimed to be) were forbidden intermarriage with Gentiles (like Mongoloids). The righteous ones would have obeyed this taboo all along. The Lamanites who repented became white and delightsome, so we can't look to them for the dark Mongoloid characteristics. And finally, all the wicked (i.e., dark-skinned) people were destroyed in A.D. 33, so any Mongoloid mixing would have to have come after that, since the inference is that all inhabitants of the Americas were white between A.D. 33 and A.D. 190.[27]

The typical Mormon dodge, though, is that any given native American could be Mongoloid alone, Semite alone, or a mixture. This reminds me of a time when I was in Oaxaca, Mexico, on vacation. In the crowded, noisy marketplace were many beggars, among them a light-skinned, hook-nosed man who appeared to be in his fifties and was extremely dirty. A Mormon companion took one look at him and said delightedly, "See! Now how can anyone say that the Indians of Mexico are not descended from the Jews?"

I wish now that I had told my friend what I was thinking—that the man looked like a vagabond, down on his luck, who had landed in Mexico in the course of his travels. Caucasian hoboes can be found in any marketplace of the world, be it Hong Kong or Quito.

Another major problem exists when the Mormon explanation of the Indians' dark skin is examined. According to Alma 3:6, the dark skin was a curse levied on the Lamanites for their transgressions, but it was to be taken away when the Lamanites accepted Christ. Perhaps some faithful Mormon Utes ought to remind their God of His promise, because their great-grandparents were baptized into the Mormon Church one hundred years ago, and their grandparents and their parents and they themselves have lived Mormonism as they have been taught. The only ones who are lighter in skin are those whose parents married Caucasians. The Mormon writer Sidney Sperry, though, said that "the process of change will be a gradual one."[28] The best with which we can credit this process is being slow in starting, because in the *Book of Mormon* it was accomplished in a single year.[29]

The Challenge of the Book of Mormon

Perhaps it was assertions like these that caused Mark Twain to describe the *Book of Mormon* as "chloroform in print." To the non-Mormon, the claims made for this book, and indeed its entire theological framework, are almost intolerable. The doctrines which are truly sacred to the faithful Mormon often appear as ludicrous to the Christian, and we must be cautious in criticizing them. After all, just because something seems humorous to us, it does not necessarily follow that it is wrong; that is, in conflict with the Scriptures. The Bible is the only reliable yardstick against which to measure seemingly false doctrine. In fact, we have been challenged by God who has commanded us to try every spirit because of the many false prophets that will try to deceive us (1 John 4:1).

A non-Mormon can read the *Book of Mormon*, marking the passages that seem to him to be outstanding in any way, and then leaf back through the book and see exactly what was going on in the mind of the writer. Just as we looked at the history or plot of the *Book of Mormon* a few pages back, let us now look at it from a doctrinal point of view.

The Doctrines of the Book of Mormon

The first few chapters set a scene that the writer hoped would put the reader into a receptive mood. By telling about Lehi, and tying the beginning of the story in with a period with which most Christians are familiar, he hoped to establish early the authenticity of this book. The first book division of this work is entitled 1 Nephi, and it is laden with prophetic dreams and visions designed to awe the reader, and disorient him so that dream and reality, truth and falsehood blend together in a dizzying swirl. We sympathize with the gentle protagonist, Nephi, and are led to mentally boo and hiss the wicked Laman and Lemuel, those embodiments of evil who tie up Nephi and mock him. We, with Nephi, are encouraged to rationalize his own cold-blooded murder of a man to steal Scripture from him—"better that one man perish than a nation should perish in unbelief."[30] We become so involved that we do not even question why such a wicked man had the holy Scriptures, and why a great prophet such as Lehi could not obtain even scrolls (which would certainly be less bulky for a transatlantic voyage), containing the Word of God, by more honorable means. We are caught up with the building of the ship, and in the glorious arrival in the "promised land." Just like in the Bible, we think.

So many mysteries we have long pondered are explained away in this *Book of Mormon*—the circumstances of the fall of Adam, for instance, and man's right to choose good from evil, the mysteries of the resurrection, and the reason for the multiplicity of religious denominations in our world.

Then the book seems to get down to serious history. This is the point at which most readers, Mormon and non-Mormon alike, will put the book down with a yawn. Wars and bloodshed spatter the pages. We are entrenched with the warriors. We see the people of Nephi rise in righteousness, and then go through cycles of prosperity, indifference, apostasy, and defeat by their enemies. Just like the Bible. All along, too, the Nephites are tantalized by the promise of a Savior, but—will they be destroyed by the Lamanites, or persevere and live to see His face?

A man is raised from the dead; a beautiful young woman dances so seductively that she is rewarded with the head of her enemy; and a persecutor of the church is struck dumb by the Lord and asked, "Why persecutest thou the church of God?" Kings are deposed and judges appointed. Just like . . . .

Then Christ comes to the Nephites—and He teaches them the same things that He taught the Jews, with a few important additions. The Nephites are righteous after His ascension, and live in peace for 150 years. Mormon and Moroni, though, record the evil that creeps into their society, and as Moroni starts to make an end to the Nephite record he suddenly remembers a few little details that really ought to be in the writings. (The author of the *Book of Mormon* wants to make sure that we understand the importance of these details—are they not the last words of a man doomed to die?)

And so the *Book of Mormon* closes with a tidying-up of several doctrinal points: how to ordain priests and teachers; the manner of administering the bread and wine; and teachings on baptism, faith, hope, and charity. Just like the Bible, or so the author hopes!

Godly and Ungodly Tenets

But an examination of the doctrines of the *Book of Mormon* in a little more depth shows that these teachings often add to those of the Bible, or worse yet, contradict it. One of the most basic tenets of Mormonism involves the fall of Adam, the necessity of opposition in all things, and the resulting free agency of man.

The *Book of Mormon* view of the fall of Adam leaves the Bible reader thoroughly confused with the definition of sin. According to 2 Nephi, chapter 2, Adam *needed* to sin for his and our own good. Without his eating of the forbidden fruit, we would never have been born. Eve would have grown old and died while he lived forever, alone. In the words of Mormon Sterling W. Sill, "Adam fell, but he fell upward." This concept is based on the Mormon premise that God put Adam in a dilemma that was literally unresolvable. He forbade Adam to eat of the fruit of the Tree of the Knowledge of Good and Evil, but he also commanded him to have children. Therefore Adam broke one law to fulfill another. In like manner, we should look forward to opposition in our own lives, that righteousness can come to pass.

The God of Mormonism is a vindictive one who makes pleasing Him impossible, giving commandments He knows men are incapable of keeping. He cannot be credited with the wisdom to resolve a situation like Adam's, only the foresight to see it coming—which makes Him doubly cruel. How different this is from the God of Christianity! "Let no man say when he is tempted, I am tempted of God: for God cannot be tempted with evil, neither tempteth he any man: But every man is tempted, when he is drawn away of his own lust, and enticed" (James 1:13-14).

If the *Book of Mormon* disagrees here with the Bible, it is certainly right on target scripturally regarding its teachings on the Trinity. Anyone who is familiar with the modern Mormon concept of the separate, anthropomorphic natures of God, Jesus, and the Holy Ghost is very surprised when he reads from the *Book of Mormon*. That's because it was written long before Joseph Smith formulated in detail his story about the first vision and the resulting doctrines on the three separate personages of the Godhead—for the *Book of Mormon* clearly teaches the unity of the Godhead. In 3 Nephi chapter 12, for example, the resurrected Christ appearing to the Nephites affirms over and over again that He, the Father, and the Holy Spirit are one. Of course modern Mormon teachings make light of this glaring discrepancy by saying that the oneness of the Godhead is only in purpose.

Another teaching that appears in the *Book of Mormon* is the prohibition of infant baptism. This was a very hot theological issue in Joseph Smith's time and it is obvious that he could not resist resolving the controversy with the *deus ex machina* of his book. In Moroni chapter 8 the writer not only condemns infant baptism as a "solemn mockery before God" (v. 9), but also condemns to hell its advocates (v. 14).

In like manner the *Book of Mormon* has the "definitive answer" on adult baptism. According to 3 Nephi 11:21-34, proper baptism has five features: (1) it is to be done for the remission of sins; (2) it is only for those of accountable age (who are capable of truly repenting of their sins); (3) it is to be accomplished by a single immersion; (4) it is to be performed only by one who has the proper authority; and (5) specific words are to be said at the time of the baptism ("having authority given me of Jesus Christ, I baptize you in the name of the Father, and of the Son, and of the Holy Ghost"—v. 25).

These instructions, as mentioned before, are found in the latter part of the *Book of Mormon,* supposedly given by the resurrected Christ. They aren't nearly so hard for a Christian to consider as the teachings of Nephi who in about 550 B.C. commanded his people to be baptized.[31] This amazing commandment is another of the startling evidences of the false nature of the *Book of Mormon* and its teachings—here Christ is consistently spoken of *in the past tense!*

Another procedure for an important ordinance of the church is found in 3 Nephi 18:5-29. Here we find the proper mode of administering the sacrament, as the Mormons refer to the Lord's Supper. Its outstanding features are: (1) it is only to be partaken of by baptized believers; (2) it is to be in remembrance of Christ; (3) it seals a covenant by the believer to do God's will; (4) it is to be partaken of often; (5) it is not to be partaken of unworthily; (6) it must be administered by someone holding the proper priesthood authority; and (7) it is to consist of bread and wine (not the water that is used in Mormon services today). These were the instructions given to the Nephites by the resurrected Christ Himself, but Moroni writing four hundred years later decided that Christ had left out an essential part of the instructions. So this Nephite prophet in Moroni chapters 4 and 5 gives the exact wording of the prayers to be said over the bread and wine (which no doubt gave Joseph Smith some problems in late 1830 when he "received a revelation" telling him to use water in the sacrament instead of wine).

The *Book of Mormon* also presents some amazing doctrines regarding the state of the soul after death. There's nothing surprising about Alma's teachings on the impossibility of repentance after death.[32] What *is* surprising is how Mormons get around this scripture and justify their baptism for the dead by saying that the "night of darkness" mentioned is not death, but a spiritual state wherein one loses the will to repent.[33]

The resurrection, according to Alma, will be a reuniting of the soul and body, and a restoration of that body to a perfect state, according to Alma chapter 40. The Mormon missionaries who baptized me said that this meant that every person would be resurrected with his body in the prime of life (as it was somewhere around the age of 25) and that all physical imperfections (blindness, lost limbs, warts, etc.) would be removed. Since as an adolescent I was a little selfconscious about my big nose (which I considered a definite physical imperfection), I often wondered if that would be corrected. That would be great, I reasoned, but would my friends be able to recognize me? Now that I am a Christian, though, I am glad that the Bible doesn't spell such things out in great detail, as does the *Book of Mormon.* I don't worry nearly so much about "mysteries" anymore.

But Joseph Smith wanted to solve them all, and, as his tool, he used the *Book of Mormon.* Alexander Campbell once noted that the *Book of Mormon* managed to comment on a surprisingly large percentage of the religious issues of their time.[34]

Some of these religious issues have been mentioned before (infant baptism, authority and ordination, the nature of the Trinity, free agency of man, the fall, the resurrection, etc.), but here is a more complete listing with representative scriptures for the reader who would like to research more: freemasonry (Helaman 6:21-29; 3 Nephi 4:7), spiritual regeneration (Alma 5:14-21), rights and responsibilities of civil governments (Mosiah 29:11-17), church government (Moroni 4:6-9), the atonement (2 Nephi chapter 9), eternal reward and punishment (Alma 41:3-7), Catholicism (1 Nephi chapters 13 and 14), fasting (Alma 17:3), repentance (Alma 5:49), "religious experience" (Mosiah 27:24-29), and transubstantiation (3 Nephi 18:28-30).

There is no doubt that Campbell himself heavily influenced Joseph Smith and thus the *Book of Mormon,* probably through Rigdon who was once one of his disciples. We see this influence in the use of the word "restoration" as regards church government and doctrine, in Joseph's insistence on the name "Church of Christ" (even though it was changed to its present title in 1838), and in a rabid opposition to a paid clergy.

In the *Book of Mormon,* too, we can see evidence of misconceptions that Joseph Smith had regarding the Indians of his day. Indians were thought of as "painted savages" who ate the flesh and drank the blood of their enemies, so it is only natural that we should find references to such things—warpaint in Alma 3:4, and cannibalism in Moroni 9:10.

It also seems that when Joseph Smith ran out of such stories in his own head, he went to convenient source books,[35] lifted a few stories, then embroidered them with extra details and changed or omitted other details. Probably his most convenient source book was the Bible, as is evident when we read in the *Book of Mormon* stories that mirror the Bible accounts of Salome, the raising of Lazarus, the conversion of Saul, and the allegory of the tame and the wild olive trees found in Romans 11. This last example is turned around by Mormon apologists who explain that Paul quoted from the Nephite prophet Zenos, instead of the obvious truth—Joseph Smith copied from Paul.

The Tanners in their research have found hundreds of parallels between the *Book of Mormon* and the New Testament, documenting in *Mormonism—Shadow or Reality?* four and one-half large two-columned pages of these parallels. And what is doubly impressive is that many of the *Book of Mormon* references, like the allegory of Zenos, were supposedly written long before their biblical counterparts—which makes many of our New Testament writers no less than plagiarists. They were so rude that they never even gave the *Book of Mormon* writers any credit when they quoted them.

The Three Nephites

Sometimes the *Book of Mormon* seems to want to be just "one up" on the Bible. An example of this is in the story of the three Nephites. Since some people have taken John 21:22-23 to mean that Christ promised John that that apostle would never die (in spite of even Christ's denial of such a thing), the *Book of Mormon* teaches that Christ promised *three* of His American apostles that they would never taste of death.

These three Nephites, who are unnamed in the *Book of Mormon,* were among the twelve disciples chosen by Christ in America. When asked by Him their hearts' desires, nine of the twelve asked to die quickly when their days of life and ministry were ended (at the age of 72), that they might rejoin Christ without delay. The other three, however, asked never to die but to stay on earth until Christ should return in His glory. Their bodies underwent a miraculous transformation that not only gave them immortality, but also immunity from pain and all sorrow except sorrow for the sins of the world. From that day forth they went out preaching and baptizing, and even though they were imprisoned and thrown into pits, dens of wild beasts, and furnaces, they escaped unscathed each time.

According to the legend, these three Nephites, along with John, are still alive today, ministering to the faithful, unbeknownst to most of the recipients of their good deeds. In fact, an aura of near-superstition has enveloped this legend, and even Mormon intellectuals speak lovingly of the three Nephites. One professor with whom I worked at BYU, Dr. Lyman Sid Shreeve, loved to tell the story about the time that he was accompanying a large group of students through the interior of Mexico. The entourage was traveling by train, and anyone who has ever ridden on a Mexican train can imagine the confusion of trying to coordinate a large group of young people, and get them all on the right cars with their baggage, cameras, and other paraphernalia. Dr. Shreeve was so involved that in the rush he misplaced his briefcase, which contained passports and many other important papers. All the students helped him comb the depot and railroad cars, but there was no sign of the suitcase. Dr. Shreeve loudly announced in Spanish to the merchants, beggars, and workers who watched nearby that he was offering "una recompensa grande"—a large reward—for the briefcase's return, but to no avail. Finally the group had to either reembark without the case or miss their train. All hope of recovering the briefcase was now gone. As Dr. Shreeve found his way back to his seat, there was the suitcase in plain sight on the chair everyone had thoroughly searched.

Dr. Shreeve to this day firmly believes that the briefcase was rescued and replaced by one of the three Nephites. Almost every Mormon, in fact, has a story of how a mysterious stranger helped a friend or relative, and they attribute many inexplicable good deeds to these three immortals. A Mormon researcher, Hector Lee, catalogued the different Nephite legends in his fascinating book, *The Three Nephites: The Substance and Significance of the Legend in Folklore.*

This is a beautiful legend, taught to children from infancy and treasured by its believers. Unfortunately, it is not true. The Mormon who would doubt this might ask himself the following questions: Where were these three Nephites during the time that the church (and its divine authority) supposedly disappeared from earth? The Mormons claim that this is what happened at the death of the last apostle (Jewish apostle, that is—excepting John).

The mission of the three Nephites was to convert souls to the truth. If they were immune to death and suffering, they should have been fearless and unsilenceable proclaimers of the gospel. Where are records of such men? The Mormons claim that authority to baptize and confirm was taken from the earth. Didn't the three Nephites and John have this authority? Why weren't the three Nephites, instead of the resurrected beings John the Baptist, Moroni, Peter, and James (along with John) chosen to "restore" the gospel ordinances? Indeed, why a need to *restore* such things at all, if they were in the possession of living men?

Archaeology and the Book of Mormon

Sometimes in speaking to people who want to know why I believe that the *Book of Mormon* is not of God, I find that the spurious nature of the ideas and the theology of the book are not the sort of thing that a stranger to its tenets can sink his teeth into. However, this is almost never the case when the subject of archaeology comes up. People of much education or little often have more than a basic knowledge of the principles of archaeological theory, and there many can begin to reason for themselves on the invalidity of the *Book of Mormon.*

Had the plot of the *Book of Mormon* been placed by its author in a more nebulous time period, and located more indefinitely as to setting, perhaps using archaeology as a tool to disprove it would not be so feasible. But Joseph Smith reasoned, and rightly so, that his nineteenth-century audience would want dates and times and places to authenticate the book in their minds. It is precisely this exact dating (time in the *Book of Mormon* is figured from either the Tower of Babel, the time of the departure of Lehi from the Old World, or the birth or death of Christ) and its geological landmarks (the Hill Cumorah, the "narrow neck of land," the "land northward," etc.) that make it so easy for the modern archaeologist to utterly atomize the foundations of this book.

Mormons claim that after the death of the last righteous Nephite in A.D. 421, the only Americans left were wicked, filthy, and ignorant (just the way the nineteenth-century reader viewed the Indians of his day). Archaeology has shown that, far from being the *end* of a period of great culture, this date marked the beginning of the emergence of the greatest pre-Columbian civilizations of the Americas.

Mormons take the great buildings and skilled artwork of these cultures as proof of the Nephite theory. In the front of older clothbound editions of the *Book of Mormon* (commonly given to proselytes by LDS missionaries), there are many beautiful color pictures of examples of the skilled craftsmanship of old American cultures. A picture of some gold tablets is inscribed with writing. The tablets were found in Persia, but no picture of such plates from either North or South America is offered. A picture is shown of bronze and copper tools which are mentioned in the *Book of Mormon,* but no tools of iron and steel such as are also described. A photograph of some small gold "plates" is obviously used for decoration and not communication. The textiles pictured are no doubt authentic, but are not of silk or wool as described in the *Book of Mormon.* A great Mexican mural is described as "Egyptian-like," but so are those of any early culture. And there are an abundance of carefully selected pictures of buildings whose cultural dates *do* fit in the *Book of Mormon* period— even though the buildings themselves are obviously not the work of any Christian civilization.

Must the faithful Mormon, though, identify the cultural achievements of American Indians before the 5th century A.D. as the work of Nephites exclusively? Yes, unless he would deny the *Book of Mormon.* While the Nephites were an industrious and creative people, the Lamanites were depicted by their biographers as being interested only in making trouble and war. Since these savages became expert at the art of killing, they managed to destroy the more peaceable Nephites and thus outlive them. This creates a dilemma. If they were by nature lazy and ignorant, they could never have achieved the high level of civilization of the Nephites. But how does one explain, for example, the advanced culture of the people of Montezuma?

Often Mormons look to their leaders for guidance in these puzzling matters. (I say puzzling with absolutely no sarcasm—imagine the plight of the poor Mormon who is asked to believe in something that has been the laughingstock of the archaeological community for years. We Christians know our anti-evolutionist teachings to be unpopular, but at least there *are* reputable non-Christian scientists who side with us!) At any rate, the authorities Mormons consult are of very little comfort to the doubting mind. The Brigham Young University archaeological society, which only recently has had the courage to come to grips with the *Book of Mormon* archaeological problem, has at various times through several spokesmen admitted that even in this advanced age that conclusive scientific proof of the validity of the *Book of Mormon* is utterly lacking.

Using Legends to Prove a Myth

Many are fond of claiming that Indian legends whose details concur with Biblical accounts of the Creation story and the great Flood are definite proof that the Indians learned these stories from their Israelite forebears. But if we accept as true the stories in the Bible, we know that since Adam was the progenitor of *every* people, then any culture could plausibly have in its folklore stories that resemble in some ways the true Biblical account. And bearing in mind the catastrophic nature of the flood which engulfed the *whole* world—why could not Indians know of this, too, being themselves as logically descended from Noah as we are?

Probably one of the greatest areas of contention surrounds a legend of the Mesoamericans, that of Quetzalcoatl, which Mormons would use to substantiate the *Book of Mormon*. From historians we learn that Quetzalcoatl was a folk hero who surfaced many times in legends and stories; so many times, in fact, that it is thought that he was not just one person but rather several people who claimed his name more as a title than as a personal appellation. This culture hero and ruler was credited by his people with the discovery of maize, and the development of the arts and sciences. According to legend, he even invented the calendar, and introduced metallurgy to his people. He was a great lawgiver and champion of justice. Ancient legends describe him as having fair hair, light-colored eyes, and a beard. When he last disappeared off the east coast of Mexico, his people anxiously looked for his return, and many years later mistakenly took the Spaniards to be his returning hosts.

Mormons claim that this old legend has its basis in fact. That much we might grant them, but the "fact" that Quetzalcoatl was Christ places Mormon apologists on a limb that futher investigation literally saws off from beneath them.

First of all, the timing of the Quetzalcoatl legend is all wrong. The first mention of him in legend occurs about A.D. 1000. If he were indeed Christ, did all Indians just suppress the legend of the Messiah until then?

79

That's not a very good way to keep a folk tradition alive! No, Quetzalcoatl was not mentioned before A.D. 1000 because that's when he, or the several people who constituted the Quetzalcoatl personage, lived. But surely, say Mormons, the fair hair, blue eyes, and beard marked Quetzalcoatl as a person from the Old World. From Europe, maybe, but I don't know of one reputable theologian who would try to maintain that Jesus Christ, who was a Jew, had blond hair and blue eyes.

But probably the one argument that would stifle the Christ-Quetzalcoatl theory is the fact that, though the American folk hero was reportedly responsible for many good deeds, he was also associated with such unsavory practices as idol worship, human sacrifice, and cannibalism. If the Mormons want to keep on with the theory that the Quetzalcoatl legend describes Christ, they're more than welcome to it.

Many Mormon writers have wisely chosen just to avoid the once-popular Quetzalcoatl issue altogether, but unfortunately have seldom chosen to correct the misconceptions of John Doe Mormon regarding the legends that he thinks "prove" the *Book of Mormon*. Surely this error of omission is as grievous as the sin of commission!

It is not only the Mormon writers who are guilty of this. It is the General Authorities, the spiritual leaders of the Mormon Church, who bear the greatest burden of guilt. They are content often to let Mormon writers make extravagant and unfounded claims for LDS scripture upon which many ignorant people base their faith and the hope of their salvation (as I did). Yet when the teachings of a writer are shown beyond doubt to be untrue, or based on false information, an edict comes out from Salt Lake City which says in effect, "This writer is not an authorized spokesman for the Church. He merely voiced his own opinions." In the past it has seemed that when writing of archaeology, a Mormon writer was allowed to write almost anything that made the Church and its books look good. Let him be proven wrong, though, and he alone is left holding the bag. Because he loves and believes in his leaders, the average Mormon writer just accepts his fate.

Fortunately, I never found myself in that position in writing for Mormon publications, but this has increasingly been the status of Mormon writer Hugh Nibley. Hemmed in on one side by the facts of archaeology which even he cannot stretch to fit the *Book of Mormon*, and on the other side by his stubborn support of Mormonism, he has resorted many times to what might be termed "negative evidence" to support the *Book of Mormon*.

Cities of the Book of Mormon

For instance, he says that there is no way of telling if any of the cities of the Nephites have been found in routine archaeological excavations.

"We have no description of any *Book of Mormon* city to compare with Homer's description of Troy. How shall we recognize a Nephite city when we find it?"[36] While it is true that no city as such has been described in Mormon writ, much appears there about Nephite, Jaredite, and Mulekite culture. Here is a checklist of what even the most faithful Mormon would agree should be evident in a *Book of Mormon* city.

1. It should by accepted archaeological standards fit in the time period covered by the *Book of Mormon* (circa 2200 B.C. to circa A.D. 425).

2. Its artwork will not be totally pagan in nature (although some non-Jewish or non-Christian artwork could be present due to some foreign inhabitants or trade with such people).

3. At least a few metal coins would be found in any Nephite city dated after the time of Alma (82 B.C.—see Alma chapter 11).

4. Some evidence of "reformed Egyptian" writing, such as that of which Joseph Smith left examples, should be evident.

5. Some trace of sheep, cattle, horses—domesticated animals—could be found.

6. We should see chariots as well as the remains of roads for them.

7. Permanent buildings such as described by the *Book of Mormon* or ruins thereof should be obvious, as even the BYU Archaeological Society maintains that the Nephites were not nomadic in nature.

8. The smelted iron, and weapons and tools made from it which are mentioned in the *Book of Mormon*, should surely have withstood the ravages of time.

9. And finally, there should be at least one example of the Old-World-type plants (especially grains) noted in the *Book of Mormon*.

Search for the Cities

Dr. Nibley should admit that no such city has ever been found. To find out why, let's examine the points on the checklist individually.

1 & 2. Though some ancient American cultures have left artwork and other evidences that indicate their civilized state as early as 100–800 B.C., such as the Tlatilcos and the Ticomans, there is absolutely no evidence that they ever reached the level of civilization ascribed to the Jaredites, who supposedly lived in the Americas from about 2200 B.C. to about 200 B.C. The Olmec civilization is dated as 800 B.C. to A.D. 100, but they had little in common with the Nephites of the same time period. The Teotihaucan people of central Mexico flourished at the apex of their civilization in the third and fourth centuries after Christ, but they too were patently pagan. Any of the other, later civilizations after the Teotihuacans were of course later than the *Book of Mormon* time period.[37]

Nowhere is there the slightest clue as to a Christian background in any artwork. Even the "tree of life" stela, a carving found in Chiapas,

Mexico, in the mid-sixties which was given a loud (but short-lived) heralding by Mormons as "proof" of *Book of Mormon* teachings, has been shown to have none of the connections to Mormonism once claimed for it.

3. The matter of Nephite coinage has consistently proved a dilemma to Mormon scholars. According to the *Book of Mormon,* the Nephites' monetary system was on a barley standard (that is, it was determined by barley, just as our paper money is backed by gold reserves). The money itself was in the form of coins ("pieces") made of silver and gold.[38] However, archaeologists tell us that not only have no native gold or silver coins been found in American excavation, but that there was no metal working at all before A.D. 400. And, *barley never grew in the New World* before the white man brought it here!

4. Many Mormons see similarities between Mayan hieroglyphics and the reformed Egyptian scribbles of Joseph Smith (which Charles Shook called "deformed English"). Most archaeologists see few such similarities. Furthermore, Mayan hieroglyphics developed independently about the time the *Book of Mormon* was drawing to a close, and had no apparent traceable etymological origins. Add to this the fact that Mayan was always inscribed on rocks (never on metal plates), even the earliest of which dates only from about A.D. 328.[39]

5. The *Book of Mormon* repeatedly refers to domesticated animals, such as cattle, oxen, sheep, swine, and goats. These supposedly were brought over on the ships with the Jaredites and the Nephites, but there is no trace of such animals before the coming of the Spaniards. Horses, too, play an important part in *Book of Mormon* warfare, but they were known in *Book of Mormon* times only as fossils of prehistoric date, as even Mormon archaeologists reluctantly admit.[40] The *Book of Mormon* mentions elephants which, too, were long extinct. (Or are we expected to believe that they came over on the ships also?) The *Book of Mormon* mentions two other animals whose existence no one can prove or disprove. They were called cureloms and cumoms, and what they were is anyone's guess—except that the *Book of Mormon* says that they, along with the elephants, were especially useful.[41]

6. The fact that Mormon teachers still try to support the unsubstantiated claims of their scripture is illustrated in the following quote from an LDS textbook: "Since the publication of the *Book of Mormon,* considerable evidence has come forth to reinforce its claims that there were horses on the American continents before the time of Columbus and that these people did know the principle of the wheel."[42] This statement is worded in a very sneaky manner. Surely, horses existed here before Columbus—*thousands of years* before him, and they were extinct long before Nephi put etching pen to plates. As for wheels mentioned in the

use of chariots—ancient Americans did indeed "know the principle of the wheel." And how did they apply this knowledge? They used rollers to move large stones, and they used spindle whorls in textile crafts, and very rarely they used a solid disc on toys. No spoked wheels; and no chariots. The great Yucatan highways many Mormons think were used for the nonexistent chariots were only for pedestrians—and even at that were built long after the *Book of Mormon* time period.[43]

7. One could reasonably expect to find some traces of the great temples and synagogues the *Book of Mormon* says existed from at least 570 B.C. to 91 B.C.[44] The temple built by the Nephites must have been a magnificent edifice. According to the account in 2 Nephi, it was patterned after that of Solomon, and its building materials included different kinds of wood, iron, copper, brass, steel, gold, silver, and precious ores. That the Nephites were able to round up all these materials just a few years after arriving in America (and, according to archaeologists, ignorant of the smelting process) is not as amazing as the contention that only seventy people were able to build it, whereas scholars estimate that Solomon's temple required the efforts of an estimated 163,300 workers and artisans for seven years.[45] While it might have been in the realm of possibility for the Nephites to have built such a temple (maybe Nephi just got carried away with describing it and exaggerated a lot), the idea of synagogues in the seventh century B.C. is implausible. The synagogue as an instution did not come into being until after the dispersion of the Jews, [46] a time after the last *Book of Mormon* transatlantic voyage from Israel, when Jews were scattered and not able to go to the Temple regularly. As we have seen, the Nephites had a temple and thus did not need the substitute of a synagogue. On top of all this, the word synagogue itself is a Greek word—how did it get on ancient American plates inscribed in 588 B.C.?

8. Another defeat for the *Book of Mormon* comes when we examine its accounts of warfare. Archaeologists assert that, during the *Book of Mormon* period, warfare was almost unknown in the Americas, except for ceremonial purposes (as practiced by the Aztecs). Inca warfare of course doesn't fall into the *Book of Mormon* time slot, and the warfare of the Mayans, which does, is characteristically disimilar to *Book of Mormon* fighting.[47] Weapons such as are described by the *Book of Mormon* simply don't exist. Steel, a substance frequently mentioned in the Mormon scripture, was unknown to Indians except as meteoric iron, and then it was treasured, not used as weapons. Metal armor[48] was likewise unknown in ancient America—there was no metallurgy in the *Book of Mormon* period. The bows and arrows mentioned in these same verses unfortunately were not invented in America until A.D. 1000.[49]

9. Using tools to "thrash" before A.D. 400 in America (as in Ether 10:25) is also an anachronism. What was there to thrash? Perhaps the

wheat, barley, neas (?), and sheum (?) mentioned in Mosiah 9:9? Archaeologists say that the first wheat and barley came to the New World with the Spaniards, and we must reluctantly pass on denying the existence of neas and sheum, and put *them* into the same category as the unidentifiable cureloms and cumoms. We are left with corn, the only native grain which did indeed grow in the Americas in the *Book of Mormon* time span, but which is not "thrashed" unless the Nephites knew of a process of which we are ignorant. Or maybe they just liked doing things the hard way.

In addition to the checklist points I mentioned that should be common to every Nephite city, the *Book of Mormon* also tells of several other features of *Book of Mormon* history that should be traceable by archaeologists. But neither Mormons nor non-Mormons can pinpoint with any security any single site mentioned in the *Book of Mormon*. The geographical descriptions, though vague, have caused Mormon geologists and archaeologists to identify the "narrow neck of land,"[50] the Hill Cumorah,[51] and the River Sidon[52] as being either in the Mexico City valley, or in Costa Rica. These are the places where they could logically exist geographically according to their descriptions. But Mormon proponents of these theories were blasted by Joseph Fielding Smith[53] who maintained to his death that the Hill Cumorah was in New York state, where Joseph Smith found the golden plates which had been deposited there by Moroni, and that the narrow neck of land is Panama. The seminary notebooks given to me contained maps which were a bit more cautious: *Book of Mormon* cities and landmarks were "tentatively" identified on two rather amorphous land bodies connected by a narrow isthmus that resembled the Americas only enough to tantalize the imagination.

This matter of the location of Cumorah is of no slight importance. According to the *Book of Mormon* over 230,000 persons lost their lives in the final battle at this hill. Why are their bones not found all over the Cumorah, New York, area? Mormons might say that Mormon 6:15 states that their bones mouldered and returned to the earth. All right, but what of their metal weapons? What of their chariots?

If Cumorah in New York state was indeed the site of so much history, the LDS Church could certainly vindicate itself and the claims of its scripture by excavating part of it. Surely the BYU Archaeology Department could be trusted by them to be respectful and thorough in their excavations—for they, most of all, have so much at stake.

Owning Up to the Truth

Why can't the Mormons own up that the *Book of Mormon* is a fraud? If any reader be still in doubt, let him send a letter to the Smithsonian Institute with the question, "Is the *Book of Mormon* confirmed by archaeological evidence?''[54] You will receive a mimeographed letter that states, in essence, that the historical picture painted by the Mormon epic is totally unlike the world of ancient Americans as they have found it in extensive excavations. Mormons have in the past claimed that many other records or inscriptions "proved" the *Book of Mormon*. Among these records were the Bat Creek Stone, the Kinderhook Plates, the Newark Stones, and the "Phoenician Ten Commandments" found in Los Lunas, New Mexico. All were highly touted, but all were forgeries. Why not place the *Book of Mormon* with them?

The answer is, of course, obvious. If the *Book of Mormon* falls, so does the entire Mormon structure. Surely the proofs presented thus far in this chapter should be sufficient to show any openminded person the false nature of this book. But let's assume, for the sake of argument, that we must not pass judgment on this book because of outside evidences offered in fields such as anthropology, archaeology, or geography. Let's look at the book alone, and with the Scripture it was supposed to complement, the Bible; for it is really not fair to judge a book of scripture on a set of secular scales only.

It must be admitted that many, many of the doctrines taught in the *Book of Mormon* would be welcome and familiar doctrine in even a conservative Christian church. Some doctrines, in fact, are exactly the same, even to the wording which matches sections of the King James Bible. What is taught in the *Book of Mormon* urges men to be righteous, to fear and honor God, and to live harmoniously with their fellow-men. This is done through direct teaching, like that of Lehi and Jacob; and it is also accomplished by showing examples of men, like Helaman, who tried to live as God would have them to live.

Contradicting the Bible

But sadly, in its efforts to supplement the Bible, the *Book of Mormon* often contradicts it. One good example of such contradiction occurs in Alma chapter thirteen, where the prophet Alma describes the priesthood. Even Mormons will admit that this chapter is one of the hardest of their scriptures to understand because of the confusing changes of tenses, and referral to the atonement of Christ and the Holy Ghost in the past tense (even though Alma supposedly lived one hundred years before the birth of our Savior). Alma got into even deeper trouble in speaking about Melchizidek whom he said "reigned under his father" (v. 18), in spite of the fact that the Bible characterizes Melchizidek and his reign as being "without father" in Hebrews 7:3. This chapter of Hebrews, when read carefully, completely negates the need for any such priesthood as is described by Alma, and says further that Christ *alone* is worthy of holding the higher priesthood—He did away with the need of sacrifice for sin with the offering of His own sinless life.

Another example of the *Book of Mormon* differing radically from the Bible is found in Alma 45:19 where it states that when Alma died "he was taken up by the Spirit, or buried by the hand of the Lord, even as Moses." At first glance it seems that the *Book of Mormon* writer was offering the reader a choice of believing *either* that Alma was taken up, or that he was buried like Moses. Not so, said Joseph Fielding Smith, who *equated* being "taken up" (or in Mormon language, "translated") with being buried by the Lord. In *Doctrines of Salvation,* he said that "Moses, like Elijah, was taken up without tasting death."[55] Contrast this to Deuteronomy 34:5-6 which states clearly that Moses died, and God buried him. Any other explanation makes mockery of God's promise to Moses that he would never enter the Promised Land. Surely God would not rebuke Moses by translating him!

Another serious error in the *Book of Mormon* appears in Alma 7:10. Here the prophet Alma in about 83 B.C. is supposedly prophesying the birth of the Savior, but he predicts that He will be born "at Jerusalem." Mormon commentaries gloss over this, saying that the whole area around Jerusalem, including Bethlehem, was called Jerusalem. But if the Nephites had, as they claimed, brought over their Jewish Scriptures with them on the brass plates, they would immediately have exposed Alma as a false prophet. Inscribed on those plates would have been the prophecy of Micah, which told of the future birth of the Savior in Bethlehem (Micah 5:2-5).

The signs which accompanied the death of Christ differ, too, when seen from the viewpoints of the Bible and the *Book of Mormon.* According to the Bible, there were three hours of darkness on "the whole land" (Mark 15:33, Luke 23:44) before the death of our Lord. Immediately after His death, there were earthquakes, and many saints were raised from the opened tombs. How different from the account in the *Book of Mormon!* The best that can be said for the signs supposedly seen by the Nephites is that they were only similar. The darkness they experienced there lasted three days, and was described as being a thick vapor that even prevented the kindling of light.[56] Instead of being followed by the earthquakes described in the Bible, this darkness came after the earthquakes which were also accompanied by torrential storms, the sinking of great cities, whirlwinds, and fires.[57] This is pretty amazing to a geologist, who knows that the Yucatan peninsula (where most Mormon archaeological efforts have been centered) has no evidence of the occurrence of earthquakes in A.D. 33—or any other time, for that matter; because earthquakes don't occur in this area of jungle that sits on a bed of solid limestone.[58]

In the Bible, the result of the signs at the time of the death of Christ was new life for some who had been dead. Contrast this concept with the actions of the vengeful god of the Nephites who destroyed—killed—every man, woman, and child whose wicked iniquities he wanted to hide from his face.[59]

How different from the gracious God of our faith who loved men enough to permit His Son to die for us! As Gordon H. Fraser pointed out,

> The whole argument of the New Testament is that men are not judged because of their acts of sin but because they will not receive Christ as their Savior. To destroy the wicked at the time of the performance of the act of redemption is to violate all the principles of the Christian Gospel.[60]

Another principle of the gospel violated by the *Book of Mormon* is its teachings on the establishment of Christ's church. In the Bible, Christ spoke of the establishment of His church always in the future tense, because it could not be established until after His death (see Heb. 9:15-16). For instance, Christ said to Peter, "Upon this rock I *will* build my church" in Matthew 16:18. But in the *Book of Mormon,* we are told that the church was established in 147 B.C.[61] In 73 B.C., believers in the New World were called Christians, according to Alma 46:15, in spite of what the Bible says about believers first being called Christians at Antioch (Acts 11:26). An anti-Mormon critic, George W. DeHoff, once asked the question, "Who is silly enough to believe there were Christians before Christ?"

The Book of Mormon *Versus the* Book of Mormon

These are only a few examples of the many ways that the teachings of the *Book of Mormon* contradict the teachings of God's Word. This is to be expected, though, from a "new revelation"—as Deuteronomy 13:1-4 tells us. We know to shun such false teachings, for they are not in harmony with the Bible. But consider the plight of the poor Mormons whose scripture not only contradicts the Bible, but also contradicts itself!

The first example of this occurs early in the *Book of Mormon* when we read in 1 Nephi chapter 8 the story of the dream of Lehi. In this dream, the waters which Lehi saw are identified as a "representation of the love of God" (11:25). Later in this same book, Nephi interprets this dream of his father's for his brothers, and changes his mind about the significance of the waters. "The water which my father saw was filthiness," says Nephi in 1 Nephi 15:27-28, "and so much was his mind swallowed up in other things that he beheld not the filthiness of the water. And I said unto them [Nephi's brethren to whom he was interpreting the dream] that it was an awful gulf, which separated the wicked from the tree of life, and the saints of God." Surely this description better fits the book in which it appears.

An almost humorous example of the human origin of the *Book of*

Mormon can be seen in Mosiah chapter 12. In order to appreciate this story, a little background information is necessary. The hero of this tale is a fearless prophet by the name of Abinadi who got himself into a lot of trouble by denouncing the evil deeds of the wicked king Noah. King Noah finally swore to kill Abinadi, so the prophet hid out for two years to escape the king's wrath. We read in Mosiah 12:1 about how he surfaced again: "And it came to pass that after the space of two years that Abinadi came among them in disguise, that they knew him not, and began to prophesy among them, saying: Thus has the Lord commanded me, saying—Abinadi, go and prophesy unto this my people . . . ." And how long do you think *that* disguise lasted?

In Alma chapter 31 we find that the prophet Alma and his brethren were appalled by the practice of the Zoramites, who had built a prayer tower called the Rameumpton which each Zoramite would ascend one at a time to pray. The worst part of this was the fact that each Zoramite offered the same prayer, word for word. Yet in chapters 4 and 5 of Moroni we are told the *exact wording* of the prayers to be said over the sacrament bread and wine (and just let one brave young priest of today try to change one syllable in a sacrament meeting!). But Alma knew the Zoramites only needed to be taught correct doctrine, so he "clapped his hands upon all them who were with him. And behold, as he clapped his hands upon them, they were filled with the Holy Spirit" (v. 36). And all this in 74 B.C.

A more serious error occurs in Mosiah 16:6-7 where the birth and resurrection of Christ is referred to in the past tense by a prophet who lived in 148 B.C. Apparently the writer of the *Book of Mormon* realized the incongruity of this, for he attempted to explain this confusion by adding that the prophet was "speaking of things to come as if they had already come" (v. 6).

Some people who read about these blunders wonder how they could have slipped under the noses of Mormons for so long. The truth is, as I will say many times, that most Mormons are like many Christians: they simply don't bother to sit down and read their scriptures often enough ever to be accused of being familiar with them. But some of the errors in the *Book of Mormon* were so obvious and so embarrassing that they were corrected after the book's first edition. On page 236 of this edition, for example, Christ was referred to as the "son of the only begotten of the Father" which of course makes Christ God's grandson. Christ was also referred to as the "Eternal Father" (later changed to the "Son of the Eternal Father"—1 Nephi 11:21), and Mary was called "the mother of God" (which now reads in 1 Nephi 11:18 as "the mother of the Son of God").

Probably one of the hottest areas of controversy rages around the

Book of Mormon's teachings on polygamy. Those unfamiliar with the teachings of this book might be surprised to learn that polygamy was flatly condemned in the book of Jacob. Jacob was a Nephite prophet who said polygamy was abominable (2:24), and equated the practice with whoredoms (2:28). Modern Mormons, though, twist verse 30 of this same chapter—"For if I will, saith the Lord of Hosts, raise up seed unto me, I will command my people, otherwise they shall hearken unto these things"—to provide an arrangement for possible future endorsement of the practice God considered so abhorrent.

The earlier Jaredites, however, had no teachings we know of on polygamy, but several things indicate that perhaps they were supposed to have practiced polygamy. The brother of Jared (the one who was so holy that he could behold the entire body of the Lord) had twenty-two children (Ether 6:20), and another Jaredite, Orihah, had thirty-one (Ether 7:2). That would be pretty hard for a monagamous man to accomplish (not to mention the wear and tear on the wife involved). In addition, Ether 14:2 states that in a time of warfare "Every man kept the hilt of his sword in his right hand, in defense of his property and his own life and of his *wives* and children" (italics mine), which certainly implies the practice of polygamy. Thus the teaching of the *Book of Mormon* on polygamy seems to be this: God permitted the Jaredites to practice it without comment; He allowed it but condemned it in the Israelites; and He forbade it to the Nephites, while saying that it might be all right some time in the future.

The writer of the *Book of Mormon* really got himself into trouble when he put Bible Scriptures into the mouths of *Book of Mormon* prophets *before* the Bible passages were written or spoken. In 1 Nephi 22:15 (written in 585-545 B.C.) the words of Malachi are quoted. Somebody should have told Malachi 150 years later that he was plagiarizing and that he should give the Nephites credit for what he was saying. But then in 3 Nephi 23:6, Jesus supposedly announced to the Nephite people that He was going to give them scriptures which He said "ye have not." What follows is a quote of the third and fourth chapters of Malachi. This is a paradox hard to resolve: the Nephites in 1 Nephi 22:15 quoted from the works of a prophet who was not yet alive, and then 585 years later are given part of this same prophet's writings because they left Jerusalem before he wrote them.

Another confusing passage is found in 3 Nephi 20:23-26, where Christ immediately after His resurrection appeared to the Nephites and described Himself as a prophet like Moses. So far so good.

Unfortunately, the passage that follows is Acts 3:22-26 (the discourse of Peter which was *his paraphrase* of Deuteronomy 18:15-19). In addition, Peter's discourse was given at least forty-one days after the resurrection of Christ.

There are many, many examples of how the *Book of Mormon* contradicts not only the Bible and itself, but also common sense. Common sense would tell us that there is something fishy about the story of the brother of Jared *telling God* how to light the barges that he and five other men would build (in an area completely devoid of timber), and in which they would sail three-fourths of the way around the world (and in which all would arrive at the same time and in the same spot on the other side of the world) as described in the book of Ether. Neither could a reasonable person be asked not to question how a decapitated man could raise up his hands and then *struggle for breath,* as described in Ether 15:29-32. We can't be criticized for doubting Nephite prophecy saying that the Lamanites would dwindle (1 Nephi 12:22). Did they dwindle? Then why are so many of them still around, and where are all the good Nephites? A lot of good their righteous behavior and white skin did them. If it were all a question of survival as a reward for choosing righteousness, then the *Book of Mormon* is a very convincing argument for a life of sin!

Praying About the Book of Mormon

In the end, though, Mormons urge proselytes to "prove" the *Book of Mormon* by prayer. This is not a unique request—the Quakers, Holiness groups, as well as all Latter-day Saint sects, encourage a personal witness that their churches are true. The *Book of Mormon* itself in Moroni 10:3-5 asks readers to test it by first reading and pondering it in their hearts, and then by asking God to manifest its truth (in other words, to give the reader personal revelation).

How different from the Bible! We are not told to pray about it. Christ never commanded us to pray about His Messiahship. His fulfillment of prophecy and the manifestations of His divine power, culminating in His glorious resurrection, negated any need to *pray about* His divinity.

Shall we light a match to find the sun? Shall God, who has given His only Son to die for us, be called upon to follow us around confirming or disproving every crackpot religious theory we contact? How much better would our time be spent in studying God's sweet Word, which would eliminate any doubts in our minds regarding the need for "further revelation"! Let us thank God for what He has given us, and not, like ungrateful children, nag Him about what He has not given.

Nor can we rely on our consciences—"feelings"—to guide us. Who can say that our consciences are a reliable guide? The Bible is replete with examples of consciences seared by sin. And we all sin.

God has given us several tools with which to fashion our spiritual lives. He has given us the master plan, the Bible. He has given us the confirming and guiding influence of the Holy Spirit. And lastly He has given us intelligence, the ability to perceive truth and evaluate falsehood.

We do ourselves a disservice and render ingratitude to God if we neglect any of these. A Mormon who is unsure about how he views the Bible, and afraid he might confuse his own selfish desires with the prompting of the Spirit *can* use his intelligence. I challenge any Mormon reader to look up all the scriptures in context which I have used in this chapter. Write the BYU Department of Archaeology and ask if there is any evidence of such things as iron, elephants, domesticated animals—any of the things the *Book of Mormon* mentions that I said didn't exist in America from 2200 B.C. to A.D. 600. And pray—not demanding that God will "reveal" truth to you, but searching the Scriptures and casting yourself upon the mercy of a just and loving God. Believe that the Bible is a sure guide. Read it without Mormon commentaries. Take the advice of James D. Bales, who said, "We cannot pray through, we must study and obey through."

A Final Look

The *Book of Mormon* has affected millions of lives, many of them for the better. So have the Koran, *Science and Health,* and the teachings of Buddha. But the *Book of Mormon* is a unique scripture which its adherents can change (and have changed) at will to suit their own purposes. Without the valuable checks-and-balances system of the many manuscripts and papyri available to the Bible scholar, the various editors of the *Book of Mormon* have through the years made additions, deletions, and corrections to their own holy writ which are much more significant in terms of doctrine than those they claim to have been perpetrated on the Bible. Even so, the inconsistencies which remain mark this book as being from a source other than God.

The *Book of Mormon* was a pioneer in the field of Mormon doctrine, the first of many scriptures which formed Mormonism as we know it today. But what is its place in modern Mormon thought? Surprisingly, it is not as important today as many of its critics think it is. In fact, most of the careful coaching that LDS youth undergo in learning about it is for the exclusive purpose of answering the objections of those who might perceive its imperfections and contradictions. For all the turmoil it has created, it contains no real earth-shaking doctrine other than its basic premise that Indians are the descendants of Israelites who saw Christ on this hemisphere. Beyond this, all the "good stuff" of Mormonism is found elsewhere in other "scriptures," where the reading is easier, the historical anachronisms less obvious, and the doctrine more personally applicable and exciting. At least that is how I saw it when I was a Mormon, and I know that my views were not uncommon.

Many people say that the proof of the *Book of Mormon*'s non-divine origin is in the fact that it is not beautiful in a literary sense. As a poet, I must disagree—in some places Joseph Smith rose above his ignorance of grammar and syntax, and in his fervor achieved a raw, wild sort of poetry. In fact, I think he himself realized the power he had with words, even early in life. In the twelfth chapter of Ether, he had one of the Nephite prophets apologize for the poor quality of his speech, but then in a burst of lyrical strength, Joseph put these words into the mouth of the Lord:

> Fools mock, but they shall mourn; and my grace is sufficient for the meek, that they shall take no advantage of your weakness; And if men come unto me I will show unto them their weakness. I give unto men weakness that they may be humble; and my grace is sufficient for all men that humble themselves before me; for if they humble themselves before me, and have faith in me, then will I make weak things become strong unto them.[62]

Joseph Smith was no John Milton, but this passage could be compared to Milton's sonnet XIX, on his blindness, which concludes:

> . . . God doth not need
> Either man's work or his own gifts; who best
> Bear his mild yoke, they serve him best. His state
> Is kingly: thousands at his bidding speed,
> And post o'er land and ocean without rest;
> They also serve who only stand and wait.

Both passages, diverse as they are in time and purpose, are "inspired" in the loose sense of the word: they are uplifting. Both strike a responsive chord in us because they provoke thought on an eternal truth.

But is the *Book of Mormon* as a whole any more inspired—any more *God-breathed-into,* to transliterate the word inspired—than the works of Milton? Which is more acceptable to a just God, the words of a humble man praising his Creator for His wisdom, or the words of a book that flouts God's Word and ascribes to *itself* His wisdom?

> Let no man deceive you with vain words: for because of these things cometh the wrath of God upon the children of disobedience. Be not ye therefore partakers with them. For ye were sometimes darkness, but now are ye light in the Lord: walk as children of light: (For the fruit of the Spirit is in all goodness and righteousness and truth;) Proving what is acceptable unto the Lord.
>
> —Ephesians 5:6-10

NOTES

[1]James D. Bales, *The Book of Mormon?* (Rosemead, California: Old Paths Book Club, 1958), p. 39.
[2]1 Nephi 19:10; Helaman 8:19-20.

[3]R. A. Torrey, *The Divine Origin of the Bible* (Chicago: Fleming H. Revell Company, 1899), p. 60.

[4]Joseph Fielding Smith, *Answers to Gospel Questions*, Vol. III, pp. 95-97, quoted in Ludlow, *A Companion to Your Study of the Book of Mormon*, p. 163.

[5]See also LeGrand Richards, *A Marvelous Work and a Wonder* (Salt Lake City, Utah: Deseret Book Co., 1950, revised 1963), pp. 66-68.

[6]Bales, *The Book of Mormon?* p. 259.

[7]Richards, *A Marvelous Work*, p. 69.

[8]Arthur Budvarson, *A Rebuttal to "The Problems of the Book of Mormon"* (La Mesa, California: Utah Christian Tract Society, n.d.), pp. 14-16.

[9]Mosiah 28:11-13.

[10]Reynolds and Sjodahl, *Commentary on the Book of Mormon*, VI, p. 87, quoted in Ludlow, *A Companion to Your Study*, p. 185.

[11]*Pearl of Great Price*, Joseph Smith 2:35.

[12]Mormon 9:32-34.

[13]As quoted in Ludlow, *A Companion to Your Study*, p. 1.

[14]Gordon H. Fraser, *What Does the Book of Mormon Teach?* (Chicago: Moody Press, 1964), p. 53. Now published under the title, *Joseph and the Golden Plates*.

[15]3 Nephi 9:18.

[16]3 Nephi 19:4.

[17]3 Nephi 19:4.

[18]Tanner, *Mormonism—Shadow or Reality?* pp. 94-95.

[19]Dr. Ross T. Christianson, *University Archaeological Society Newsletter* (Provo, Utah, January 30, 1960), Number 64, pp. 5-6.

[20]Jarom, v. 14.

[21]As quoted in Ludlow, *A Companion to Your Study*, p. 179.

[22]Ether 3:6-20.

[23]Ether 2:1-2; 6:4.

[24]Ether 8:18-26.

[25]Fraser, *What Does the Book of Mormon Teach?* p. 49.

[26]Ibid., p. 44.

[27]4 Nephi 1.

[28]Sidney Sperry, *Problems of the Book of Mormon*, pp. 222-228. (Now published under the title, *Answers to Book of Mormon Questions*.) "In a move that astounded Mormons and critics alike, the LDS Church released its 1981 edition of the *Book of Mormon* with the phrase, "white and delightsome" omitted in 2 Nephi 30:6, which referred to the change that would take place in converted Lamanites' skin in these, the last days. New editions now read, "pure and delightsome." LDS officials say this is a correction of an early printing error. (How did this error go undetected for 150 years with 12 prophets—including Joseph Smith who examined the 1837 edition personally, as its preface states—all claiming the *Book of Mormon* was correct?)

[29]3 Nephi 2:11-16.

[30]1 Nephi 4:13.

[31]2 Nephi 31.

[32]Alma 34:31-35.

[33]Ludlow, *A Companion to Your Study*, p. 103.

[34]Tanner, *Mormonism, Shadow or Reality?* pp. 63-64.

[35]Ibid., p. 88.

[36]Hugh Nibley, *An Approach to the Book of Mormon* (Salt Lake City: Deseret News Press, 1957), p. 373.

[37]All dates given are from *Precolumbian Art* by Francesco Abbate, general editor, Octopus Books, London, 1972.

[38]Alma 11:4-19.

[39]Fraser, *What Does the Book of Mormon Teach?* p. 54.

[40]Ludlow, *A Companion to Your Study,* p. 24.

[41]Ether 9:19.

[42]Ludlow, *A Companion to Your Study,* p. 95.

[43]Fraser, *What Does the Book of Mormon Teach?* p. 62.

[44]2 Nephi 5:16; Jacob 1:17; Alma 16:13; 23:2.

[45]Fraser, *What Does the Book of Mormon Teach?* p. 75.

[46]Orrin Root, *Training for Service: A Survey of the Bible* (student edition) (Cincinnati, Ohio: Standard Publishing, 1964), p. 56.

[47]Victor Wolfgang Von Hagen, *The Ancient Sun Kindoms of the Americas* (Cleveland: The World Publishing Company, 1961) pp. 159-161, 347-351.

[48]At least implied in Alma 43:18-21.

[49]Fraser, *What Does the Book of Mormon Teach?* p. 61-62.

[50]Alma 50:34; 52:9; 63:5; Mormon 2:29; 3:5.

[51]Mormon 6:2; 6; 8:2.

[52]Alma 4:4; 22:29; 43:22; Mormon 1:10.

[53]*Deseret News,* Church Section, February 27, 1954, pp. 2-3.

[54]Address: National Museum of Natural History, Smithsonian Institute, Washington, D.C. 20560.

[55]Joseph Fielding Smith, *Doctrines of Salvation,* II, p. 107.

[56]3 Nephi 8:19-23.

[57]3 Nephi 8:5-19.

[58]Fraser, *What Does the Book of Mormon Teach?* p. 81.

[59]3 Nephi 9:2-12.

[60]Fraser, *What Does the Book of Mormon Teach?* p. 84.

[61]Mosiah 18:17.

[62]Ether 12:26, 27.

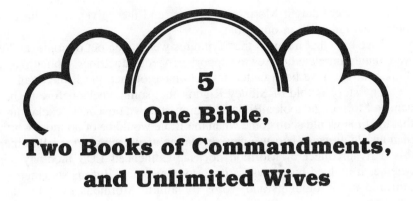

5

One Bible,
Two Books of Commandments,
and Unlimited Wives

For behold, I reveal unto you a new and an everlasting covenant; and
if ye abide not that covenant, then are ye damned; for no one can
reject this covenant and be permitted to enter into my glory.
—*Doctrine and Covenants* 132:4

It was still warm at the end of August, 1973. I sat in the crowded
classroom and looked at the other students who surrounded me. Some
were talking excitedly of their summer activities, of jobs, engagements,
and returning and departing missionaries.

I hoped no one would talk to me. I was only taking this religion class
because each full-time student at BYU is required to take at least one per
semester. It was hard enough for me to return to BYU with a tentative
decision that Mormonism was wrong. But I thought I had made a wise
decision in taking a New Testament class to fulfill that requirement. I
hoped thereby to avoid the issues that would arise in other classes, such as
"Pearl of Great Price" or "Teachings of the Living Prophets."

When I saw the teacher enter, I began to relax. He introduced him-
self, recognizing by name former students and smiling. "Welcome to
class," he said. "In this course we'll study the first four books of the New
Testament. Our text for the class will be *Jesus The Christ* by James E.
Talmadge. Of course, you'll need your *Book of Mormon, Pearl of Great
Price,* and Bible as supplementary texts."

How Mormons View the Bible

Nowhere else could you expect to find the Bible used as a "supplementary text" for a New Testament class. This incident is indicative of the way Mormons regard God's Word in the Bible. In looking
back at the instructions I received in seminary classes on the Bible, I
realize that we never studied, say, the Book of Ephesians or the Gospel of

John. We were taught Mormon concepts, and then given Scriptures to memorize and mark in our Bibles.

I see now that many of the Scriptures were taken out of context. We were taught unrelated verses to support erroneous doctrines. Sometimes I think it might have been better never to have opened the Bible at all.

The story is told of Sidney Rigdon that some weeks before he became a Mormon he took a Bible and threw it down on a desk, exclaiming that the time would soon come when the Bible would be of no more worth than an old almanac because new revelation would supplant it.[1] Whether this early architect of Mormon doctrine influenced LDS theology, or whether it molded his views, is open to conjecture. But his statement is mirrored in the thoughts and words of faithful Mormons from his day until ours.

When I was a Mormon, I didn't hate the Bible. But it wasn't my favorite Book of Scripture! It wasn't very definitive on Mormon doctrine, though it was often dependable as a back-up. I never reached the mental depths of the young Mormon missionary who, after a long discussion threw a Bible across a table to an ex-Mormon friend of mine and screamed at him, "Well, you can just *have* that stinking book!"

This missionary's point of view, though unfortunate, isn't too hard for a reader of the *Book of Mormon* to understand. Second Nephi 29:3 mocks the trust of the Bible believer by having him say mindlessly, "A Bible! A Bible! We have got a Bible and there cannot be any more Bible," with the Lord responding by calling such a man a "fool" (v. 6). Actually, says the *Book of Mormon,* the Bible is so imperfect that, instead of leading men to God, it actually causes them to stumble.[2]

The Eighth Article of Faith formulated by Joseph Smith states that the Bible is the word of God as far as it is translated correctly. To this might be added, "And as far as it seems to agree with Mormon theology." Wherever God's Word can be twisted to seem to prophesy the coming forth of Mormonism, or to support its theories on the "great apostasy," then Mormons accept it as true. Usually any Bible statement that flatly contradicts the ideals of their faith has either been publicly "explained away" by a Mormon leader or flatly changed or deleted in their other scriptures.

Mormons say that the many variations in different Bible manuscripts "prove" that Holy Writ is not above being corrupted. They don't take into account that the variations in Bible manuscript readings involve only one one-thousandth of the entire text, if we discount variations in spelling, punctuation, etc. And of this one-thousandth disputed part, there is no real doctrinal question left unresolved. As Luther A. Weigle said in *An Introduction to the Revised Standard Version of the New Testament,* "No doctrine of the Christian faith has been affected by the revision for the simple reason that, out of the thousands of variant readings in the manuscripts, none has turned up thus far that requires a revision of Christian doctrine.''

The Mormon Church looks at the denominationalism and religious division of the last few hundred years, and heaps it like useless garbage upon the doorstep of Christians, saying, "Your mistranslated Bible has caused all this. You took out important parts of the gospel, and have no prophets to give them back. You poor fools!"

But religious division can't be blamed solely on different interpretations and translations of the Bible. Is the present-day Bible responsible for the errors of Buddhists and Taoists? What about Moonies and Satanists?

Nor do living prophets guarantee religious unity. In First Kings 19 Elijah cried to the Lord, that of all the children of Israel, he, alone, was left to serve God. (Of course he learned later that actually seven thousand Israelites remained faithful; but even at that the number represented only a small part of the Israelite nation.) Let's face it, religious division has always existed—even when living prophets headed Israel. And no Mormon with his eyes open can deny the divisions over doctrine that exist in his own "prophet-guided" church. Walk into a crowd of Mormons and ask what each thinks of blood atonement, or the marriages of Christ, if you want to see religious division!

Furthermore, as Dr. James D. Bales has noted, "The majority of believers are not divided over what the Bible says, but they are divided over what the Bible does not say."[3] Both Mormons and Christians would agree that the Bible does not say anything about what formulates distinctively Mormon doctrine. The casual observer might wonder if the Mormons use the Bible at all. They do, but more in debating with Christians than in searching for doctrinal truth.

Bible Versions Used by Mormons

Mormons are limited to one single version of the Bible, the so-called King James Version. There are numerous reasons for this. First, many doctrinal tenets of Mormonism are built upon the foundation of the Mormons' peculiar affinity for and interpretation of Elizabethan English. Mormon missionaries are sent out with instructions to use only the King James Version when quoting from the Bible. Joseph Fielding Smith stated candidly that the only reason missionaries use this version is that it "gives a common ground for proselyting purposes."

Another reason Mormons cling to the King James Version so tenaciously is that it is quoted verbatim in many Mormon scriptures, especially in the *Book of Mormon*. Even the angel Moroni in speaking to young Joseph Smith used the language of the King James Version.

Joseph Smith sanctioned the use of this version through his example of using it, but he said that the German translation of his day was actually the most accurate in the world. That was of course before Joseph finished his own "translation" of the Bible. The official title of this marvelous work is *The Holy Scriptures Translated and Corrected by the Spirit of Revelation by Joseph Smith the Seer.* It is more popularly known as "the Inspired Revision," or the "Joseph Smith Translation." The official title brings up many questions in the mind of an observer. If the Scriptures were corrupted, were they still "holy"? From what language did Joseph "translate" them? And if they were in such need of being corrected, why didn't Joseph just do that to begin with, without bringing in the complicating factors of the *Book of Mormon?*

It seems that the *Book of Mormon* had pretty well served its purpose in Joseph Smith's doctrinal plans up until 1830. But at that time Joseph felt that he needed some Biblical authentication for the ideas on priesthood that he and Sidney Rigdon were in the process of formulating. His "inspired" Bible was the perfect vehicle. The Book of Genesis, with its familiar stories of the patriarchs and their open communication with God, was the section of the Bible most mutilated by Joseph Smith. The *Book of Mormon* idea of the "fall upward" of Adam was expanded upon, and the concept of a pre-existent state of all men was forced upon the Creation story. Adam was identified as a great priest, and the story of Enoch was stretched out into an entire chapter which would later provide the basis for "the United Order of Enoch," the Mormon Church's unsuccessful attempt at communistic living.

The idea of the Melchizidek Priesthood was validated by Joseph Smith's padding of the story of Melchizidek in both Genesis and Hebrews, wherein a priesthood succession from Melchizidek through Christ to modern man was implied—totally destroying the original intention of both Bible passages.

In Genesis 50, Joseph Smith could not resist the temptation of adding a "prophecy" foretelling that a descendant of the Biblical patriarch Joseph would arise in the last days. He would be named Joseph, and would be the son of a man named Joseph . . . just like Joseph Smith . . .

The mainstream Latter-day Saint Church has not in the past recognized the "Inspired Version" as doctrine, claiming that it was never completed by Joseph Smith, and that what was finished was later corrupted by uninspired persons. In recent years, its influence in Mormon thought has grown.

But according to Joseph Smith's own statement in the *History of the Church,* he did indeed complete the translation.[4] *Doctrine and Covenants* 124:89 commands that the translation be printed. I knew several faithful Mormons at BYU who read the Inspired Version to the complete exclusion of the King James Version, reasoning that the Bible had been corrupted for thousands of years, whereas the enemies of Joseph Smith had only a short time in which to do their damage.

Since, then, the Mormon Church is by its own admission left without a reliable Bible, surely one of the most pressing needs of the church would be to correct the errors in that Book. The job of course would ascribe itself to the present-day "prophet, seer, and revelator" of the church. Is there a need for true Scripture? Does the Mormon prophet have the power to so correct and translate? If he does, why have he and past presidents of the Mormon Church deprived their people of truth? Could not their time be better spent in revising the Bible than in signing temple divorces and entertaining Mormon beauty queens?

Joseph Smith did not include the Song of Solomon in this "translation" of Holy Writ, saying that it was "uninspired." Many Bible scholars might agree with him. But if it were totally secular and sensual as Mormons claim, why did Joseph Smith quote chapter 6 verse 10 from it in *Doctrine and Covenants* 5:14, 105:31, and 109:73? As if to deny this, the cross-references to these verses in the *Doctrine and Covenants* ignore their Bible origin.

Even after he completed his Inspired Version, Joseph Smith himself continued to quote almost exclusively from the King James Version. Even when it differed from the King James Version, he would not quote from his own translation.

The Mormon Church does not encourage Bible scholarship by the average member. They have too much to lose if their members learn to understand and love the Bible. A person who trusts in God's Word more than in the teachings of men is not easily manipulated by a bishop or priesthood leader. Psalm 119:160 tells us that God's Word is true from the beginning, and verse 140 tells us to love it because of its inherent purity. But Mormons call the Bible corrupted and misleading.

Common sense alone tells us that God would not leave mankind with an unreliable guide upon which to base both our faith and our judgment of future revelations, should there be any. A just storekeeper would not punish his clerks for selling underweight produce when he himself had provided them with an inaccurate set of scales. In the same way, our God is just and wise; He has not left us without inspired Scripture to teach us doctrine, to rebuke and correct us, and to teach us righteousness unto perfection (2 Timothy 3:16-17). We cannot blame the religious conflicts of the world on God's Word, but on the conflicts that exist within the darkened heart of man. Our lack of understanding of the mind of God actually prevents us from "proving" Scripture through feelings and sensations, as Moroni encouraged his readers to do. God's Word doesn't have to prove itself to anyone—it is inherently true. It is not the cloth to be measured—it is the unerring, finely-wrought yardstick of truth itself.

History of the Doctrine and Covenants

But the Bible was not where I sought truth when I was a Mormon. I often remarked to friends and roommates that the *Doctrine and Covenants* was my favorite book of scripture. It was so practical, so contemporary. Indeed, it is the only standard work of the LDS Church to be written in modern times. (Though I believe that the extra-Biblical scriptures of Mormonism were all products of the mind of Joseph Smith, the Mormons claim both the *Book of Mormon* and most of the *Pearl of Great Price* to be modern translations of ancient documents, whereas the *Doctrine and Covenants* is the record of recent revelations.) Mormons cherish the *Doctrine and Covenants,* regarding it as an accurate, chronological record of the adding of revelation upon revelation for the formulating and perfecting of the young church.

The first edition of the *Doctrine and Covenants* was published in 1833 under the title, *Book of Commandments.* This little volume, containing sixty-five revelations, is today a rarity since most of the copies of it were destroyed when a mob burned the printing office where they were stored. Ten thousand copies were originally intended for publication, but obviously only a small fraction of this number was actually printed. It was printed again in 1835 under the title *Doctrine and Covenants of the Church of Latter-day Saints.* This change of name was a great surprise to many members of the church, who maintained that God had Himself named the collection of revelations *Book of Commandments* in Section 1, verse 6. Church leaders justified changing the name by putting the former title in lower-case letters in later editions, making it seem like a description rather than a title.

The book was printed again in 1844, 1876, and 1921. Today's edition is basically the same as the 1921 edition, but differs *radically* from the *Book of Commandments.* A Mormon commentator on the *Doctrine and Covenants* says euphemistically of the *Book of Commandments* that it was "not complete, and its readings frequently differ from corresponding sections in later editions."[5] It would be more accurate to say that the *Book of Commandments*—supposedly God's Word to His infant church—was so changed, added to, and mutilated as to be almost unrecognizable when compared to today's *Doctrine and Covenants.* Melvin J. Petersen documented no fewer than 2,643 changes in the 1835 edition of the *Doctrine and Covenants* as compared to the 1833 *Book of Commandments.*[6]

Recently the LDS Church suppressed photocopies of the *Book of Commandments* which were prepared by a faithful member of the church. The Mormon Church is still afraid of the contrast between the *Book of Commandments* and the modern *Doctrine and Covenants.* They claim that additions to the *Book of Commandments* were due to Joseph Smith's adding of explanatory material to the revelations, and the deletions were those of non-essential parts. But contact with a *Book of Commandments* is bound to raise questions in the mind of a Mormon. Who gave Joseph Smith the right to add to God's Word, even if only to make it easier to understand? Or how could he cut out parts of scripture, calling them "nonessential"? It is a variable god, indeed, who gives a revelation that needs major revision two years after its publication.

Although much material has been added to the *Doctrine and Covenants* since its inception, seventy-five pages of material was deleted from the 1921 and all subsequent editions. This material was known as the "Lectures on Faith" and is now published in a separate volume with the explanation that it was never accepted as doctrine equal with the revelations in the *Doctrine and Covenants,* though they are "profitable for doctrine."[7] (Second Timothy 3:16 uses the phrase, "profitable for doctrine" as a definition of Scripture, but Mormons apparently see a difference in the two.) At any rate, many Mormons breathed a sigh of relief when the "Lectures on Faith" were removed from the *Doctrine and Covenants,* for they are surely some of the most boring reading ever produced by Joseph Smith.

Contents of the Doctrine and Covenants

Much more has been written about the *Book of Mormon* and the *Pearl of Great Price* by non-Mormon critics than has been written about the *Doctrine and Covenants.* One reason is that the *Doctrine and Covenants* makes no claims to antiquity, as do the other books which can be so easily disproven in this day of the modern sciences of archaeology and linguistics. The bulk of the *Doctrine and Covenants* is usually studied as much for history as for doctrine by non-Mormons. Sometimes, though, it is nearly ignored. In his book, *Joseph Smith, Seeker After Truth,* John A. Widtsoe once stated that

> This book itself is a witness for the truth of the Prophet's claims. The explanation of old doctrines and presentation of new ones are convincing evidence of their divine origin. Enemies of the Church have rather carefully avoided the discussion of this book. They have been afraid of it.[8]

To take issue with Apostle Widtsoe, I must point out that anti-Mormon writers aren't afraid of it at all. Most are bored by its oppressive style, as are many Mormons. But the *Doctrine and Covenants* is a veritable storehouse of proof of the falseness of Latter-day Saint revelation. True, Mormonism's critics give more emphasis to the other "scriptures," but this often arises out of the non-Mormon's exaggerated view of the importance of the *Book of Mormon* to the average church member. However, it bears repeating that more of today's practices and doctrines within

Mormonism arise from the teachings of the *Doctrine and Covenants* than from either the *Book of Mormon* or the *Pearl of Great Price*. Ask the average Mormon to tell you the outstanding doctrines of the *Book of Mormon,* and he'll get to "opposition in all things" and stop. Ask him the same about the *Pearl of Great Price* and he'll probably be stumped after the Joseph Smith story and the concept of the pre-existence. But every LDS child knows the *Doctrine and Covenants* to be the source of such teachings as the Word of Wisdom, the three degrees of heaven, revelations on polygamy, baptism for the dead, priesthood ordination, how to tell a good angel from a bad one, etc., etc., etc.

But the truth is, most of the *Doctrine and Covenants* is just plain uninteresting. Early sections especially seem like a hodge-podge of Bible verses picked indiscriminately from the Old and New Testaments, interlaced with commands, cajolings, and scathing rebukes, all aimed at anyone who crossed the path of Joseph Smith. Overall, the *Doctrine and Covenants* covers a wide assortment of subjects, ranging from personal instructions to doctrinal teachings on the Holy Ghost, the fall, the atonement, salvation for the dead, eternal marriage, repentance, baptism, the priesthoods, other scriptures, the economic status of man, and our final destiny. It is a book of instructions and invectives, of pleas and unbelievable promises.

All of this is shown, in the *Doctrine and Covenants,* as the result of revelation from God. A question many non-Mormons ask is, "What sort of revelation? Voices, or visions, or what?" Actually, the revelations in the *Doctrine and Covenants* came through four different methods. One way that Joseph Smith said he received revelation was directly: that is, the Lord spoke directly to him. He also claimed that some of the revelations came through the Urim and Thummim. A notable example of this is his use of the magic spectacles to translate an original document written by John the Beloved (recorded in Section 7). The Urim and Thummim, however, was not used after 1829 when Joseph Smith claimed to have received the Melchizidek, or higher, Priesthood. Joseph Smith said some of the revelations came through visions. Another method for receiving revelations was through direct conversation and visual contact with a heavenly messenger, such as Peter or Moroni.

What the Doctrine and Covenants *Teaches*

It is very difficult to provide a simple "overview" of a book as complex as the *Doctrine and Covenants.* What follows here is a roughly chronological outline of the high points of this book. An entire book could be written on its doctrinal ramifications. A discussion of the effects of some of these revelations on modern Mormonism will follow in later chapters.

The *Doctrine and Covenants* is divided not into chapters, but into "sections." Each section is numbered and divided into verses, and has a short heading that describes briefly the circumstances surrounding the receipt of the revelation, including the date and a synopsis of its contents. Almost all modern editions of the *Doctrine and Covenants* are bound together with the *Pearl of Great Price* in one volume. The *Doctrine and Covenants* has a short concordance, a chronology of the revelations, and introductory material attesting to their validity.

It is obvious to even the most casual reader of the book that its first sections—notably 3, 5, 10, and 17—have as their outstanding purpose the *Validation of the Book of Mormon,* and through it, the standing of Joseph Smith as a prophet. Other introductory sections—2, 13, and 27—purport to be the *words of angels.* In Section 2 Moroni spoke concerning the Aaronic Priesthood, and in Section 13 John the Baptist ordained Joseph and Oliver Cowdery to the Melchizidek Priesthood. In Section 27 Joseph was told by another angel that he was to use water, instead of wine, in the church's sacrament services.

The *parchment record written by John the Beloved* and translated via the Urim and Thummim as Section 7 has already been mentioned. Later, in Section 93, verses 16-18, it says that "the fullness of the record of John" is yet to be revealed. Just what was this record and where is it now? The *Doctrine and Covenants Compendium* gives the reader two options. Either God actually gave John's parchment to Joseph Smith to translate; or Joseph Smith simply looked into the Urim and Thummim, and the parchment and its words became visible there. "It would seem natural . . . to assume that the parchment was still hidden in a safe place, possibly somewhere in the Near East."[9] Of course, it is obvious why Joseph Smith never produced John's parchment. Its authenticity could have been immediately ascertained by the Greek scholars of his day. Whereas Joseph could be a little more daring with Egyptian (which he believed to be untranslatable), and with "reformed Egyptian" (which everyone knows to be untranslatable), he couldn't afford to try to fake ancient Greek. So it stayed "hidden away," and the translated portion tells us that Christ did indeed promise John eternal life, and that he, like the three Nephites, is alive and well among the Jews, preparing them for the great "gathering" when they shall regain their fatherland.[10]

Of more than passing interest are Sections 13, 65, and 109, which are *prayers.* The last two illustrate especially well Joseph's gift with words, and his use of "revelation" to jab at his enemies (see 109:29).

Revelations

A great many of the revelations of the *Doctrine and Covenants* are *addressed to certain individuals,* some of whom went on to be leaders of

103

the church, and some who left it completely. Mormons see these revelations as a great example of a personalized gospel. In them, the God who knows men's hearts is said to give specific instructions to each one who needed it.

But a non-Mormon sees other things in these individualized revelations—they come across as tongue-lashings backed up by threats of divine and eternal punishment. A prime example of this is found in Section 10, wherein *Book of Mormon* witness Martin Harris, who lost a part of the Nephite manuscript, was called "wicked," and later, by implication, a liar (vv. 1, 28).

Did Joseph Smith *use the revelations he received to exalt himself?* Section 21 commanded him to keep a record wherein he would be called "a seer, a translator, an Apostle of Jesus Christ, and an Elder of the Church" (v. 1). (A Christian might compare such gasconade with the modest statements of Paul about himself.) Joseph Smith even used the revelations of the *Doctrine and Covenants* to command a house to be built for himself (41:7).

Joseph Smith also *used the revelations to "answer" questions* he had about the Bible. Section 77 purports to be no more and no less than a question-and-answer quiz of God. Joseph asked questions about the meanings of several of the symbols of the Book of Revelation. The literal interpretations he ascribed to many of these symbols betrays his lack of understanding of figurative language as used by John.

Sections 74, 86, and 113 also claim to be *explanations of Bible verses.* The question of just how an unbelieving spouse is sanctified by the believing one, and how their children are made holy is dealt with in Section 74. In Section 86 the parable of the wheat and the tares is made to apply to priesthood holders (wheat) and the blessings promised to them. Section 113 also forces the concept of priesthood onto several unsuspecting, isolated verses from Isaiah. In fact, much of the *Doctrine and Covenants* has to do with the concept of priesthood, but that whole issue is so complex that it will be dealt with in detail in another chapter.

The *mechanics of how to run a church* is the subject of many sections of the *Doctrine and Covenants.* Section 20, for example, speaks definitively on baptism, how to administer the sacrament, the duties of elders, priests, teachers, deacons, and members; the function and timing of conferences, and the blessing of children. Section 27 authorizes the use of water instead of wine in the sacrament. Section 42 deals with church discipline, and 107 with priesthood offices and duties.

Four of the sections of the *Doctrine and Covenants* are records of visions. Section 76 is perhaps one of the most basic in LDS theological teachings on Satan, hell, and heaven, and must be read if one is to understand the official Mormon belief on these subjects. The vision in

Section 110 records the appearance of Christ, Moses, Elias, and Elijah in the Kirtland temple. Joseph Smith's "Vision of the Celestial Kingdom," and Joseph F. Smith's "Vision of the Redemption of the Dead" were made canonical in 1976 and added to the *Doctrine and Covenants.*

Section 78 is of great interest because of the *foreign-sounding names* which were assigned to the persons mentioned in this section and in Sections 82, 92, 96, 103, 104, and 105. Such names as "Baurak Ale" for Joseph Smith prevented the church's enemies from knowing the intentions of plans such as Section 103 detailed—the recovery by force of the land they'd left in Missouri.

The famous *Civil War prophecy* of Section 87 has for years been touted by Mormons as proof positive of Joseph's powers as a prophet. However, the force of this assertion is lessened considerably when one considers that even Mormons admit the prophecy was not put into print until 1851. Besides, a careful and objective reading of the entire "prophecy" would lead one to believe that the coming Civil War would mark the beginning of an era of continuous war on "all nations"—which has certainly not proven to be the case.

Health

Probably the most famous and far-reaching revelation to touch the Mormon people as a whole since its introduction is found in Section 89. Here the Word of Wisdom—the *health law*—is found. A lot of misunderstanding surrounds the non-Mormon's concept of what the Word of Wisdom entails. Originally, it was not given as a commandment (v. 2), but as "a principle with a promise" (v.3), a sort of bargain with God for health. Because of the restrained language of the section, many Latter-day Saints have regarded it as optional. But any modern-day Mormon who wants to enter a temple must practice its principles.

Basically, the Word of Wisdom forbids the use of "wine or strong drink" for any purpose other than in the sacrament or for washing one's body; it forbids tobacco for any purpose other than as a poultice for bruises, and for "all sick cattle"; and it says that "hot drinks" are neither for the body nor the belly. It encourages the use of fruits and herbs in season, but cautions man to use meat sparingly. It says that wheat is for mankind, corn is for oxen, oats is for horses, rye is for swine and birds, and barley is for "all useful animals." Those who keep the Word of Wisdom are promised many things: health, wisdom, knowledge, freedom from fatigue, and protection from the destroying angel.

The background for this revelation is an interesting one. Brigham Young said that it was precipitated by Emma Smith's complaining about the mess she had to clean up after Joseph's friends got together and spat tobacco all over the floor. Joseph, too, was disgusted by the clouds of smoke from the men's pipes, so he "inquired of the Lord" as to the use of tobacco.

The resulting revelation dealt with more than just tobacco. But it also raised some questions. In 1842 Hyrum Smith defined the "hot drinks" mentioned in Section 89 as coffee and tea. Thus, the average Mormon's concept of the substances forbidden by the Word of Wisdom is limited to liquor, tobacco, coffee, and tea.

Modern scientific research has indeed borne out Joseph Smith's contention that alcoholic beverages, as well as coffee, tea, and tobacco are devastating in their effect upon the human body. The Word of Wisdom has become the badge of faithful Mormons of all ages, and it is not merely coincidental that Mormons live longer, healthier lives than their Gentile counterparts. I thank God for their health, and fervently desire that Christians would become as sensitive to the care of their "temples" (1 Cor. 3:16) as our Mormon friends. Too often, though, the emphasis in observing the Word of Wisdom is focused on the "four forbiddens." The definition of "hot drinks" as coffee and tea in particular opens several questions.

Can one drink iced coffee and iced tea? The answer is no. In addition, Heber J. Grant, a former president of the church, advised against the use of another hot drink, cocoa. Many Mormons do not use chocolate in any form. I did not use it for eight of the ten years I was a Mormon, though it was served freely in the dormitory cafeterias at Brigham Young University. Most faithful Mormons do not drink cola drinks, either.

So what do chocolate, cola, and iced coffee have in common? None are hot drinks. But all contain caffeine. Thus, the measure of a food's prohibition is not its being a hot liquid, but its caffeine content. Thanks, Joseph Smith, for the Word of Wisdom, but I don't think you can be given full credit for recognizing the harmful effects of caffeine in all its manifestations! Only the most accommodating person could extract a prohibition against caffeine from the phrase, "hot drinks." Faithful "temple-recommend" Mormons can drink hot Postum or herb teas, but have shamed their families by drinking a Coca-Cola.

No one would argue with the Word of Wisdom's condemnation of the poison, alcohol. But in the Word of Wisdom its use is encouraged as an agent in washing the body. I am as much puzzled by this as by the Word of Wisdom's advocating the use of tobacco on bruises, and for all the diseases of cattle. A great emphasis is placed on what Mormons should *not* eat or drink, but the profitable use of these substances as advised in the *Doctrine and Covenants* is virtually ignored (maybe because they don't work?). Also often passed over is the Word of Wisdom's warning against the over-use of meat. As a Mormon, I would eat meat at only one meal a day, but of all my many acquaintances in the densely-Mormon population of Brigham Young University, there were only a few who consciously limited the use of meat because of the Word of Wisdom.

Church leaders were adamant in their condemnation of the liquor and tobacco industries. The Word of Wisdom, according to its own admission, was given "in consequence of evils and designs which do and will exist in the minds of conspiring men" (89:4). Dr. Sperry, in his *Doctrine and Covenants Compendium,* characterized the directors of the tobacco industry as "men without conscience . . . moral cowards,"[11] and mentioned the "lack of ethics and morality"[12] of the liquor industry. But it is a documented fact that Joseph Smith sold liquor in Nauvoo, and Brigham Young in Utah built a distillery and sold alcoholic beverages.[13] At one time, the largest liquor business in the state of Utah was run by the Mormon Church-owned department store, Zion's Cooperative Mercantile Institution (ZCMI).[14] Joseph F. Smith confirmed the fact that ZCMI sold liquors but excused it by saying that if any unfortunate who depended upon liquor didn't buy it at ZCMI, he would just go somewhere else.[15] So much for being your brother's keeper!

Section 93 is perhaps the most definitive in LDS scripture on *the relationship of truth, knowledge, and intelligence;* and the source of the famous assertion that "the glory of God is intelligence" (v. 36). It is also one of the few statements by Joseph Smith on philosophical tenets that makes any sense at all to a non-Mormon.

A revelation of unusual form is found in Section 102. This consists of the *minutes of a meeting.* Unlike other revelations which say, "thus saith the Lord," this section's only pretension to inspiration is the fact that it *is* included in the *Doctrine and Covenants,* and is thus scripture. It is signed by two clerks, and deals with the organization of a high council, and discipline therein.

Prophecies

Another distinctive organization spoken of in the *Doctrine and Covenants* is the *United Order.* Also known as the Order of Enoch, the United Order was an altruistic, communistic venture in which all participants were "to have equal claim upon properties, for the benefit of managing the concerns of your stewardship" (82:17). It was patterned after the Mormon concept of the people of Enoch, who with him were taken up to heaven without tasting death because they all shared equally amongst themselves. The United Order was described in Section 78 verses 8-16 as an "eternal" covenant that could never be broken. It was a considerable failure for the many causes previously discussed in Chapter Three.

Much of the *Doctrine and Covenants* is devoted to the concept of a *new Jerusalem.* In section 57, Missouri is designated as "the land I have appointed and consecrated for the gathering of the saints . . . the land of promise, and the place for the city of Zion" (vv. 1 and 2), Mormons were encouraged to buy all the land they could around Independence ("the center place"). Section 84 prophesied (with two "verilies") that a temple would be built there "in this generation" (vv. 4 and 5). In spite of the obvious failure of this prophecy, Mormons still look to Missouri as the site of the new Jerusalem, even with the knowledge that the site dedicated for the temple by Joseph Smith is now tenaciously owned by a Latter-day Saint splinter group.

An area in Daviess County, Missouri, is identified in Section 116 as "Adam-Ondi-Adam," the site where Adam supposedly built the first altar after the expulsion from Eden, and where he blessed his children before his death (107:53). This will also be the place where a great council meeting will be held just before the second coming of Christ, which will be attended by Michael, Gabriel, and other holders of the priesthood keys who will relinquish those keys to Christ.

Conflicts

One thread that runs consistently through the *Doctrine and Covenants* is the *theme of persecution* and the Mormon response to it. The beginning of Section 98 commands courage and patience in regard to their enemies. Section 122, which is surely one of the classic examples of Joseph Smith's artistry with words, advises him that persecution is for the good of the one persecuted, for it always results in valuable experience.

Two sections of the *Doctrine and Covenants,* 127 and 128, are in the form of *letters* from Joseph Smith to the church at large. In Section 127 verse 2 he comments that "deep water is what I am wont to swim in," and then he plunges into the doctrine of baptism for the dead. He details the need for witnesses and recorders of such baptisms, and even gives exact instructions for the location of the fonts in the temples.[16] The remainder of Sections 127 and 128 are taken up with Joseph Smith's twisting of Bible verses to make them seem to support baptism for the dead, and is an excellent example of the unfettered magniloquence of the literary prophet.

Since most of the *Doctrine and Covenants* was composed during the time that Mormons were experiencing *conflicts with the state and federal governments,* it is interesting to note Sections 98 and 134. Section 101 states that God Himself established the American Constitution (v. 80), and the people of the Church were encouraged in Section 98 to uphold it. A more detailed statement on the church's beliefs regarding its responsibilities to the government and the government's duties to the church is found in Section 134, which was composed by Oliver Cowdery.

Sections 129, 130, and 131 are *gems of Mormon doctrine.* Section

129 tells the vision-prone Mormon people how to know if a supernatural being who appears to them is from God or from Satan. (Offer such a being your hand. If he takes it, and you don't feel anything, you're in trouble.) Section 130 deals with the dwelling place of God and the angels, identifying it as a faraway planet, and speaks of the importance of gaining knowledge. It also deals with the physical nature of the bodies of God and Christ, and other matters. Section 131 describes the three degrees of glory in heaven, and defines spirit as "refined matter." It also deals with a little-understood (even by Mormons) doctrine known as having one's "calling and election made sure," as a result of what is called "the more sure word of prophecy." This is an absolute assurance from God of salvation, and guarantees that one's soul cannot be lost, unless one commits murder.

Section 135 was written by John Taylor, and is a *narration of the events surrounding the deaths of Joseph Smith and his brother Hyrum.* The bitterness and loss felt by Joseph's bereaved followers can be read even between the lines, and no one, no matter how little divinity he might impute to the life and works of Joseph Smith, can read this moving account without wishing that Joseph Smith had died a more peaceful death.

Section 136 was written by Brigham Young, and is his only contribution to the book. It contains *instructions for the trek westward* and definitely reflects the personality of Young, even though it is supposedly the Word of the Lord. It gives practical, definitive directions for the organization of the traveling companies; with a minimum of the scripturalistic verbiage that characterizes Joseph's writings tucked in at the end so that no one would mistake it for anything less than *A Revelation.*

Polygamy

I have saved until last the most controversial section of the *Doctrine and Covenants* because its final culmination comes at the end of the volume. Section 132, though, started the whole issue, and purports to be God's explanation of why ancient prophets were allowed to have more than one wife and concubines. The revelation is in the form of an answer to Joseph's question. Verse 1 sets the tone for the entire section by assuming that God approved heartily of the "doctrine" of *polygamy:*

> Verily, thus saith the Lord unto you my servant Joseph, that inasmuch as you have inquired of my hand to know and understand wherein I, the Lord, *justified* my servants Abraham, Isaac, and Jacob, as also Moses, David, and Solomon, my servants, as touching the principle and doctrine of their having many wives and concubines (italics mine).

Thus, with no prefatory argument, Joseph Smith resolved for the Mormon mind the question of whether or not God approved of the Old Testament practice of plurality of wives. Joseph bypassed the whole issue by saying that not only did God tolerate it, but that He *required* it.

This argument is suspended (securely, some Mormons think) from Joseph Smith's version of the story of Abraham. According to Section 132 verse 35, God commanded that Abraham take Hagar the handmaid of his wife as a concubine so that he could have the seed that God had promised him.

But anyone who reads Genesis 16 can see the holes in this argument. God didn't tell Abram to take Hagar, Sarai did; and in verse 5 of Genesis 16 she admits that this, in hindsight, wasn't a very good idea.

The *Doctrine and Covenants* says that the plural wives of Isaac, Jacob, Moses, and Solomon were also commanded of God (vv. 37-38), and that all of David's wives except the wife of Uriah were given to him by God. But in no modern translation of the Bible can we find an example of where God commanded a man to take more than one wife. There is a possible exception to this in the case of a levirate marriage, wherein the next of kin of a man who died childless would marry his kinsman's widow (Deut. 25:5-6; see also Gen. 38:1-26 for the story of Tamar).

Of course, the practice of concubinage was as widespread in the Old Testament as the practice of polygamy. In contrast to a polygamous wife, who was legally married to her husband, a concubine simply lived with him.[17] According to Section 132, God was supposed to answer Joseph's questions about concubinage too—but this practice as pertaining to modern times is neither condoned nor condemned.

Section 132 does not make polygamy an optional marital relationship. It is called a "new and everlasting covenant" in verse 4, which states that "if ye abide not that covenant, then ye are damned, for no one can reject this covenant and be permitted to enter into my glory." The earthly marriage union, which we Christians regard as blessed and approved of by God, is "of no efficacy, virtue or force in and after the resurrection of the dead; for all contracts that are not made unto this end have an end when men are dead" (v. 7).

One underlying principle of Mormon polygamy is that anyone who refuses it will receive an inferior inheritance in heaven, and will be appointed to be servants of those who did accept it (v. 16 and 17). Polygamous saints are promised great blessings. In verses 19 and 20 we learn that if "sealed" Mormons shed no innocent blood, they will be raised in the first resurrection, or as soon afterwards as possible. They shall inherit thrones, kingdoms, principalities, powers, dominions, and all heights and depths. They will be able to pass unscathed by angels and gods, and their family relationships (marital, parental, and filial) will be eternal. Finally, they are promised that they will become gods, with angels in subjection to them.

The brunt of the *Doctrine and Covenants* section on polygamy is that no one can be exalted without it, and that only Joseph and his successors have the "keys" to this ordinance. Anyone who rejects it is damned; as is any man or woman who commits "adultery" by having marital relations outside the covenant having once entered into it. The wife of any such adulterous man would be given to another, faithful man, who will "be made ruler over many" (v. 44).

The last dozen or so verses of the revelation are transparently aimed at those who would oppose these teachings, most specifically at Joseph's wife Emma. It is obvious that this revelation, like the Word of Wisdom, was written with her in mind. She is told to accept all of Joseph's plural wives (v. 52), though she is threatened with destruction (v. 54) if she cannot "abide this commandment."

Furthermore, she is told that Joseph will be given even more wives if she fights against the revelation (v. 55). Poor Emma! Damned if she did, and humiliated if she didn't! Joseph tried to soften all this by saying in verse 61 that a first wife would have to give permission for her husband to take a second one, but he himself repeatedly took wives without Emma's knowledge or consent, claiming that he was exempt from this provision of the commandment (v. 65).

Apparently polygamy as a whole never went much smoother than what we see in the *Doctrine and Covenants*. Emma fought the doctrine of plural wives with every psychological weapon at her disposal, but lost. Brigham Young had dozens of wives, one of whom rebelled so violently and expressively against the slavery of polygamy that her book, *Wife Number 19,* is a classic among books about polygamy. Mormon lore is full of stories of childless "aunts" who lived with grandmother and grandfather in uneasy cohabitation.

Some of the most unsavory, heartbreaking stories in print were detailed in Kimball Young's book, *Isn't One Wife Enough?* In fact, many people have wondered why a man would want more than one wife anyway. The Bible's first polygamist, Lamech, is remembered mainly for the fact that he, besides being the first to have two wives, was also a murderer (see what two wives can drive you to!). We're all familiar with the contentions between Abraham's wives Sarah and Hagar, Jacob's problems with Leah, Rachel, Bilhah, and Zilpah, and the mess that King David's household was always in. Solomon's one thousand foreign wives leeched Israel's money from him to build altars to their heathen idols; and his son, Rehoboam (also a polygamist), let pagan worship prevail in the by-then divided Israel. In short, far from being a symbol of kingly power, polygamy in the Old Testament signified moral decay.

The revelation commanding polygamy was not published for the church as a whole until 1852, eight years after the death of Joseph Smith. It was not until 1876 that it was added to the *Doctrine and Covenants* and assigned the section number 132. Up until that time, though, there was another revelation (numbered 109 in the 1854 edition) which flatly denied that polygamy was practiced among Mormons, stating:

> Inasmuch as this church of Christ has been reproached with the crime of fornication and polygamy; we declare that we believe that one man should have one wife; and one woman but one husband, except in the case of death, when either is at liberty to marry again.[18]

This revelation was dropped from the *Doctrine and Covenants* when that on polygamy was added. Therefore, there existed a forty-five year gap between the receipt of the polygamy revelation and its inclusion in the doctrinal canon. During twenty-one years of that time, too, the church was denying publicly that they had anything to do with the practice of polygamy.

It's easy to see why Mormons don't delve too deeply into the history of Section 132, and if they do, why they want to avoid the issue altogether. Utah Mormons maintain that Joseph Smith introduced the doctrine of polygamy before his death, which doctrine was brought to fruition under the auspices of his successor, Brigham Young. Members of the Reorganized Church deny that the Prophet Joseph ever even thought of the doctrine because he denied it so vehemently before his death. Others, like Isaac Sheen, said that Joseph did indeed preach and practice polygamy, but that he "repented of his connection" with it, claiming that it was of the devil.[19]

Probably Sheen was closest to the truth. By the time he died, Joseph probably wished he'd never mentioned the word polygamy. Just when he first formulated the doctrine will probably never be known. But it is obvious that by the time he got around to asking God about it (remember, Section 132 is supposed to be God's answer on the matter), he already had more than two wives: In verse 52, God told Emma to "receive all those who *have been given* unto my servant Joseph" (italics mine). Mormons say that a certain number of women were promised, or "given," to Joseph before he actually married them. But history tells us that Joseph was married to at least twelve women before July 12, 1843, the date of the recording of Section 132.

In addition, Joseph Fielding Smith, a former president of the Mormon Church, in his book *Blood Atonement and the Origin of Plural Marriage* quoted an affidavit which verified that not only did Joseph have plural wives, but that he "cohabited with them as wives."[20] Worst of all was that Joseph Smith married women who were married to other men; besides committing adultery himself, he used his power and influence as a supposed prophet to coerce married women to join him in sin.

Joseph Smith claimed that he did not introduce polygamy to God's people, but that he merely restored it. But the Nephites of the *Book of Mormon* abhorred the idea of plural wives. Early Christians didn't practice it, either. Even if Joseph Smith claimed to be living Old Testament polygamy, he didn't do a very good job of it. An Old Testament polygamist couldn't marry his wife's sister (Levi. 18:18—bear in mind that Jacob lived before this law was given.). Nor could he have two wives who were mother and daughter (Lev. 20:14). Yet Joseph Smith married five pairs of sisters, as well as a mother and her daughter.[21]

When polygamy was first introduced, many men were appalled when commanded to take an additional wife (or in the case of Heber C. Kimball, commanded to *surrender his own first wife* to Joseph Smith in marriage). Most either accepted the doctrine or left the church. The doctrine of polygamy had as one virtue its ability to separate believers from unbelievers, and left few fence-sitters in its tumultuous wake.

In fact, some of its adherants actually claimed that it was vastly superior to monogamous marriage. George Q. Cannon, an early apostle, said that the children of patriarchal (polygamous) marriages were healthier and more vigorous and intelligent than others.[22] Brigham Young put the blame for civilization's problems with prostitution and adultery squarely on the shoulders of monogamy, saying that polygamous societies had no place for such sins.[23] He regarded extra wives as a sort of escape valve for the poor suppressed monogamous man who could not otherwise control his passions. Such men as polygamy would thus best serve, however, would have to do a lot of changing in order to qualify as Christians!

Some Mormon apologists shrug off polygamy by claiming, as I did, that less than three percent of the Mormon men ever practiced polygamy. But others, like T. Edgar Lyon, have admitted that the real figure might have been as high as ten percent.[24] Non-Mormons have estimated an accurate figure to be as much as twenty percent. A standard explanation of the necessity for polygamy is that there were many more women than men in the early church and that plural marriage was a good way to absorb the surplus women of the population. I grew up thinking that polygamous men married old or homely women just to give them a home and (if they weren't past childbearing age) a family. But John A. Widtsoe, a Mormon writer, affirmed that "there seems always to have been more males than females in the Church."[25]

Polygamy Rescinded

Whatever the statistics, polygamy became an attraction to some men and an outstanding feature of the church of that time. An institution which even today affects many Mormons who are themselves second or third generation descendants of polygamous unions. They, understandably, often have more trouble reconciling the commandments in Section 132 than do any others. The fact is that when it was given, the commandment to practice polygamy was *not* optional. Nor was it temporary—it was described as a "new and everlasting covenant." As practiced by Mormons, it certainly was new to the world. But everlasting it was not. History records that polygamy as an approved and practiced tenet of the Utah Mormon Church came to a halt in 1890, when the President of the Mormon Church, Wilford Woodruff, issued a document that appears at the end of the *Doctrine and Covenants*, titled "Official Declaration."

Whereas for thirty years Mormon leaders had been telling their members that they would be cursed by God if they didn't practice polygamy,[26] now Woodruff cited the constitutionality of the 1862 federal laws against polygamy, and said, "I hereby declare my intention to submit to those laws and to use my influence with the members of the Church over which I preside to have them do likewise."[27]

How could this be? How could an "eternal" principle, essential to salvation, be suddenly revoked? Many Mormons thought Wilford Woodruff had lost his mind or his priesthood authority, and continued living in polygamy. Some went to court for their right to practice the doctrine they continued to maintain was of God. Many went to prison. A number took their wives and went "underground," or to Mexico. Still others left the church and tried as best they could to undo the damage done in their lives by polygamy.

Many a polygamous wife claimed that her marriage was never happy after the coming of other wives, even according to Brigham Young.[28] But the situation was even worse for plural wives when polygamy was declared by the church to be wrong. What did a man do with his other wives, if cohabitation with them was illegal? What of his children by them? Many bitterly blamed the U. S. Government for their "cruel" treatment of such marriages. But was it the fault of the government?

The laws prohibiting polygamy only voiced the views of Christians who *knew* polygamy to be wrong. If the revelation were as irrevocably true as Brigham Young said it was,[29] and as divine as Orson Pratt said,[30] and as necessary as George Teasdale said it was,[31] then a person would have to be crazy to abandon it!

This is precisely the view of "Fundamentalist" Mormons who even today live in polygamy, both outside the United States and inside our borders. They had their beginnings when Wilford Woodruff issued the Manifesto. They claim that the "everlasting" covenant of marriage is just that, and feel that they would rather face imprisonment and fines from the government than to abandon their families and face God after rejecting one of His commandments. They claim, and quite correctly so, that Wilford Woodruff "sold out" to the federal government on the matter of polygamy.

Utah, at the time polygamy was at its apex, was desirous of becoming a state of the Union. With this as a lever, the government exerted such financial and legal strictures on the Mormon Church that its very being was threatened. When President Woodruff issued the Manifesto, he claimed that polygamy was to be suspended as a practice, not as a doctrine. He cited "bitter persecution" as the reason for this. But whatever the persecution, Mormons can't rightfully lay the blame on others. The blame must lie with those who formulated and preached this doctrine. Their deception and wilfullness must be seen behind the tears of every abandoned plural wife and her children.

But even after Mormon leaders told their people to abandon polygamy, some of those in high positions continued to practice it. For instance, Joseph F. Smith, sixth president of the church, fathered no less than eleven children by plural wives *after* the issuing of the Manifesto, according to his own sworn testimony before a federal investigating committee. This behavior exemplifies an issue that still burns in the hearts of Mormons who are courageous enough to ask themselves two questions. *If polygamy was eternal, why was it rescinded?* Some Mormons will shrug their shoulders and say that what God gives, He can take away; and perhaps He was just testing His people anyway. But it is a cruel God indeed who would set up a family system and then deprive innocent children of their fathers. *If polygamy were not eternal, why was it called such, and why did Mormon leaders continue to practice it while repudiating it?*

In the end, polygamy is a dead issue with the majority of Mormons. Most know little about it, and care less. Their attention is very rarely directed to Section 132 or to the Manifesto, and except for an occasional "rude" reference to it by a Gentile, they don't even think about it.

Perhaps the polygamy issue, with its many unanswered questions, is most typical of all the issues in the *Doctrine and Covenants*. Here, most obviously, can a reader see the inconsistencies in the processes behind Mormon "revelation." Mormons are fond of attacking the Bible to show its alleged contradictions. But a Christian doesn't have to look very long in the *Doctrine and Covenants* to find confusion and error.

Problems Within the Doctrine and Covenants

In Section 27, for instance, the reader is introduced to the idea of an office of "Elias." In the Mormon mind, Elias is a title, not a name. (Of course, the Bible scholar knows that Elias is just the Greek form of the name Elijah, but we're not supposed to know that. Joseph Smith obviously didn't know it—he claimed in Section 110, verses 11-13, that he saw both Elias *and* Elijah.) According to Mormon doctrine, people who have held this title include John the Baptist and Noah.

Joseph Smith also showed his ignorance of Bible language in Section 4. In verse 5, he lists the qualifications for service in the kingdom as: faith, hope, charity, and love, with an eye single to the glory of God. Joseph would have been better off if he had kept his eye single to a Greek-English Bible. Anyone who reads only the King James Version, as do most Mormons, might accept "charity" and "love" as separate concepts, but modern translations recognize that "charity" is the Elizabethan translators' attempt to find an English word that would approximate the "agape" love Paul spoke of in First Corinthians 13.

In *Doctrine and Covenants* Section 95 we have another example of just how little Joseph Smith knew about Hebrew. Here he took the liberty of transliterating a scriptural phrase, "Lord of Sabaoth." He said it was "by interpretation, the creator of the first day, the beginning and the end." It is apparent that he confused this phrase with the one found in Mark 2:28, where Christ spoke of the "Lord of the Sabbath," which does indeed have reference to a day of the week, though not the first day. "Lord of Sabaoth" refers to God's kingly role as commander-in-chief of the heavenly host, and of all living things. It cannot reasonably be stretched to refer to the creation of the first day.

Joseph Smith also seemed to have a lot of trouble keeping straight the gods who gave him the revelations of the *Doctrine and Covenants*. In Section 29, for example, the speaker in the revelation says that he is Jesus Christ, and then later in verse 42 speaks as the Father. In Section 49 the reverse occurs: the speaker says that he is the Father of Christ in verse 5, but later in verse 28 identifies himself as Christ. Since the Mormons assert that God and Christ are totally separate personages, they don't even have a Trinity doctrine to fall back on after Joseph Smith bobbled like this.

The list could go on and on, relating one example after another to illustrate the false nature of the *Doctrine and Covenants*. But before we leave the subject of this amazing book, let's consider one section of it that perhaps better than any other shows its inherent spirit.

Section 19 might pass unnoticed by Mormon and critic alike—in the beginning it seems to have little to offer to distinguish it from others like it. Its introduction affirms that it is "A COMMANDMENT OF GOD, and not of man" (just in case anyone would think otherwise), and the first twenty verses pound that idea point by point into the head of Martin Harris, the object of the revelation. He is told to repent lest God punish him endlessly, humble him with almighty power. But here is where the revelation begins to differ from the norm. It tells Martin he is to preach nothing but repentance and then uses the same strong-arm methods to command the affluent and gullible Harris to pay all the debts incurred in printing the *Book of Mormon*, to liquidate and give to the church all his lands and property except that needed to support his family, and finally, to leave house and home except to visit occasionally with his loved ones. He is told that the blessings he will so obtain will be greater than the "corruptible" riches he will give to the church.

And then Joseph Smith, masquerading as the god of this revelation, grandly asks the soon-to-be homeless and destitute Martin, "Behold, canst thou read this without rejoicing and lifting up thy heart for gladness?" (v. 39).

NOTES

[1]Cowdrey, Davis, and Scales, *Who Really Wrote the Book of Mormon?* (Santa Ana, California: Vision House Publishers, 1977), p. 109.

[2]1 Nephi 13:29.

[3]Bales, *The Book of Mormon?* p. 32.

[4]Joseph Smith Jr., *Documentary History of the Church,* I, p. 368.

[5]Sidney B. Sperry, *Doctrine and Covenants Compendium* (Salt Lake City: Bookcraft, Inc., 1960), p. 763 footnote.

[6]Jerald and Sandra Tanner, *The Case Against Mormonism* (Salt Lake City: Modern Microfilm, 1967), Vol. 1, p. 188.

[7]B. H. Roberts, *A Comprehensive History of the Church of Jesus Christ of Latter-day Saints,* II, p. 176.

[8]Widtsoe, *Joseph Smith—Seeker After Truth,* p. 254.

[9]Sperry, *Doctrine and Covenants Compendium,* p. 66.

[10]Joseph Smith Jr., *Documentary History of the Church,* I, p. 176 footnote.

[11]Sperry, *Doctrine and Covenants Compendium,* p. 451.

[12]Ibid.

[13]Tanner, *Mormonism: Shadow or Reality?* pp. 406-412.

[14]Editorial in *Salt Lake Tribune,* July 14, 1908.

[15]*Conference Report,* April 1898, p. 11.

[16]See also *Doctrine and Covenants* 124:29-42.

[17]Edith Deen, *Family Living in the Bible* (New York: Harper and Row, 1963), p. 12.

[18]Tanner, *Mormonism: Shadow or Reality?* Photoreprint, p. 202.

[19]Isaac Sheen, *True Latter-day Saints Herald,* Vol. I, No. 1, p. 24.

[20]Joseph Fielding Smith quoted in Tanner, *Mormonism: Shadow or Reality?* p. 221.

[21]Brodie, *No Man Knows My History,* p. 336.

[22]*Journal of Discourses,* XIII, p. 202.

[23]Ibid., XI, p. 128.

[24]Tanner, *Mormonism: Shadow or Reality?* p. 225.

[25]John A. Widtsoe, *Evidences and Reconciliations* (Salt Lake City: Bookcraft, 1960), p. 390.

[26]See statement by Heber C. Kimball in *Journal of Discourses,* XI, p. 211.

[27]*Doctrine and Covenants,* 1952 edition, p. 257.

[28]*Journal of Discourses,* IV, pp. 55-57.

[29]Ibid., V, p. 203.

[30]Ibid., XVII, pp. 224-225.

[31]Ibid., XXV, p. 21.

6
The Perils of the Pearl

There is nothing hidden but what shall be brought to light, and
nothing secret but what shall be discovered.
> —Parley P. Pratt, Mormon leader,
> speaking of the *Pearl of Great Price*
> in the *Millenial Star*
> July 1, 1842, p. 46.

Through my life as a Mormon, I knew little about the *Pearl of Great
Price*. It is quoted less than other LDS scripture, and has few exciting
stories in it to compare with the adventures of Nephi or Alma in the *Book
of Mormon*. Many of its doctrines were so deep or so controversial that
they were rarely discussed in public meetings. In ten years of Mormonism
I was never asked to read this, the shortest of all books of Mormon
scripture. When I did read it, it was on my own initiative.

It was this book, which I was looking at in the fall of 1973, that
rocked my foundations as a Mormon. Those illustrations shocked me into
the recognition that Joseph Smith was no translator of Egyptian. It was
not until much later, though, that I went back and objectively examined
the *Pearl of Great Price*.

Now, whenever I start to think that maybe Mormonism wasn't all
that bad, or that Joseph Smith could have just been a misunderstood
altruist, I go to my *Pearl of Great Price*. I get a slap in the face—and
thanks, I needed that.

The Contents of the Pearl of Great Price

It is not easy to talk about the *Pearl of Great Price* as an entity
because its contents, like those of the *Doctrine and Covenants,* are so
divergent. Whereas the *Book of Mormon* purports to be the records of the
ancient Americans, and the *Doctrine and Covenants* the revelation given

to early Mormon church leaders, no such blanket statement of contents will suffice for the *Pearl of Great Price*. It includes a listing of the Mormon "Articles of Faith," a sort of creed upon which LDS doctrine is based, formulated by Joseph Smith. The *Pearl of Great Price* contains other writings of the prophet, a book called Writings of Joseph Smith. This tells of his first vision, the coming forth of the *Book of Mormon,* the visit of John the Baptist, and the rise of the church. Writings of Joseph Smith also contains an extract from his Inspired Version of the Bible, a passage from Matthew. In April of 1976 the Mormon church authorized the inclusion of two additional revelations in the *Pearl of Great Price*. One was the record of a vision Joseph Smith said he received in January of 1836. The other was the record of a vision supposedly given to Joseph F. Smith, the sixth president of the church, in 1918. Both "visions" were later transferred to the *Doctrine and Covenants*.

The other two-thirds of the *Pearl of Great Price* are supposed to be from the writings of two Old Testament patriarchs, Abraham and Moses. Abraham's writings record details of that prophet's life not found in the Bible, as well as information about the pre-existence, the council in heaven, and divine principles of astronomy. Moses' writings detail the events that led to the Creation of the world and the history of mankind from Adam to Noah.

This book of scripture, which includes so many divergent parts, was first compiled by Franklin D. Richards of the Council of the Twelve. He published it under the title, *Pearl of Great Price,* in Liverpool, England, in 1851. It underwent "various adjustments" before being canonized as scripture in 1880. It was revised again in 1902 when all the material incorporated into the 1876 *Doctrine and Covenants* was dropped from its contents so as to avoid duplication. Then, too, it was divided into chapters and verses with references. It was accepted as a "standard work," joining the Bible, the *Book of Mormon,* and the *Doctrine and Covenants,* in its revised form in 1902. But all in all, this short book has undergone thousands of word changes since its 1851 edition.

Articles of Faith

One of the most oft-quoted parts of the *Pearl of Great Price* is known as the Articles of Faith. These thirteen doctrinal statements were composed by Joseph Smith after Wentworth, a newspaper editor, wrote to Joseph Smith in Nauvoo, asking for a brief statement of the doctrinal beliefs of the Latter-day Saints. They are considered as scripture.

A Christian casually observing the Articles of Faith would find few quarrels there. But as we shall see in later chapters, the distinctively Mormon doctrines hinge upon the meanings that Mormons assign to the Christian terminology of the Articles of Faith. For instance, such concepts as being "saved" or "punished," and the idea of "authority," are uniquely Mormon as Mormons interpret these words.

Joseph Smith's inclusion of his own "inspired" translation of Matthew 23:39 and all of Matthew chapter 24 has raised questions in the minds of many, Mormons and non-Mormons alike. That Joseph Smith considered this passage important is implied in the fact that for years it was the only New Testament part of his Inspired Version to be singled out as scripture by the Utah church. (The Reorganized church, you will recall, has always accepted the whole Inspired Version as scripture.) But when I was a Mormon I never heard why this particular passage was so important. It was rarely quoted. It is a mysterious monument to Smith's ability to conglomerate scriptures for his desired effect, and its name, Joseph Smith Chapter 1, is fitting.

Also included in the Writings of Joseph Smith is a short autobiography of his early life, known as Joseph Smith Chapter 2. I discussed the main elements of this writing when I dealt with Joseph's story earlier, showing the discrepancies between the actual events and Joseph's memory of them, which he wrote down much later, in 1838. Of particular interest is Joseph Smith 2:14-20 which details the appearance of God and Christ to the boy Joseph. This is the most relied-upon passage by which Mormons justify their doctrine that God and Christ possess separate physical bodies.

Joseph Smith's "Vision of the Celestial Kingdom," which was added to the *Pearl of Great Price* in 1976, is regarded by some Mormons as a "new" revelation, but it can hardly be regarded as such since the event supposedly occurred almost 150 years ago. This short, ten verse section assured Joseph Smith that he was not to worry about people who died without hearing the Mormon gospel, because God would judge their hearts, and if He knew they would have accepted it had they the chance, then they would be "heirs of the celestial kingdom" (v. 7). The same would apply to people living in the future, and to children who died before reaching the "years of accountability"—age eight.

Joseph F. Smith's "Vision of the Redemption of the Dead," which was also canonized as part of the standard works in 1976, is a much longer passage. It tells of how Christ went into the spirit world after His death, and with the help of certain righteous men, preached "faith in God, repentance from sin, vicarious baptism for the remission of sins, the gift of the Holy Ghost by the laying on of hands" (v. 33). Those who were dead had the option of accepting these principles and paying the penalty of their transgressions (v. 59). Then they were treated just like those who had accepted the Mormon gospel on earth. In addition, righteous Mormons of today will have the opportunity after death of preaching to heathen peoples.

Nothing in either of these two "revelations" held any surprises for the Mormon of 1976, for they were already the basis of much doctrine about the dead. The only puzzle is why they were added to the *Pearl of Great Price,* from which they were recently dropped. They are now part of the *Doctrine and Covenants* (see chapter 5.)

The Book of Moses

These writings of Joseph Smith—the Articles of Faith, the Matthew "translation," Joseph Smith's early history, and his "vision"—as well as the "vision" of Joseph F. Smith, make up a little over one-fourth of the *Pearl of Great Price.* The rest of this book is taken up with what Mormons believe to be the writings of Moses and Abraham. Moses' writings were "revealed" to Joseph Smith in 1830 when he was working on his translation of the Old Testament. This "Book of Moses" is supposedly the unabridged story of the Creation and mankind down till Noah, upon which our "incomplete" Genesis account was based. It was first published in six installments printed at irregular intervals from August 1832 until January 1844. Basically the Book of Moses is a revision of the Genesis account that includes a heavy injection of "Christian-type" doctrines into the old-covenant writings. A scan of the teachings of this book reveal the following doctrinal points.

1. Man can talk to God literally face to face (1:2; 7:4) and see Him with spiritual eyes (1:11).

2. This record of Moses is not included in our Bible because of the wickedness of men (1:23) and is to be shown only to those who believe (1:42).

3. There are many "earths" that God has created (1:29, 33).

4. Joseph Smith is considered by God to be one "like Moses" (1:41).

5. The speaker, God (Elohim), created by Himself everything but man (2:1-25), but He was helped in man's creation by His Only Begotten (2:26).

6. All living things were first created spiritually before being created physically (3:7).

7. Trees are living souls (3:9); thus, by implication, all living things have souls.

8. Satan was a son of God (5:13), brother to Christ and to all mankind. He rebelled when his plan promising compulsory, universal salvation was rejected by God (4:1-4).

9. Adam received the Holy Ghost (5:9).

10. Adam rejoiced after and as a result of his transgression (5:10-11; compare to Gen. 3:10).

11. Cain was cursed because he made a secret pact with Satan for gain (5:29-33—note that priesthood is not mentioned).

12. The first polygamist, Lamech, covenanted with Satan (5:49), and kept not God's command (5:52).

13. The "Gospel" was preached in antediluvian days, and was confirmed by the Holy Ghost (5:58-59).

14. The priesthood is said to have originated with Adam (6:7).

15. Genealogies were kept in Adam's day as they should be kept now (6:8).

16. Christ atoned for original sin (6:54).

17. Adam was given the Comforter (6:61).

18. After receiving the Holy Ghost, Adam was baptized—with water (6:64) and with fire and the Holy Ghost (6:66).

19. Canaanites were cursed with a blackness that caused them to be despised by all men (7:8).

20. Enoch built a city called Zion (7:18-22) which was taken up to heaven with him (7:69).

21. The seed of Cain was black (7:22).

22. A purgatorial prison was built for those who perished in the flood (7:38).

23. The earth is female in gender, and has a soul and a voice (7:48).

24. An actual one-thousand-year millenial reign by Christ upon this earth is promised (7:65).

25. Noah taught repentance and baptism for the gift of the Holy Ghost (8:24).

26. Noah, not God, was sorry that man had been created (8:25-26; compare to Gen. 6:6-7).

It is interesting to know that this section of the *Pearl of Great Price* has undergone 1,195 word changes since first being published in 1851. How this can be justified is beyond my understanding, in view of the fact that Mormons claim Joseph Smith received this by direct revelation from God. I can see the LDS point of view when they say that God can give modern-day revelations to individuals which need to be revised or revoked as situations change. (I can see it, though I don't agree with it.) I *cannot* see why their deity could not accurately relay to Joseph Smith the contents of a record written by Moses thousands of years ago.

History of the Book of Abraham

Since the original record does not exist, we cannot check Joseph Smith's version of the Book of Moses except against the Genesis account—MENE, MENE, TEKEL, to Joseph Smith.

But the remainder of the *Pearl of Great Price*, the Book of Abraham, *can* be checked, for the original records are available today.

There are, in the possession of the Mormon Church, several papyrus fragments, from one of which the Book of Abraham was *translated* by Joseph Smith.

Here is another tribute to the resourcefulness of Joseph Smith, who could use anything that came his way to further his own purposes. Early in his life Joseph found a smooth rock that became a "seer stone." Later he used a workman's carving on one of his temples to show what the face of God looked like—except, he observed, the nose was just a *little* too broad. And when a man traveled to him with mummies and papyrus, why, Joseph couldn't resist building some of his most fantastic doctrines around the history and contents of those scrolls.

So that we can understand the situation in which Joseph Smith thus found himself, we need to appreciate the times in which he lived. The end of the eighteenth century was the era of Napoleon's visits to Egypt, and the obelisks and artwork he brought back from the fabled Nile kindled the world's interest. Everyone those days knew *something* about Egypt—but no one knew much, because their mysterious ancient hieroglyphic language was a locked door. Then, just six years before the unheralded birth of one Joseph Smith in Vermont in 1805, an equally unappreciated stone was discovered. But when someone noticed that this two-thousand-year-old black rock contained three passages in three different languages—Greek, hieroglyphics, and demotic (a simplified hieroglyphic writing)—then the Rosetta Stone, as it was named, began to receive the notice it deserved.

During the time that Joseph Smith was supposedly receiving the first vision, a young man named Jean François Champollion theorized that if the names in all three passages were equivalent, then the other information probably was. In America, Joseph Smith began writing the *Book of Mormon,* and during the organization and early years of the Mormon Church, many scholars pored over the Rosetta Stone, wondering if this basalt slab could realize the possibility of reading all the silent writings on the walls of tombs and temples. In the same year, 1832, that Brigham Young became a Mormon, Champollion died, and it wasn't until after his death that the scholarly world recognized and appreciated his work. In 1837 the herculean task of assembling the first ancient Egyptian dictionary was completed. No one had ever supposed that such a thing could be done—least of all, Joseph Smith.

In June of 1835 a frustrated young man by the name of Michael H. Chandler sought out the famed Mormon prophet. Chandler had inherited eleven Egyptian mummies. His disappointment at finding that the bodies carried no jewels was barely compensated for by the fact that there was a papyrus roll on the breast of one of the mummies, and a few scraps of papyrus on the others. Chandler had earned a little money traveling around the country exhibiting the curiosities. When he met Benjamin

Bullock III, a relative of Joseph Smith's friend Heber C. Kimball, he was told that the "Mormon prophet" could translate anything.

Chandler drove 250 miles to Smith's home in Kirtland, Ohio, where he was well rewarded for his efforts. As soon as Joseph laid eyes upon the papyrus fragments that Chandler had had examined by other "experts," the Mormon sage asked to be excused, and retired into his "translating room." When he returned a short while later, he carried a written translation in English of the fragment's writing. What the "translation" said, we may never know, but it so impressed Chandler that he presented Joseph with a certificate stating:

Kirtland, July 6, 1835

This is to make known to all who may be desirous, concerning the knowledge of Mr. Joseph Smith, Jun., in deciphering the ancient Egyptian hieroglyphic characters in my possession, which I have, in many eminent cities, showed to the most learned; and from the information that I could ever learn, or meet with, I find that of Mr. Joseph Smith, Jun., to correspond in the most minute matters.

(signed) Michael H. Chandler
Traveling with, and proprietor of,
Egyptian mummies[1]

Soon afterwards, Joseph Smith offered to buy the papyri, but Chandler refused to sell them without their owners, the mummies. The sale was consummated to the tune of $2,400.00.

Joseph identified one of the mummies as King Necho[2] and another time he said one of the mummies was that of a king's daughter. But the mummies were of only peripheral interest to Joseph Smith—the scrolls were what fascinated him. He said that one scroll had on it the "autograph of Moses" and additional writings by his brother Aaron.[3] Unfortunately we do not have Joseph Smith's "translation" of this record.

Nor do we have the translation of what Joseph Smith in his journal called "the writings of Joseph of Egypt." Joseph Smith, speaking as Nephi in the *Book of Mormon*, mentioned the prophecies of Joseph of Egypt (2 Nephi 4:2). Though some Mormon authorities say that Joseph Smith *did* translate Joseph's writings on the Chandler papyri,[4] the translation has never been published. This is because its prophecies were "too great for the people of this day."[5]

However, Joseph Smith *did* translate and publish a portion of the scrolls he bought from Chandler. Joseph said that one portion of the papyrus was written in the handwriting of Abraham himself—which made it much older than the Bible account of Genesis which was recorded long after the fact by Moses. Dr. Sidney Sperry, Mormon authority, has even gone so far as to say that the "Book of Abraham" (like the Book of Moses) was an original document upon which Genesis was based.[6]

It was not until 1842, though, that the translation was completed. It was published in the Nauvoo, Illinois, *Times and Seasons* between March 1 and May 16, 1842. Joseph Smith oversaw the printing, and commissioned a young woodcarver, Reuben Hedlock, to reproduce sections of the scrolls' illustrations for printing to accompany the translations.

Joseph Smith promised further extracts from the Book of Abraham (indicating that what he had published hardly covered the entire document), but before he was able to do so, he was killed in Carthage Jail. After his death, Joseph's mother Lucy Mack Smith took over the scrolls and mummies. She kept them and exhibited them to curious visitors who were fascinated by her colorful descriptions of them. Lucy was living with Joseph's widow Emma and her second husband, Charles Bidamon, when the elderly Mrs. Smith died in 1855. One year later Emma and her son Joseph III sold the Egyptian artifacts to a Mr. A. Coombs. The sales receipt of this transaction is still in existence.

By 1859 the scrolls had been loaned or donated to the St. Louis Museum. In 1863 they were on catalog in the Chicago Museum. It was long assumed that the scrolls were burned in the fire that destroyed a great deal of the Chicago Museum in 1871.

Doctrines of the Book of Abraham

That part of the *Pearl of Great Price* which is known as the Book of Abraham was translated from these scrolls, and is the basis for many doctrines of Mormonism. If we were to scan it quickly as we did the Book of Moses we would find it teaching that:

1. The Mormon priesthood was first held by Adam and passed down to Abraham, the writer of this record (1:3).
2. Pharaoh's wicked priest tried to sacrifice Abraham (1:6-15).
3. The land of Egypt was settled by the descendants of Ham (1:23-24).
4. Pharaoh did not hold the priesthood because he was "cursed as pertaining to the priesthood" (1:26-27).
5. The priesthood was promised to Abraham's seed (2:9).
6. The "Gospel" was preached in Abraham's time (2:10).
7. Abraham possessed the Urim and Thummim (3:1).
8. The star named Kolob is near to God's throne (3:2-3).
9. Since Kolob revolves once in each one thousand years, one of its days is equal to one thousand of our years in God's perspective (3:4).
10. All spirits are eternal and incapable of being created (3:18-19).
11. Certain persons were fore-chosen by God, before the world was formed, to be His rulers (3:23-24).
12. Satan rebelled when he was not chosen to accomplish God's aims (3:27-28).

13. "The Gods" organized and formed the heavens and the earth (4:1), as well as collectively carrying out the entire creation process as outlined in Genesis 1 and 2.

14. When the Gods decreed that Adam would die the same day that he ate of the forbidden fruit, they were speaking of the one-thousand-year days of God (5:13).

The record of Abraham as translated by Joseph Smith was by his own admission incomplete. Mormon leaders have theorized that on the basis of some of the Book of Abraham's illustrations, subsequent translation would have told about Abraham's further adventures in Egypt.

The Book of Abraham Under Fire

While most Mormons of the last half of the nineteenth century and the first half of this one engaged in speculating on what Joseph Smith would have written if he had lived longer, the experts of the Egyptian language scoffed at Joseph's translating abilities. The certificate that Mr. Chandler had given Joseph attesting to his abilities as a translator of ancient Egyptian was worthless because neither Chandler nor the other men he had consulted could read enough ancient Egyptian to certify *anyone* else's translations.

The attacks on the Book of Abraham began in earnest in 1860 when Louvre expert M. Theodule Deveria examined the facsimiles which were printed in the *Pearl of Great Price*. Since Joseph Smith had claimed to translate several names and some of the information on the scrolls from which the woodcuts were copied, Deveria was able to make his own translations and then compare them to those of Joseph Smith. Though hindered in several places by the poor quality of the woodcut reproductions and by untranslatable sections, Deveria was nonetheless able to ascertain categorically that not only were Joseph Smith's translations incorrect, but also that Joseph Smith had apparently altered the original documents themselves. Of course all Deveria had to base his opinions on were the facsimiles printed in the *Pearl of Great Price,* but these were also the facsimiles presented as part of the Word of God by Joseph Smith.

The flame of controversy was fanned again in 1912 when Franklin S. Spaulding, the Episcopal Bishop of Utah, published a book called *Joseph Smith Jr. as a Translator*. In researching for this book, Spaulding approached several of the most emminent authorities of the science of Egyptology and asked them their opinions of the woodcuts of the *Pearl of Great Price* and Joseph Smith's interpretations of those woodcuts. The list of experts consulted by Spaulding reads like an honor roll of the best Egyptologists, and included Dr. W. M. Flinders Petrie and James H. Breasted. When their verdicts came in, every expert had the same thing to say: Joseph Smith had no idea of even the basics of translating ancient

Egyptian. A sampling of their comments on Joseph's translations: "an impudent fraud," "pure fabrication," "the work of pure imagination."

The Mormon Church was stunned by this publication, and lost no time in coming out with a reply to it. They chose a man to write their "answer" who worked as a professional writer and who at one time in his career wrote a book defending the liquor industry. This man, J. C. Homans, wrote under the pen name of Robert C. Webb, and gave himself the title of Ph. D.—an honor never bestowed upon him by any university. His book was a confusing mass of circumlocution that alternated between generalizations about the culture of ancient Egypt and attacks on the credentials of the experts quoted by Spaulding.

In 1965, Modern Microfilm Company, operated by Jerald and Sandra Tanner of Salt Lake City, reprinted Spaulding's work, which was by now out of print. This reprinting could have caused as big a stir as its first, but an event of much greater importance intervened.

Atiya's Discovery of the Scrolls

A professor of Middle Eastern Studies at the University of Utah was visiting the New York Metropolitan Museum in the early spring of 1966, doing research for a book he was writing about eastern Christianity. This man, Dr. Aziz S. Atiya, was Egyptian by birth and Coptic by faith, but working as he had at a university in the middle of Mormon Country, he was familiar with Latter-day Saint doctrine and scriptures. As he was looking through a large box of Egyptian documents brought to him by a museum attendant, one particular piece of papyrus attracted his attention. Upon closer examination, he saw that the papyrus, which had some parts missing, had been glued onto a piece of more modern paper, and the missing parts drawn in pencil onto the newer paper. What made this so unusual was the fact that whoever had drawn in the missing sections had done so in a very peculiar manner—and the completed vignette looked just like Facsimile No. 1 in the Mormon *Pearl of Great Price*. Atiya's suspicions were confirmed when he found ten more pieces of papyrus along with the bill of sale signed by Emma Smith Bidamon and her son Joseph Smith III, in a storage file.

The history of the scrolls soon came to light. Apparently the Mr. Coombs who bought the scrolls from Emma had given them to his housekeeper. The housekeeper's son-in-law sold the scrolls to the New York museum in 1947. There they had been ever since, with the full knowledge of the museum officials.

It is not therefore strictly accurate to say that Atiya "discovered" the scrolls, since the museum knew of their whereabouts and significance for almost twenty years. Nor could it be said that Atiya was the first to tell members of the Mormon Church of the scrolls' location. One Mormon later co-authored a book, *From the Dust of Decades,* about the "discovery" of the papyri. This man, Walter Whipple, himself knew of the location of the papyri and actually had photographs of them back in 1962, but kept this information quiet until a non-Mormon with the credentials of Dr. Atiya "found" them.

I am not implying that Dr. Atiya cooperated with the LDS Church in faking the find. It was probably only due to circumstances that he was the one who stumbled across the scrolls. But those Mormons who before Dr. Atiya's find *knew* about the scrolls—and there were more than just Whipple—were no doubt relieved when a non-Mormon came across them.[7] Why did the Metropolitan Museum not notify the Mormons? (An official of the museum said tactfully, "Frankly, we didn't know what the Mormon Church's wishes were."")[8] It wasn't because the papyri weren't genuine. Atiya and other qualified experts have not argued with the fact that the scrolls are uncontested examples of ancient Egyptian papyri. When Atiya found the scrolls and notified the Mormon Church, they expressed great appreciation. The New York Metropolitan Museum, realizing the importance of the scrolls to the Mormons, presented them to LDS officials in a formal ceremony on November 27, 1967. But the Mormon Church, I am sure, wishes it had never seen those scrolls again.

Why? Because in 1967, the Egyptian language was no longer the barrier it was in Joseph Smith's day. Today a competent Egyptologist can read the *Pearl of Great Price* papyri and tell you the one thing that Mormons don't want to hear: the papyri say absolutely *nothing* about Abraham, or Joseph, or God, anything even remotely related to Mormonism. When Atiya found the scrolls, those who had known for years of their existence—and their implications—swallowed hard and accepted them as gracefully as they could.

Translating the Scrolls

As soon as the news of the scrolls came to light, some Mormons began to rejoice that here, finally, could Joseph Smith be vindicated as a translator. But the church warned members that, pending a new translation by a Mormon Egyptologist, no one should depend upon the scrolls to "prove" Joseph Smith's abilities as a translator. Hugh Nibley, the archaeologist to whom most of the church looked for assurance, was not very comforting. "LDS scholars are caught flatfooted by this discovery," he confessed in Brigham Young University's newspaper.[9]

Many Mormons felt confident that the president of the church, the "prophet, seer, and revelator," would be able to translate the papyri. These were surprised when the documents were given to Hugh Nibley, who kept them for a long time and only translated *one* word from them—and that incorrectly.[10]

Nibley began writing a series of articles for the church's periodical, *The Improvement Era,* which stretched over a two-year period from January, 1968, until May, 1970. He used over two thousand footnotes and quoted from such sources as old Rabbinical writings to try to find parallels between ancient Egyptian culture and that portrayed in Joseph Smith's translation of the Book of Abraham. Even though I was very interested in the whole issue, Nibley's ponderous display of unrelated facts only served to bore me. I decided that the whole matter was too deep for anyone who didn't have a doctorate in ancient languages. In retrospect, I think that was probably the express purpose of Nibley's writings, for I know that he is more capable of coming to the point than he showed himself there. Once I got waist-deep in his circumlocution, I, like most other Mormons, forgot to ask the cogent question of the whole issue: What do the papyri *say?*

In 1968 Nibley had given the papyri to a Mormon Egyptologist, Dee Jay Nelson. (Although unquestioned at the time, Nelson's degrees were later shown to be from a "diploma mill." His findings, however, have been substantiated by many renowned Egyptologists, including Dr. Klaus Baer.) Nibley felt confident that fellow-Mormon Nelson could vindicate the prophet's translation.

But when Nelson finished a translation of the text and labeled illustrations, the Mormon Church refused to print it. Nelson was disturbed by this, and feeling an obligation to let other of his brethren know of the true meaning of the papyri, he took his translation to Modern Microfilm for publication. When Nelson's translation was published, it became obvious why the church had handed it back like a hot rock. Nelson had, after careful examination and extensive research, concluded that the eleven fragments found in the Metropolitan Museum and presented to the Mormon Church, when translated, bore no resemblance to any of the writings of Joseph Smith.

Were These the Joseph Smith Papyri?

This and subsequent research by qualified Egyptologists outside the Mormon Church have shown that those eleven papyrus fragments made up the following elements:

1. A "Book of the Dead"—and ancient funerary text—for a deceased woman by the name of Ta-Shere-Min.

2. An illustration of a judgment scene from another "Book of the Dead," made for a female musician named Amon-Re Neferinub.

3. A "Book of Breathings" (a late Ptolemaic Period version of the "Book of the Dead"), also called Sen Sen because of the repetition of this word throughout the text—made for a deceased man named Hor.

Of course, some Mormons who heard of the undeniably pagan nature of the texts of the papyri thought that perhaps a mistake had been made; perhaps these weren't the same papyri once owned by Joseph Smith. With some of the papyri there was no question—Reuben Hedlock had copied their illustrations—even preserving the ancient Egyptian scribe's misspelling errors intact in the *Pearl of Great Price* woodcuts. (The LDS Church agreed from the beginning that the papyri were the source of at least one of the *Pearl of Great Price* woodcuts.) Part of the Metropolitan Museum papyri hadn't been used as a basis for the woodcuts, it is true, but they fit exactly the descriptions given by contemporaries of Joseph Smith, who had seen and described the scrolls. The Reverend Henry Caswell, for instance, visited Nauvoo and was shown the papyri by Joseph Smith.[11]

In an open letter, Dee Jay Nelson stated of the LDS papyri:

> That these were the papyri used by Smith cannot be honestly denied because some of the fragments were glued to pieces of heavy paper with handwritten notations on the back linking them to the "Prophet." They also display the original counterparts of hieratic characters which had been copied by Smith (and/or) his scribes into three handwritten notebooks. These notebooks are still in existence, owned by the church.[12]

The "notebooks" referred to by Nelson lie at the crux of the whole Mormon dilemma of the relationship between the papyri and the Book of Abraham. These notebooks show, beyond any doubt, that Joseph Smith went through the motions of a deciphering process so that his people would think that he had actually translated the hieratic characters.

Joseph Smith began these notebooks, which are referred to by Mormons as "The Kirtland Egyptian Papers" or by their more descriptive title, "The Egyptian Alphabet and Grammar," in the year 1835. They are now in the possession of the Mormon Church.

What the Egyptian Alphabet and Grammar consists of is sheets divided into three columns. In the first column Joseph Smith or a scribe copied a character from the small Sen Sen papyrus. The second column contained the English pronunciation of the character opposite it. The third column contained Joseph Smith's translation of that symbol. Thus, one line would have a symbol, its pronunciation, and its English equivalent.

One section of the Egyptian Alphabet and Grammar had a portion of the Book of Abraham—chapter 1, verses 4 through 28—"translated" using this method. A great number of English words were assigned to each Egyptian symbol, which the Grammar indicated was due to the fact that each hieratic character could be broken down into individual strokes (just as the English letter "A" could be broken down into three strokes). Each stroke was assigned a weird-sounding name and a meaning.

Some Mormons, including Hugh Nibley, have said that the

Grammar is just an illustration of how Joseph Smith liked to play around with other languages for his own amusement. They cite as evidence the fact that Joseph Smith never publicized the Egyptian Alphabet and Grammar, but rather kept it to himself. But in considering this explanation, it must be remembered that Joseph Smith didn't think he would ever be found out. Though Champollion was finally getting recognition for his decipherment of hieroglyphics (unfortunately posthumous recognition), the science of Egyptian translation was still young. Certainly Joseph Smith had no access to a complete Egyptian hieroglyphic dictionary, so he made up his own. The fact that he did not publish it doesn't matter as much as the fact that he went to all the trouble to formulate it.

Problems with the Papyri

Some Mormons have zealously maintained the veracity of Joseph Smith's bizarre translating methods by means of several complex arguments. Many feel forced to defend his translations because the introduction to the Book of Abraham as printed in the *Pearl of Great Price* does, after all, state that the scripture was "translated from the Papyrus, by Joseph Smith." Also, Joseph Smith actually quoted some of his made-up Egyptian in public.[13] It is obvious that Joseph Smith took his "experimenting" very seriously.

In attempting to clear up this confusion, some Mormons have evolved complicated systems whereby they claim that Joseph Smith used deeper, second-level or third-level meanings of the Egyptian words to find the story of Abraham hidden in the pagan "Book of Breathings." Some claim that the funerary text was a memory-jogging device to help a reader remember the elements of the Abraham story, which one critic compared to memorizing the book of Jonah by tying it to the French National Anthem.[14]

Isn't it silly the lengths to which people will go to get around the fact that Joseph Smith only pretended to know Egyptian in order to foist some of his ideas off on his people in the guise of scripture? People who are not under obligation to defend the Book of Abraham can see clearly the book's origins. The King James Version of the book of Genesis was undoubtedly the primary source used by Joseph Smith.

In addition to the problem of the papyri not saying what Joseph Smith said they did, there is the additional trouble involving the age of the papyrus which Joseph Smith used. The Sen Sen was defined by Dee Jay Nelson as a type of funerary text which was not even developed until the seventh century B.C.[15] Other experts have placed the particular Shaiten Sen Sen used by Joseph Smith for the Book of Abraham as a product of the Ptolemaic Period of Egypt—after 332 B.C. The papyri were supposedly the source of "the Book of Abraham, written by his own hand, upon papyrus"[16] and added to by Joseph, Moses, and Aaron. Even Mormons must now admit, though, that the scrolls do not date from the time of Abraham at all.

The fact is that the scrolls could date to very near the time of Christ. Mormons generally offer this explanation: Joseph Smith's boast to an observer that the scrolls contained the "autograph of Abraham"[17] was not accurate—what he meant was that the scroll he had in his possession contained a copy of Abraham's signature. They say that Abraham did indeed write the original papyrus manuscript, but it was passed down and altered by individuals who did not understand it, until it was finally buried with a princess who may or may not have realized its significance.

Translations of the Papyri

The small Sen Sen papyrus connected with the Book of Abraham was not written in hieroglyphics, the formal and bulky writing used in inscriptions, but in hieratic, the cursive business script which was a simplified form of hieroglyphics. From the symbols on this papyrus, Joseph Smith fashioned 5,470 words of the text of the Book of Abraham. It seems strange that he could have given Mr. Chandler an immediate "while you wait" translation, but had to go to all the trouble in a busy time of his life to formulate an Egyptian grammar.

Joseph Smith rendered one single symbol (which in Egyptian is *Khon*, the moon god) into the following passage:

> And his voice was unto me: Abraham, Abraham, behold, my name is Jehovah, and I have heard thee, and have come down to deliver thee, and to take thee away from thy father's house, and from all thy kins-folk, into a strange land which thou knowest not of;
>
> And this because they have turned their hearts away from me, to worship the god of Elkenah, and the god of Libnah, and the god of Mahmackrah, and the god of Korash, and the god of Pharaoh, king of Egypt; therefore I have come to visit them, and to destroy him who hath lifted up his hand against thee, Abraham, my son, to take away thy life. Behold I will lead thee by my hand, and I will take thee, to put upon thee my name, even the Priesthood of thy father, and my power shall be over thee.
>
> As it was with Noah, so shall it be with thee, but through thy ministry my name shall be known in the earth forever, for I am thy God.   —*Pearl of Great Price,* Abraham 1:16-19

How Joseph Smith could get all this—with the proper names of Abraham, Jehovah, Elkenah, Libnah, Mahmackrah, Korash, Pharaoh, Egypt, Priesthood, and Noah—out of a one-syllable word is hard to believe. At another point he "translated" the sixty-one words of Abraham 1:11 from the Egyptian symbol meaning "the" or "this," and Mormons have been elated that this passage contains both words.

Dee Jay Nelson in his book, *The Joseph Smith Papyri,* calculated that the proportion of English words in the Book of Abraham as compared to its source, the small Sen Sen, to be twenty-five words to each hieratic character. The forty-six symbols used by Joseph Smith in a 1,125-word passage from the Egyptian Alphabet and Grammar wouldn't even cover the vocables in the proper names in the passage under investigation, and would have left an additional 1,060 words unaccounted for.

When faced with this sort of evidence, most Mormons will agree that Joseph Smith could not have "translated" the Book of Abraham from the small Sen Sen papyrus; at least not by any process that could properly be called translating. But this just leads Mormons to further specu-lations—that the Book of Abraham was translated with the Urim and Thummim (in spite of what Joseph Fielding Smith said about that instru-ment never being used after the receipt of the Melchizidek Priest-hood)—or that the Book of Abraham was translated by means of a seer stone which the church possesses even today—or that Joseph Smith was simply "inspired" to bring forth the Book of Abraham using the papyri in a manner we cannot understand. (I'm not sure I can understand any of the proposed methods.)

This uncertainty has led to caution in recent LDS publications. Many Mormons refuse to use the word "translation" in referring to the Book of Abraham any more. They refer to the Sen Sen as "an aid to inspiration" and some speak of the symbols thereon as "super-cryptograms," claim-ing that if Christians can get a spiritual meaning out of the Song of Solomon, then the same should be true of the Book of the Dead. But behind this stands the irrefutable fact that Joseph Smith stated that the Book of Abraham was *translated* from the writings of Abraham himself, written on the papyrus purchased from Chandler.

When truly translated, this is what an Egyptologist has said that the small Sen Sen says:

> Osiris shall be conveyed into the Great Pool of Khons—and likewise Osiris Hor, justified, born to Kikhebyt, justified—after his arms have been placed on his heart and the Breathing Permit (which [Isis] made and has writing on its inside and outside) has been wrapped in royal linen and placed under his left arm near his heart; the rest of his mummy-bandages should be wrapped over it. The man for whom this book has been copied will breathe forever and ever as the bas of the gods do.[18]

The underlinings in the above translations occurred when the translator came to illegible parts of the papyrus. But when Joseph Smith came to such places, or even to holes in the scroll, he just made up his own symbols, put them into the Egyptian Alphabet and Grammar, and "translated" on with no interruption.

The Facsimiles

The translation done by Joseph Smith must be considered to be printed exactly as he wrote it, because he was the editor of the *Times and Seasons* when the Book of Abraham was printed therein. The woodcuts which were illustrations of some of the pictures on the scrolls must have met with his approval, too, for we read in *History of the Church* that Joseph inspected and corrected the work done by the woodcarver Hedlock.[19]

Even Mormon scholars, though, admit the quality of the woodcut illustrations has worsened with each printing of the *Pearl of Great Price*. But it is not hard for me to understand why the LDS Church does not publish new editions of the *Pearl of Great Price* with photographs of the papyri illustrations upon which the woodcuts were based. The reason is that the papyri betray even worse than the woodcuts the fact that Joseph Smith was completely unfamiliar with the things the papyri depicted. One Mormon apologist, Nephi Jensen, tried in the early 1940s to prove that Joseph Smith had been able to interpret some of the symbols on the facsimiles. But usually the nearest that Joseph Smith could get to a true interpretation of the illustrations was when he labeled a great percentage of the elements as "gods." By the law of averages and considering the fact that papyri depicted obviously supernatural beings, he was right at least part of the time. But Mormons of today insist that the facsimiles contain two levels of meaning. There is the obvious meaning that any Egyptologist could extract, they say. But there is also a deeper meaning that the illustrations suggested to the prophet, a meaning understood only by the priest class, that would convey the true meaning.

There are three facsimiles printed in the *Pearl of Great Price*. The first one was identified by Joseph Smith as a representation of an attempt by a wicked Egyptian priest to sacrifice Abraham on an altar. The only things in the woodcut which look strange—that is, uniquely un-Egyptian—do not appear on the original papyrus. For instance, part of the papyrus where the jackal head of the god of embalming, Anubis, once appeared had flaked away, even in Joseph Smith's day. Some nineteenth-century person, probably Joseph Smith, simply glued the papyrus to a piece of paper and penciled in a new head—that of a human—and labeled it "the idolatrous priest of Elkenah." He also drew a knife into the "priest's" hand to reinforce his assertion that this was a sacrificial scene. Joseph Smith called the representation of the dead man's "ba" or soul, which hovered over his body, the Angel of the Lord—which blows all kinds of holes in the Mormon argument that angels don't have wings.

Facsimile Number Two is a poor copy of what Egyptologists would call a hypocephalus. This was a disc placed under the head of a mummy. Unfortunately, the original hypocephalus was not in the collection found in the New York Metropolitan Museum, and its whereabouts are unknown. There are enough extant copies of authentic hypocephali, though, to ascertain what one should look like. Egyptologists were puzzled for many years when they tried to determine the translation of the inscription written around the rim of Joseph Smith's copy of his hypocephalus. Then a few years ago researcher Grant Heward discovered that some of the hieroglyphic writing had been replaced by a few lines copied from the Hor Sen Sen fragment. This was evidently done by someone who couldn't read Egyptian—which makes Joseph Smith a prime suspect!—because the hieratic (cursive) Sen Sen characters were copied in upside down, alongside the hieroglyphic (formal) characters, complete with the spelling errors of the scribe who wrote the Sen Sen.

On the inside portion of the hypocephalus, another missing portion was filled in with a boat containing the hawk-headed god Ra. This god was apparently copied from the papyrus fragment commonly known as the "Trinity" fragment because of the three-headed god represented on it. In addition, Joseph Smith identified a god with an obviously erect phallus as the Holy Ghost.

An additional problem associated with Joseph Smith's use of a hypocephalus is the fact that no such thing existed until late in Egypt's history—at least a thousand years after Abraham. Some Mormons have concluded that Abraham began the hypocephalus drawings, and that later scribes completed them and put them into the form of a hypocephalus. This is stretching the whole issue far too much for comfort.

Facsimile Number Three has also been a great problem for Mormons, because the figures that Joseph Smith labeled as (1) Pharaoh, (2) Abraham, (3) a prince, (4) Shulem, a waiter, and (5) a slave have their real names written above them on the papyrus. They are accurately identified as (1) the goddess Isis, (2) the god of the dead, Osiris, (3) the goddess of truth, Maat, (4) a dead man named Hor for whom the scroll was written (obviously the focal point of the whole picture, for all the others are looking at him), and (5) the god Anubis (part of whose head was missing in the original papyrus). This was the facsimile which so disturbed me when I realized that the women were all identified by Joseph Smith as men. Critics of Mormonism have also noted that Abraham 1:27 states that Pharaoh was a descendant of Ham (and thus a Negro), yet the figure that Joseph Smith labeled as Pharaoh is white.

Blacks, the Priesthood, and the Papyri

The whole issue of denying priesthood to blacks has come from this Egyptian Book of the Dead. Even the verse in the Book of Abraham

(1:26) which talked of blacks and the priesthood came from a *hole in the papyrus*. But in stubbornly defending this impious fraud, the Mormon Church has, for over a hundred years, given blacks a second-class status in their organization.

The Bible has been clear on who is entitled to God's grace and blessings:

> God has shown me that I should not call any man impure or unclean
> . . . I now realize how true it is that God does not show favoritism
> but accepts men from every nation who fear him and do what is right.

—Acts 10:28, 34-35 NIV

Even the *Book of Mormon* echoed the same idea:

> For none of these iniquities come of the Lord; for he doeth that which is good among the children of men; and he doeth nothing save it be plain unto the children of men; and he inviteth them all to come unto him and partake of his goodness; and he denieth none that come unto him, black and white, bond and free, male and female; and he remembereth the heathen; and all are alike unto God, both Jew and Gentile.

—2 Nephi 26:33

The *Book of Mormon* was first published in 1830. How could the LDS Church make such a complete turnabout in doctrine? Wallace Turner, in trying to analyze the evolvement of the anti-Negro policies, noted that the early Mormons were mainly from New England, New York, and Ohio—all abolitionist areas. But when the Mormons moved to Missouri, a slave state, problems began to erupt between them and Missourians, who thought the Mormons wanted free blacks to immigrate to their state. The Missourians got this impression from an imprudently-worded editorial printed in the LDS periodical *Evening and Morning Star*, July, 1833. Mormons overreacted in trying to remove that impression, and by 1836 the LDS publication *Messenger and Advocate* was saying it was fine to free slaves after purchasing them from their owners—just so you put the freed blacks on another continent. The publication of the completed Book of Abraham in 1842 finally provided the scriptural meat Mormons were hungry to sink their teeth into.

Policies of the Church Concerning Blacks

Negroes were defined by Brigham Young as those having a "flat nose and black skin."[20] He enlarged upon this by making a statement which has haunted Mormons ever since. He said that no man with even a single drop of Negroid blood in his veins could hold the Mormon priesthood.

Of course Mormon leaders have not been willing to bear the entire burden of answering those who would want to know why they denied the priesthood to blacks. After all, even the "prophet" David O. McKay once commented that the whole issue was based upon only the one verse in the Book of Abraham. With such a thin foundation for such a controversial issue of doctrine, Mormons look to God to show that He is the great Segregator, for did He not place the first blacks way over there in Africa?

In Brigham Young's day, anyone of the "chosen race" who was found "mixing his blood with the seed of Cain" would be subject to an immediate death penalty. I wasn't aware that Brigham intended this as an eternal principle, but he stated that this "law of God" would "always be so."[21]

The Mormon historian, B. H. Roberts, said that Cain, because of his murder of his brother, was cursed with a black skin. His Negro blood was passed down and preserved during the flood through Egyptus, the black wife of Ham.[22] Other Mormons believe that Egyptus was pregnant with child by another black man when she entered the ark, and thus her son Canaan was a full-blooded black while all her other children by Ham were half black.[23] Therefore, all the descendants of Ham were Negroid.

The question might arise as to why God would allow such a cursed race to continue through the flood. Brigham Young taught that Cain recognized that if he killed his brother Abel, all his own posterity would be cursed, but he, and the pre-existent spirits who would become his descendants agreed to share the burden together.[24] (Such premeditation is uncharacteristic of the Cain I read of in Genesis!) President John Taylor said in the *Journal of Discourses* that it was necessary for the posterity of Cain to continue through the flood so that the devil could be represented on the earth through them, and through their influence help provide the "opposition" Mormons believe is so necessary.

According to the *Pearl of Great Price,* Ham and the Negress Egyptus had a daughter whom they also named Egyptus. Her son, Pharaoh, was the first ruler of the land of Egypt, which his mother had discovered. Pharaoh, being of the blood of Egyptus and Ham, was "cursed . . . as pertaining to the priesthood" (Abraham 1:26; see also v. 27). Here, then, is the entire scriptural basis upon which Mormons have built the anti-Negro teachings they held for so long. You can look through the *Doctrine and Covenants* and the *Book of Mormon* and never find anything else to substantiate this view—and of course, the Bible teaches that the gospel—in its fulness—is for all people with no regard for their race.

As early as 1843 Joseph Smith was advocating "national equalization" for blacks while restricting them by law to marry only those of their own race.[25] Brigham Young went even further with his rabid abhorrence of black-white relations, insisting that Negroes, because of inherent stupidity, were *meant* to serve whites. He stated: "The Canaanite cannot have wisdom to do things as the white man has."[26] The *Juvenile Instructor,* a Mormon publication, spoke of the Negro's intelligence as being "stunted."[27] A recent president of the LDS Church, Joseph Fielding Smith, once spoke of Negroes as being "an inferior race."[28] Smith later tried to soften his hard public stand against Negroes with the equally insulting remark in *Look Magazine* that " 'darkies' are wonderful people, and they have their place in our church."

What Joseph Fielding Smith objected so much to, and why he was so adamantly opposed to Negroes, was the thought of white Mormons marrying blacks—Mormon or not. Mormon apostle Mark E. Petersen went so far as to say in 1954 that Negroes had as a primary objective in life the mingling of their race with whites through intermarriage. Though I realize that this statement was made before the saying, "Black is beautiful," I am sure there were blacks even twenty-five years ago who had no intention of "breaking into" the white race by marriage.

Alex Haley's *Roots* has only intensified an overwhelming racial pride that has existed among Negroes for generations, and Mormon leaders have inordinately flattered themselves by presuming that Negroes would *want* to intermarry with them. After all, how many Negroes are masochistic enough to want to associate with people whose leaders have declared that Negroes are inferior?

Here, again, Mormons are not willing to bear the responsibility for their racial views alone. Whereas they blame earthly segregation of Negroes on the God who placed Negroes in Africa, they blame the Negroes themselves for their years without the Mormon priesthood. According to Alvin R. Dyer and many other LDS authorities, Negroes before 1978 did not have the priesthood because they themselves *rejected* it in the pre-existence. In the time before the world was created, Negroes were: "not faithful,"[29] "less valiant,"[30] "indifferent in their support of the righteous cause,"[31] and "less worthy."[32]

All these remarks have to do with the theory that when Christ and Satan squared off in the pre-existence, one-third of the spirits there went with Satan (and were cast down to earth), and of the remainder, some sided enthusiastically with Christ, and the rest just kind of dragged along with the Savior. For this lack of devotion, these last spirits were sent to earth in black bodies that would be a sign to priesthood holders that they should not pass on their priesthood to these sluggish spirits. Negroes could be baptized, but could not hold the priesthood. Now, the implications of being a black Mormon man were these: Unlike your white counterparts, you were barred from receiving any vital inspiration for anyone except your wife and children, since you could hold no priesthood responsibility over anyone else. Your wife and children were yours for life only, because you couldn't be married "for eternity" in a Mormon temple. Without such higher ordinances, you had no hope of being exalted in the celestial kingdom as your white brothers were—though you could go there as a servant to them. (In fact, a Negro woman was once formally "sealed" to Joseph Smith as a servant. Mormon leaders seemed piqued that this "did not satisfy her, and she pleaded for her endowments.")[33]

A friend of Joseph Smith, a Negro man by the name of Elijah Abel, was ordained an elder, and later a seventy. He served a mission in Canada, too, before his death in 1884. Mormons say this was done "before the word of the Lord was fully understood," and they consider Abel's ordinations as a fluke in their history. However, they deny that Abel's son Enoch and grandson Elijah were ordained to the priesthood—the younger Elijah as late as 1934, in Logan, Utah.[34]

Lester Bush, writing in the liberal publication, *Dialogue: A Journal of Mormon Thought,* related that a recent president of the church, David O. McKay, let a young Negro be ordained to the priesthood because the blessing the young man received from his patriarch said that, despite the outward appearances of the young man and his relatives, he was not of the "cursed" lineage. McKay also authorized the sealing in a temple of two Negro children to the white Mormon couple who had adopted them.[35]

David O. McKay also stated privately once that he, unlike most other Mormons, didn't believe that Negroes were under any curse. In fact, he thought the whole Negro issue within Mormonism hinged on a practice, not a doctrine, which he hoped would be soon discontinued.[36] The Negro problem was surely burdensome to Mormons during McKay's presidency, for that was the time that many Western Athletic Conference schools boycotted athletic events with Brigham Young University. Pressure from black organizations was levied on the Mormon Church, but to no avail. The church's stand on Negroes and the priesthood could only be changed, Mormons insisted, by a revelation from God.

The Reorganized Church, meanwhile, had managed to avoid all these problems almost before they began. Joseph Smith's son, Joseph Smith III, in 1865 announced that he had received a revelation (now in their scriptural canon) which cleared the way for ordination of blacks.

Blacks in the Church

In the absence of a like revelation, the Utah church tried to make visible changes that would appease its critics. In 1970, for instance, the first black singers were admitted to the Mormon Tabernacle Choir. The church made a big hullabaloo over the blacks who joined the church, too. The one with whom I was most familiar was Alan Cherry, a convert to the church who was a popular speaker at BYU. Before he became a Mormon, he was overweight, and had problems with drinking, smoking, the use of marijuana, immoral behavior, and anti-white attitudes. He embarked on a search for truth, a self-concept, and Christ. Unfortunately he settled for Mormonism. Alan Cherry became famous because he was an exception—one happy black Mormon willing to say so in a church population of four million.

Mormons would have you believe that its black members have always been meek and patient, content to work hard for the church and wait for the day when they would have their "curse" removed. But many weren't happy without the priesthood, and said so. And non-LDS Negroes living in Utah know how the Mormon doctrine has clouded the atmosphere in that state for them. D. R. Oliver, a black lawyer, wrote a book, *A Negro on Mormonism,* in which he said that Utah was worse than the South for blacks who wanted employment other than menial labor.

Though Mormons have claimed to welcome blacks into their church as members, they have never actively proselyted among black people. While Mormons were claiming on the one hand that they loved their Negro friends, and on the other hand avoiding them with the message Mormons consider to be essential for salvation, some very strange things were going on in the background. Polynesian men who had joined the Mormon Church were given the priesthood, because they were on the "isles of the sea."[37] The *Book of Mormon* story forced Mormons into the assumption that the islanders, too, were of the chosen race. Of course, anthropologists know that most people of, say, the Fiji Islands are Negroid and not Semitic. Mormons, then, have been bestowing their priesthood on certain blacks for many years.

Mormon sociologist Lowry Nelson was consulted in 1947 to ascertain the plausibility of sending LDS missionaries into Cuba. Nelson replied that, from his professional observations, there had been so much racial mixing in that country that he doubted there were any "pure" whites. Brigham Young, you will remember, had taught that even "one drop" of Negro blood in a man's veins would disqualify him from receiving the priesthood. Lowry Nelson was disturbed, as have been many Mormons who value their religion, and he could not understand why the gospel should be denied to someone because of his ancestry.

In 1963 the Mormon Church announced that it would send missionaries to eastern Nigeria. But the Nigerian government refused to give visas to missionaries because of the church's racist policies. Black Nigerian Mormons continued to write to Salt Lake City for instructions and books on doctrine for their newfound religion. By 1965 *Time* magazine reported a Mormon membership of seven thousand Ibibio, Ibo, and Efik tribesmen in Nigeria.[38] Then the whole Mormon system started to crumble. The Nigerian Mormon leader, Anie Dick Obot, set himself up as bishop over a council of seventy-five elders, not knowing that the priesthood was "necessary" for such an organizational move. The Utah leaders meanwhile were appalled by this, and by the publicity that the Nigerians were getting over their practice of the Mormon tenet of polygamy. The whole Nigerian Mormon empire disappeared almost without a trace, like the wicked cities of the Old Testament, when the Nigerians belatedly learned of the LDS Church's teachings of the "inferiority" of the black race.

The New "Revelation"

It was about 1963, too, that Church leaders began openly discussing a possible change in their Negro policy. Hugh B. Brown, a general authority, said that the "problem" was being "considered."[39] But then as people forgot about Nigeria, the whole thing was quietly dropped.

Pressure continued, from within the church—angry white and black members who sensed the unfairness of the church's stand—and outside the church. Each time a Mormon leader was asked when Negroes could receive the priesthood, the reply would be: "When God reveals that the time is right."

As a Mormon, I never thought I'd see the day that a Negro would hold the priesthood. Brigham Young had said many times that God would never allow a black to rule over a white in government or religion. He also said that the seed of Cain (who had supposedly rejected the priesthood in the first place) wouldn't have the priesthood until after death[40] and after *all* of Adam's other children's seed had "had the privilege of receiving the priesthood and having received their resurrection from the dead."[41] A recent president of the church, the late Joseph Fielding Smith, explored the implications of Young's teachings on when Negroes could receive the priesthood and concluded that Abel, Adam's son, must be resurrected, achieve godhood, and raise up posterity "on some other world" before any faithful descendants of his murderer could receive the priesthood.[42]

On June 9, 1978, I was driving down the street on my way to meet my husband for lunch. I was listening to the radio when I heard an announcement from the national news service that the Mormon Church had introduced a new policy regarding Negroes and their priesthood. I shook my head. There had to be some mistake. As a Mormon, I had regarded such an eventuality in the same way I'd viewed death, and the second coming—they'd all happen sooner or later but too far away time-wise to worry about. As a Christian, I had come to the conclusion that Mormons were much too stubborn to ever back down on the Negro issue. But as the radio continued, I saw I was wrong both times. The First

Presidency had released a statement saying that "the long-promised day has come." He said that the Lord had revealed that Negroes could now hold the priesthood. Unlike the revelations of the nineteenth century church, the exact text of this revelation was not given. If President Kimball received some sort of unearthly message in that upper room, I know its source, and it was not of God. Someone might ask if I don't think it good that the Mormon Church finally gave its priesthood to blacks. Though I hope that this would be a good beginning to the breakdown of traditional prejudices, I cannot be happy with any cosmetic change that this organization might effect to make itself and its ungodly doctrines more attractive to my black brethren.

But I don't think Kimball received anything more in that upper room than a realization that he had to make a decision between revelation and the loss of revenue. The Internal Revenue Service had begun examining the tax-exempt status of the multimillion dollar investments of the LDS Church, the admission policies of Brigham Young University and other Mormon schools, and the notorious lack of "affirmative action" in Mormon-owned firms. The church saw in this the beginning of the kind of pressure that the United States government put on it before the polygamy "manifesto" was issued.

Smoldering, too, was the issue of Doug Wallace, a young Mormon who had passed his priesthood on to a black friend. For this, and trying to get speaking time at a Mormon conference, he was excommunicated. He brought suit against the Mormon Church which was unsuccessful, apparently because of poor preparation. But when he came up with what ex-Mormon writer Bob Witte called "an ironclad case," and presented it to a judge, the judge apparently contacted President Kimball and told him that there'd better be a new revelation on the way giving the priesthood to blacks or Wallace would win this new case, with disastrous financial and publicity results for Mormondom.

Then in early June of 1978 the Las Vegas jury came to its decision on the famous "Mormon will" which if validated would have given the LDS Church $150,000,000 of the Howard Hughes fortune. (Incidentally, I don't think that the Mormon Church was behind the forging of this will. They don't need the money that badly. But had the will been verified, I don't think the church would have refused it, either.) At any rate, the will was pronounced a fraud. If you had forgotten all about that will verdict coming out just before the "Negro revelation," that was exactly the way Mormon leaders had planned it.

I'm not sure, actually, that there was any limited number of "reasons" for the timing of the announcement about blacks and the priesthood. Maybe the LDS Church finally realized just how unlikely it is to expect "pure" blood from anyone!

143

The Seed of Ham in the Bible

From the text of Genesis 10:6-20, and from Mormon's identification of Ham's descendants as Canaanites, Philistines, Egyptians, and most early Africans,[43] an ex-Mormon writer by the name of Melaine Layton has shown that all these people were, according to Mormon doctrine, cursed as to the priesthood. Not only could such people not hold the priesthood, but any white man who mixed his blood with them was, according to Brigham Young, subject to an immediate death penalty.[44] This was because the product of any such union could never hold the priesthood.

But if we look at the Bible, we see that Abraham mixed his blood with Hagar, an Egyptian woman (Gen. 16:2-4). Judah married the daughter of Shua, the Canaanitess (1 Chron. 2:3-4). And Joseph married an Egyptian woman through whom he begat Ephraim and Manasseh (Gen. 41:45, 50-52). All white (non-Negro) Mormons are descended from either Ephraim or Manasseh, according to their patriarchal blessings. Therefore they could not even hold their own priesthood, because they are descendants of an Egyptian who was the descendant of Cain![45]

Joseph Fielding Smith denied that Joseph married an Egyptian, saying that she was a Hyksos,[46] but glossed over the fact that she was a Canaanite (a descendant of Ham through Canaan). So it all ends up the same—Mormons themselves come from what they call a "cursed" lineage. Furthermore, Christ was of the lineage of Ham, as the following illustration shows:

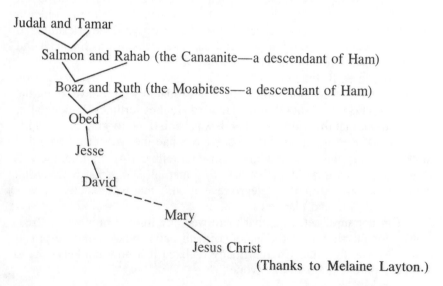

Judah and Tamar

Salmon and Rahab (the Canaanite—a descendant of Ham)

Boaz and Ruth (the Moabitess—a descendant of Ham)

Obed

Jesse

David

Mary

Jesus Christ

(Thanks to Melaine Layton.)

If Mormons couldn't hold their own priesthood until June 9, 1978, and if Christ himself was disqualified from it, who would want it? My black brothers in Christ certainly would not!

The Mormon Church has, by giving Negroes their priesthood, undoubtedly removed financial, social, and governmental pressure from itself. But as was the case in the polygamy issue, Mormons haven't changed the *doctrine*, only the *practice*. And according to that doctrine, blacks are still cursed—unless we are to believe that the last of the "unvaliant" spirits that were born into this world died on June 9, 1978. Mormonism has denied its past "prophets" with this so-called revelation.

I pray to God that more Mormons will have the courage, through the revelation of God in the Bible, to deny the false prophets of Mormonism today.

NOTES

[1]Joseph Smith Jr., *Documentary History of the Church*, II, p. 235.

[2]Keith Terry and Walter Whipple, *From the Dust of Decades* (Salt Lake City: Bookcraft, 1968), p. 68.

[3]Ibid., p. 76.

[4]Ludlow, *A Companion to Your Study*, p. 35.

[5]Ibid.

[6]Dr. Sidney Sperry, *Ancient Records Testify in Papyrus and Stone* (Salt Lake City: Bookcraft, 1938), p. 81.

[7]Terry and Whipple, *From the Dust of Decades*, p. 114.

[8]Ibid., p. 113.

[9]*Daily Universe*, December 1, 1967.

[10]Tanner, *The Case Against Mormonism*, II, p. 140.

[11]Reverend Henry Caswell, *City of the Mormons; or, Three Days at Nauvoo* (London: 1842), pp. 22-23.

[12]Cowdrey, Davis, Scales, *Who Really Wrote the Book of Mormon?* p. 195.

[13]Brodie, *No Man Knows My History*, p. 292.

[14]"Joseph Smith Among the Egyptians," Reprint of an article that appeared in *The Journal of the Evangelical Theological Society* by Wesley P. Walters (Salt Lake City: Modern Microfilm, 1973), Winter, 1973, Vol. XVI, No. 1.

[15]Tanner, *The Case Against Mormonism*, II, p. 163.

[16]Introduction to the Book of Abraham, *Pearl of Great Price*, p. 29.

[17]Tanner, *Mormonism: Shadow or Reality?* p. 320.

[18]Klaus Baer translation quoted in Tanner, *Mormonism, Shadow or Reality?*, p. 317.

[19]Joseph Smith Jr., *Documentary History of the Church*, IV, p. 519.

[20]*Journal of Discourses*, VII, p. 291.

[21]Ibid., X, p. 110.

[22]Tanner, *The Case Against Mormonism*, II, p. 171.

[23]Tanner, *Mormonism: Shadow or Reality?* p. 584.

[24]Ibid., p. 583.

[25]Joseph Fielding Smith, selected and arranged, *Teachings of the Prophet Joseph Smith* (Salt Lake City: Deseret News Press, 1956), p. 270.

[26]Wilford Woodruff, quoted in Jerald and Sandra Tanner, *Mormonism Like Watergate* (Salt Lake City: Modern Microfilm, 1974), p. 15.

[27]*Juvenile Instructor,* Vol. III, p. 157.

[28]Joseph Fielding Smith, *Way to Perfection,* p. 101, quoted in Jerald and Sandra Tanner, *Mormons and Negroes* (Salt Lake City: Modern Microfilm, 1974), p. 2.

[29]Joseph Fielding Smith, *Answers to Gospel Questions,* II, p. 186.

[30]Bruce R. McConkie, *Mormon Doctrine* (Salt Lake: Bookcraft, 1966), 476.

[31]B. H. Roberts, *The Contributor,* Vol. VI, pp. 296-297.

[32]John J. Stewart, *Mormonism and the Negro,* Part 1, p. 50, quoted in Tanner, *Mormons and Negroes,* p. 6.

[33]Tanner, *Mormonism: Shadow or Reality?* p. 584.

[34]Tanner, *Mormons and Negroes,* p. 11.

[35]Lester Bush, *Dialogue: A Journal of Mormon Thought,* Spring, 1973, p. 45.

[36]Tanner, *Mormonism: Shadow or Reality?* p. 290, quoting David O. McKay.

[37]2 Nephi 10:20-21.

[38]*Time,* June 18, 1965, p. 56.

[39]*Newsweek,* June 17, 1963, p. 60.

[40]*Journal of Discourses,* XI, p. 272.

[41]Ibid., II, p. 143.

[42]Joseph Fielding Smith, *Answers to Gospel Questions,* II, p. 188, 1958 edition.

[43]*Juvenile Instructor,* III, p. 157.

[44]*Journal of Discourses,* X, p. 110.

[45]Melaine Layton, "Can the Descendants of Ham Hold the Priesthood?" (Concord, California: Pacific Publishing Company, 1977).

[46]Joseph Fielding Smith, *Answers to Gospel Questions,* I, pp. 169-171.

7
The Precarious Summit
of Continuing Revelation

And whatsoever they shall speak when moved upon by the Holy
Ghost shall be scripture, shall be the will of the Lord, shall be the
mind of the Lord, shall be the word of the Lord, shall be the voice of
the Lord, and the power of God unto salvation.

—Doctrine and Covenants 68:4

Whatever its effects upon the religious world, Mormonism has not,
as it originally purposed, done away with religious division. Its aberra-
tions of Scripture and liberties with the Word of God, though, have
caused Christianity to continually solidify against it. In that sense, Mormonism has unified many otherwise disassociated religious elements. But
it has added its own share of splinter groups to the denominations of the
world, too—and all claim to be the "true" church of Jesus Christ of
Latter-day Saints.

Since the death of Joseph Smith, many denominations claiming authority from him have come into being. Some estimates run as high as one
hundred such groups; a conservative estimate is about sixty. Of that
number, at least sixteen are still in existence.[1] Most of these groups were
founded soon after the death of Joseph Smith. Members of the second-
largest group, the Reorganized Church of Jesus Christ of Latter Day
Saints (note that there is no hyphen between the seventh and eighth words
of the name) are also known as "Josephites," or "Reorganites." They
claim a membership of about 250,000

The Reorganized Saints

The RLDS Church claims that before Joseph Smith died, he ordained his son, Joseph Smith III, to be his successor as prophet, seer, and
revelator. This office has continued to be a hereditary one for them.

The Reorganized Church of Jesus Christ of Latter Day Saints was formally organized in 1859, fifteen years after the death of Joseph Smith. Joseph Smith III was only a young boy when his father died, and after such an experience, it is no wonder that it took him so long to be persuaded by his father's friends to accept the responsibilities of the presidency. He and his successors claim their authority from Joseph Smith and the church that he founded in 1830, but they regard Brigham Young and the subsequent Mormon presidents as false prophets. They are particularly bitter toward Brigham Young, because they claim that he formulated the doctrine of polygamy and ascribed this doctrine of his own to Joseph Smith to give it validity. To support this, they cite Joseph Smith's public denials before his death of the practice. The Utah Mormon doctrine of men progressing to become gods, too, Reorganites attribute to Brigham Young. They say that he caused the records of the church to be falsified to make it seem that Joseph Smith had also taught this during his lifetime.

The Reorganized Church has its headquarters in Independence, Missouri. Their own editions of the *Book of Mormon* and the *Doctrine and Covenants,* along with Joseph Smith's Inspired Version of the Bible, make up their canon of scripture. They deny the revelations of the *Doctrine and Covenants* which they say were written after the death of Joseph Smith (notably the section on polygamy and those writings of Brigham Young and Wilford Woodruff), and continue to add new material to their *Doctrine and Covenants* and to publish such new revelations as they are "received." They reject utterly the "ancient" writings in the *Pearl of Great Price.*

In all deference to the RLDS Church, there is nonetheless a wealth of documentation to prove to the serious student that Joseph Smith did indeed preach the plurality of gods who were once men, and the doctrine of polygamy—even though he publicly denied the latter. Persons who were appalled by these teachings were attracted to the Reorganized Church since it maintained the truth of things like the *Book of Mormon* but rejected those doctrines to which they objected, a sort of half-way house between false doctrine and *falser* doctrine.

Since the Reorganized Church does not have the elaborate temple rites of the Mormon Church, their temple services are open to the public. They maintain a missionary force, but their workers, unlike the Mormon missionaries who might come to your door, are salaried.

Strangites

Another splinter group is known as the Church of Jesus Christ of Latter-day Saints, Strangite. It is named after James J. Strang, one of the Nauvoo convert followers of Joseph Smith. Strang claimed that the very day that Joseph Smith died an angel appeared to him, Strang, and anointed him to be the successor. Strang also produced a letter from

Joseph Smith that supposedly designated him as the next president of the church in the event of the death of the prophet. Many, many of the influential Mormons of the day followed Strang when he went to Wisconsin, including two of the apostles and William Smith, the brother of Joseph. His position was strengthened by his "vision," which had all the hallmarks of divine authority such as Joseph Smith had. He also "found" a clay receptacle buried in the ground which contained brass plates inscribed with strange characters. When he "translated" them with the aid of a Urim and Thummim, they named him as Joseph's true successor. Later, he received some plates he called the plates of Laban, which when translated by him advocated polygamy. Of course he could not be lax in following God's commands, and among the wives he took was one who had toured the East with him disguised as a male secretary until her pregnancy gave her away.

This odd-looking little redhead was known to his followers as "King James," and the Strangite group once numbered almost 3000. They established themselves in the Beaver Island area of Lake Michigan as "The Kingdom of Saint James."

The *Book of Mormon,* the *Doctrine and Covenants,* and the *Law of the Lord* (translated from "the plates of Laban") are the scriptures Strangites live by. Strang himself, like Joseph Smith, died a martyr to his cause, assassinated by some members of the church he had founded. He left behind five pregnant grieving widows and a crumbling kingdom.

There are very few Strangites today. They deny the virgin birth, the atonement of Christ, and the authority of the Utah Mormon prophets. They worship on Saturday, and attempt to keep the Law of Moses by, among other things, circumcising their males and by offering animal sacrifices.

Hedrickites and Fettingites

The Church of Christ, Hedrickite, also known as the Church of Christ, Temple Lot, is centered in the Independence, Missouri, area like their Reorganite cousins. They number about 1500. Their one most outstanding feature is the fact that they own the very spot that Joseph Smith dedicated as the site of the New Jerusalem temple to be built in Independence. Despite lawsuits, attractive financial offers, and additional stringent efforts by other LDS groups to take this land from them, they still own it. They make it plain that they have absolutely no intentions of giving it up. They once started construction on a temple but, because of their limited finances, were unable to get any further in the building process than the excavation of a large hole, which the city of Independence finally filled up again. This small group does not believe in nor do

149

they practice polygamy nor baptism for the dead, and they reject the Utah Mormon doctrine of men progressing to become gods.

A Hedrickite by the name of Otto Fetting formed another group, known as the Church of Christ, Fettingite, after he claimed to have been visited by John the Baptist in 1930. This and subsequent messages from this heavenly being through Fetting had as their prime objective the building of the temple on the two-and-one-half-acre Hedrickite plot. They differ doctrinally very little from their mother church, the Hedrickites.

Bickertonites

The Church of Jesus Christ of Latter Day Saints, Bickertonite, was founded in 1862 by Sidney Rigdon and one of his ex-Mormon followers. This man, Bickerton, was told by God to center his people in St. John, Kansas, in 1874. Six years later he himself was disfellowshiped from the church and was succeeded by William Cadman. Another man by this same name now heads the Bickertonite Church, which in its one-hundred-year history has endured four splits. It has only a few hundred American adherents, most of whom live in Monongahela, Pennsylvania. They do claim, however, to have 3500 black African members. They do not practice polygamy, nor baptism for the dead, nor do they believe in more than one God.

Fundamentalists

Perhaps the splinter group of Mormonism about which most is rumored and least known is the Fundamentalists. There are several sects which come under this heading. They are distinguished by their adherence, against all odds, to the doctrine and practice of polygamy. *Newsweek* in 1955 estimated that Utah polygamists numbered about twenty thousand, which number included wives and children. A conservative modern estimate is thirty thousand.

Mainstream Utah Mormons will often lie to cover up for polygamous neighbors under federal investigation because, though they themselves can't practice plural marriage on earth, church doctrine requires that they accept the principle. Most third- or fourth-generation Mormons have polygamous ancestors in their family tree. These two factors will cause them to protect those whose actions they cannot condone.

Most Fundamentalists are among the more faithful of all LDS group members because they consider themselves defenders of the true faith, who are willing to suffer any persecution for their beliefs. Some Fundamentalists feel they are actually a part of the mainstream LDS Church, which they think only issued the Manifesto to ease government pressures on itself. Others are bitter about the Manifesto and feel that if the Utah church doesn't believe in Section 132 of the *Doctrine and Covenants* enough to practice it, they should "tear it out of the book."[2]

Most Fundamentalists live in Salt Lake City and Bountiful, Utah, near the Utah-Arizona border, and in northern and southeastern Arizona. These live in constant fear of exposure. Others who would escape such pressure have moved to Mexico, where they live in "colonies."

Plural marriages, with the sanction of the Utah church, were performed in Mexico for at least fourteen years after the Manifesto, according to Stanley S. Ivins, the son of Anthony Ivins, who performed such marriages.[3] Many Mormons in Mexico are products of polygamous marriages, and many follow the example of their fathers in taking plural wives. It is the most faithful mainstream Mormon, in fact, who would be tempted to practice polygamy. Samuel Taylor observed, "Modern Mormons believe in plural marriage, but not its practice. The more deeply immersed a Mormon becomes, the thinner the line may become between belief and practice. The threat of Fundamentalist doctrine is to the most devout."[4]

So who is right among these sects? All claim authority from Joseph Smith, and all are founded upon "revelation." Who is to say that James Strang's anointing by an angel has less authority than Brigham Young's selection as prophet by his friends? Why should the "Law of the Lord" be less important than *Conference Reports* of last April's general conference of the Utah Church? If John the Baptist told Otto Fetting, who believed in the *Book of Mormon* with all his heart, to build the New Jerusalem temple, why aren't missionaries of all LDS sects doing it?

Now, I was a member of the Utah Mormon Church. What I've said about the other sects I know primarily from what I've read about them. Mormon splinter groups are the illegitimate stepchildren who are pushed into closets and forgotten until someone is rude enough to mention their names. The fact that they even exist as descendants of a church founded on perfect revelation is a blemish on its reputation.

The Nature of Revelation

To understand Mormon doctrine, you must understand the nature of revelation as the Mormons understand it. Man must be as active a participant as God. Man's part in revelation is this: (1) he must desire and seek revelation, (2) he must have faith, (3) he must be worthy in character, (4) he must have an objective need or purpose, and (5) usually he must be aware of this need.[5]

Basically, Mormon doctrine delineates six basic types of revelation. The first is a direct message from a heavenly being, such as Joseph Smith received when Moroni appeared to him. The second kind is a vision, such as is recorded in *Doctrine and Covenants* Section 110, wherein Joseph Smith and Oliver Cowdery saw the Savior standing on the breastwork of the pulpit in the Kirtland Temple. A third type of revelation is that received by means of a physical object, such as a peepstone, the "rod of Aaron,"[6] or the Urim and Thummim that Joseph Smith used to translate the *Book of Mormon*. Dreams are a fourth type of revelation. They are exemplified by the dream experience of Heber C. Kimball in his journal, where he saw the soon-to-be opened mission field of England represented by a field of diseased wheat. This signified the area's lack of spiritual depth. A fifth type of revelation is typified by this story about Joseph Smith: "At times the inspiration of the Holy Ghost came upon him with such force he knew the ideas that had entered his mind were of divine origin."[7] The last and most commonly experienced type of revelation is that which comes through a spiritual confirmation, and was defined in *Doctrine and Covenants* 9:8-9:

> But, behold, I say unto you that you must study it out in your mind; then you must ask me if it be right, and if it is right I will cause that your bosom shall burn within you; therefore, you shall feel that it is right. But if it be not right you shall have no such feelings, but you shall have a stupor of thought that shall cause you to forget the thing which is wrong.

This "burning in the breast" is the type of revelation relied upon by most Mormons. It is differentiated from the "force of revelation" just discussed by the fact that this is the confirmation of what could be an otherwise "uninspired" idea or purposed course of action.

Mormons recognize the broad use of the word "inspiration" to pertain to the fields of music, art, physics, geometry, and house-training a puppy. It would be accurate for a Mormon to say sincerely that a profligate like Lord Byron was "inspired" because he wrote good poetry, as was Paul Gauguin who left his wife and family so he could paint. I would not deny that these men were masters of their arts, but would question if God inspired them in their works or their lives.

The importance of "inspiration" in Mormon life cannot be overestimated. Christians believe the Word of God, in the Bible, is revelation to us. But Mormons, who believe that direct revelation is available to them, must of necessity view scripture as "secondhand revelation."

This is borne out by a Mormon apologist who said, "In spiritual knowledge, I must say that my own experiences with prayer, the Spirit, and revelation are *Primary* evidence, whereas the evidence and testimony of the scriptures, of the prophets, and other good, believing people, and of the historical record of mankind are secondary."[8] From this quote it is easy to see that personal revelation is put on one level, while the scriptures, opinions of sincere persons (even if they're wrong), and secular history are put below. Mormons are therefore encouraged to seek revelation for themselves.

The Mechanics of Revelation

Mormon revelation is by its very nature iconoclastic. Joseph Smith, in Mormon eyes, *had* to receive direct revelation to organize the church because "the doctrines and disciplines of other churches would not suffice; in effect, new wine could not be put into old bottles."[9] But this revelation, though revolutionary, was also perfect. Joseph Fielding Smith, a recent president of the church, stated categorically that there was "no need for eliminating, changing, or adjusting any part" of revelation to make it harmonize with previous revelations.[10] Mormon leaders speak glowingly of how new revelation "dovetails" into old, fitting as exactly as die-cut jigsaw puzzle pieces.

In Mormon theology, there is no "revelation" that is more authoritative than another, because all are the Word of God. Brigham Young once said, "I have never yet preached a sermon, and sent it out to the children of men, that they may not call it Scripture."[11]

Today the doctrine is well defined which specifies who can receive revelation about what. A member of the Mormon Church can receive revelation for himself and his subordinates. Thus, a mother can receive revelation for herself and her children; a man for himself, his wife, and children. A bishop is entitled to revelation for himself, his counselors, his family, and the members of the ward over which he presides. Only the president of the church, therefore, can receive revelation for the church or the world at large. In keeping with the "dovetail" idea, any revelation must concur with previous revelation to be acceptable—unless it comes from a prophet.

Joseph's Successors

Joseph Smith's death in 1844 marked the end of the age of visions. Subsequent "prophets" never seemed to reach the heights of revelation that Joseph did. Brigham Young, the second president of the Mormon Church, was no dreamer; he was a doer. His reign over the church was characterized by marked numerical and financial growth. At the time of his death he presided over 140,000 people who had scratched 360 towns out of the arid southwestern dirt. He is remembered for his gruff manner, his many wives and children, and his hatred for anyone or anything that got into the way of his dreams of Mormon independence. No matter what his faults, he was loyal to his prophet to the end. His dying words were, "Joseph! Joseph!"

John Taylor, the Church's third prophet, had as his hardest task the job of living up to the leadership qualities and force of character of his predecessors. He was present in the Carthage jail with Joseph Smith when he was killed, and, like Brigham, was loyal to Joseph all his life. Taylor died in exile because of government pressure due to his views on polygamy, which he staunchly defended all his life.

His successor, Wilford Woodruff, is remembered by Mormons almost solely for the Manifesto. But though he was only president of the Church for nine years, under his direction the Salt Lake Temple was completed, Utah achieved statehood, and most important—he was able to hold together the crumbling shambles of a Mormonism shaken by the polygamy issue.

Successor to Woodruff was Lorenzo Snow, president from 1898 until 1901. He is remembered by Mormons almost exclusively for his emphasis on tithing whereby "the windows of heaven" were opened, along with members' pocketbooks. The interpretation of the law of tithing as a strict ten percent of one's gross income is the reason that the Utah church is so much wealthier than the Reorganized church, which requires ten percent of one's "increase"—what is left over after living expenses.

The next president of the Mormon Church was also the first near relative of Joseph Smith to hold the office. His name was Joseph Fielding Smith, but because there was a later president (his son) by the same name, he is referred to as Joseph F. Smith. He was only five years old when Joseph Smith died and was the son of Hyrum Smith, the prophet's brother who with him was killed in Carthage jail. Under the leadership of Joseph F. Smith, the great debts under which the church had struggled were paid off in 1907, and a new era of prosperity for the Mormons began. During his presidency, however, the Church was shaken by the investigation of an LDS Senator. The issue at hand was whether this man, Reed Smoot, could discharge his duties as a U. S. Senator with the conflicting demands his religion might make on him. (Patriotism was not an outstanding characteristic of the Mormons of that day.) Smoot was exonerated, but in the course of the "Smoot hearings" Joseph F. Smith was called as a witness. Here the "prophet" made the amazing admission that during his presidency, "I have never pretended to nor do I profess to have received revelations."[12]

When Smith died in 1918 he was followed in the presidency by Heber J. Grant. Grant had grown up close to Brigham Young, and his own extreme poverty as a boy made him particularly concerned with this problem in the Church. In 1936 he initiated the program of two-year storage of food and that same year the Welfare Plan was organized. Both are today outstanding features of the LDS Church.

George Albert Smith, the eighth president and also a relative of Joseph Smith, served from 1945 until 1951. A scholarly-looking man, he encouraged Church involvement in the Boy Scout program and authorized the first printing of the *Book of Mormon* in Braille. He was also known for his wry sense of humor. Once a member wrote to ask him what he thought of two controversial issues, cocoa and cremation. He thought a moment and then replied to his secretary, "Write and tell him that they're both hot."

David O. McKay presided over the Church during a period of unparalleled peace and prosperity. Problems over the Church's position on Negroes, however, were intensified when the *Pearl of Great Price* papyri were discovered, casting doubt on the ability of latter-day "prophets" to translate. McKay emphasized missionary work, and one of his favorite sayings was, "Every member a missionary." He encouraged a weekly "Family Home Evening" for members, and many temples were dedicated or begun during his presidency. He was active politically and tried to influence his subordinates to oppose both the repeal of right to work laws and liquor by the drink in Utah. But he made no dramatic statements of doctrine, no great public prophecies, in his many years of leadership. In only one thing did he break radically with tradition: he was the first president since Joseph Smith who didn't wear a beard.

Much controversy within the Church was stirred up when Joseph Fielding Smith became president. Son of President Joseph F. Smith, he was the most authoritative spokesman on church doctrine in recent years. Though his succession to the office of "prophet, seer, and revelator" was inevitable (the president of the Council of the Twelve Apostles always becomes president of the church upon the death of the previous president), many Mormons were upset when he became Prophet. I was taught that he was a shy, kindly, gentle old man, but truthful persons more in the know described him as narrow-minded and authoritarian. He was as strict with himself as he was with others, however. Once his secretary, Brent Hafen, asked him why he didn't go home for lunch instead of eating alone at the church office building. "President Grant did it, and so did George Albert Smith, and President McKay," pleaded Hafen. "Yes," said Joseph Fielding Smith, "and now they're all dead!"

He was followed by Harold B. Lee, who was only president for a short time before his death, though he was much younger than most of his recent antecedents. A humble man, he worked in the welfare programs of the Church and placed special emphasis on the place of youth in the future of the Church. He was the president of the Church when I left it.

Spencer W. Kimball, a descendant of one of Brigham Young's counselors, was the next president of the Mormon Church. He was well acquainted with trouble in his personal life, for during the course of it he suffered a near-drowning, facial paralysis, typhoid fever, heart disease, and the removal of vocal chord tissue which necessitated that he relearn the process of speech. He assured himself immortality, at least in the annals of religious leaders, by being the Mormon president who declared in June of 1978 that blacks are now eligible to receive the priesthood.

After Kimball's death in 1985, he was succeeded by Ezra Taft Benson. Benson is familiar to many Americans because he served as secretary of agriculture in the Eisenhower cabinet. He is politically an ultra-conservative, though his extreme outspokenness seems to have been tempered by his advanced age (87) and what many see as the increasing power of the Council of the Twelve Apostles.

Continuing Revelation

All the recent presidents of the LDS Church have had as one of their greatest duties the management and distribution of the millions of non-taxable tithe and investment dollars that pour into the Church's brimming treasury. It is because of this that critics of the Church have charged that the "revelation" received by twentieth-century prophets is more of the "spirit of Dow-Jones" than of God. Indeed, revelation has surely changed since the days of Joseph Smith's bold (and incautious) prophetic utterings. Parley P. Pratt once said that Joseph dictated revelations slowly, never backtracking or correcting. (Why bother when he could get away with wholesale revisions of revelations even after printing them?) Today's prophets issue terse little press releases and meandering conference addresses that refer to past doctrines and glowing principles of righteousness, rarely ever putting the divine stamp of "thus saith the LORD" as Joseph Smith seldom hesitated to do.

Previous Mormon prophets have promised the Mormon people not only a continuing stream of revelation from God to prophet to church member, but have for years tantalized their anxious followers with the promise of new scriptures. Part of the plates from which the *Book of Mormon* was translated, for example, was "sealed" and taken back by the angel Moroni. This portion, which amounted to between one-third and two-thirds of the total volume of the plates, is yet to be revealed and given to faithful Mormons as scripture. Mormons also cite second Corinthians 13:1 which says that two or three witnesses establish the truth, and say that the Bible (the record of the Jews) and the *Book of Mormon* (the record of the Nephites) will be joined by a third record, that of the Ten Lost Tribes.

These promises thrilled me when I was a Mormon. New scriptures! I could hardly wait. But I know now that such scriptures will never come forth. Why? Because the Mormon Church has lost its nerve. Though I anticipate future bows to financial and public pressure like the Manifesto and the black-priesthood announcement, no "new" scriptures will be translated from ancient records. In the early days of the Church, when the sciences of archaeology and linguistics were in their infancies, Joseph could recklessly turn out volume after improbable volume like the *Book of Mormon,* the *Pearl of Great Price,* and the records of Ham and Joseph (ancient documents supposedly translated by Joseph Smith but never published). But no Mormon "prophet" is that incautious in this modern age. The mythical remainder of the mythical *Book of Mormon* will stay in the safekeeping of the mythical Moroni. The record of the Ten Lost Tribes will stay lost too. Nor will the Church ever bring out of hiding the "records of Ham and Joseph," which are probably gathering dust in a vault in the Church Historian's office, a potential bonfire of controversy and certain embarrassment. Mormons will have to be content with the continuing history of their church in the "Church News" section of the *Deseret News,* in the *Ensign,* and in *Conference Reports.*

The prophet alone can contradict scripture, according to Harold B. Lee.[13] This is in the eyes of a Christian a paradoxical statement. But Mormon leaders like Brigham Young have always placed much more emphasis on the teachings of the "living oracles" than on written scripture of any kind. Of course, aberrant behavior in the lives of men like Joseph Smith and Brigham Young have caused a considerable tempering of this position with more caution. A Mormon when faced with irrefutable evidence of the moral vices of early Church presidents will have a pat answer: "A prophet is a prophet only when he is acting as such." This provides a convenient "out" when a prophet in speech or in action blunders. But I, as a faithful Mormon, did not believe that a prophet *could* blunder. The teachings I received led me to believe with all my heart that the prophets were nearly perfect.

Of course the higher the man in the Mormon hierarchy, the more vocal he will be in supporting and building up Church leaders. The leaders realize that they can only achieve the high offices to which they aspire by continually exalting these positions. It becomes a process of continually scratching the backs of the men whose offices they covet, and waiting patiently until someone dies so that they can move up.

If, therefore, Mormons cannot judge their leaders by how they practice the principles they teach, and if a prophet can change and/or countermand scripture at will, how then can the Mormon ascertain the authority of his prophet-leader? Harold B. Lee said, "There is one safety, and that is that we shall live to have the witness to know."[14] This puts us right back to Moroni's challenge to *Book of Mormon* readers: our own volatile consciences serve as judge.

But Mormons are also promised that their prophet must be obeyed, for he can *never* teach false doctrine.[15] Theodore M. Burton, a General Authority, said in the October, 1961, conference, "The Lord will never permit the great prophet, our seer and revelator, to fall or lead the people astray. Before this could happen, God must of necessity remove that man from the earth."

The Voice of Senility

Sadly, this is not the case. I know of one time when this principle proved to be false. In 1971, I was rooming at Brigham Young University with a girl whose uncle worked near the office of President Joseph Fielding Smith. One day this friend came to me to unburden herself of something that was troubling her deeply.

Our conversation began with a discussion of how feeble and wizened the nonagenarian prophet of the church had become. When he spoke before groups, he was helped from his chair to the podium and back again, and when he spoke he read directly from a written text, rarely lifting his eyes from the paper and speaking almost breathlessly. We had been told that he was so shy that few strangers were allowed to see him. One of his secretary's jobs, in fact, was to stand so that if anyone unexpectedly tried to kiss the prophet, the secretary would intercept the kiss on his own cheek. "Bless President Smith's heart," we would say, "that sweet old man."

But my friend pitied him even more than ever, and, as she spoke, I began to understand why. She told me, with horror and doubt in her voice, that her uncle had explained to her the reason for all this protection of the president. According to him, Joseph Fielding Smith was so senile in his last years that "outsiders" who might detect this were kept away from him. His mind wandered so badly that all his speeches had to be prepared for him, and as soon as he finished reading them, he was ushered quickly back to his seat because otherwise he would ramble on aimlessly.

Were my friend not an honest and dedicated Mormon, and were not her source so reliable, I would have had reason to doubt her story. It troubled me as deeply as it had her. When I told my boyfriend about what my friend had said, he insisted that there had been a mistake made either on the part of my friend or her uncle, because God would take a prophet from the earth before He would allow him to become senile.

Actually, I think that he was as concerned as we were by the prospects of a leaderless church; but I think what really scared us all was the fact that someone else was preparing speeches that claimed to be the words of God, and putting them before a figurehead prophet who had only to read them aloud to authenticate them.

If Joseph Fielding Smith could suffer "mental failing," why could this not have been true of Joseph Smith, or Brigham Young? When does a prophet become less than a prophet—without ceasing to be a prophet? Though many Mormons in ignorance will deny this story about Joseph Fielding Smith, those who were close to him know the truth, and their testimony (which I am sure will remain unspoken) would be the most powerful argument ever voiced against the idea of a prophet who supposedly "cannot fall" and who is bound to the office until separated from it by death.

The Test of a Prophet

But one would not have to accept even this admittedly apocryphal story of one of the prophets of Mormonism to be assured that none of them are God's spokesmen. In the Bible God gave us the infallible test of a prophet:

> And if thou say in thine heart, How shall we know the word which the Lord hath not spoken? When a prophet speaketh in the name of the Lord, if the thing follow not, nor come to pass, that is the thing which the Lord hath not spoken, but the prophet hath spoken it presumptuously: thou shalt not be afraid of him.
>
> —Deuteronomy 18:21-22

We should stop and notice several things about this Scripture. First of all, it doesn't condemn men for questioning the right of any person to speak in the name of God. In First Thessalonians 5:20-21 Paul told Christians that they should not despise prophetic utterances, but in the next breath he told them to *prove all things* and to hold fast to those things that are good.

Secondly, the Deuteronomy passage doesn't allow for just a good batting average on prophecies. For instance, it doesn't say that you should accept a man as a prophet if most of what he prophesies comes to pass. This Scripture passage encourages us to look at *each* thing a would-be prophet might say, and to reject him if he prophesies falsely.

Lastly, Deuteronomy 18:22 teaches a truth that it took me a long time to come to, even after my conversion. We are told that a false prophet—one who has failed the test that God outlined—should have no power over us. We should not fear him. When we are afraid of such a man, we are enslaved by our own minds and not by any power the man himself might have.

It is the fulfilled predictions of Mormonism that are touted so much. Surely Mormon prophets must be of God, a proselyte might think, if they could prophesy the coming of Columbus to America, the Revolutionary War, and the Civil War (all of which are, like much other Mormon revelation, at least partially "prophesied" after the fact). But even the dime-store astrologists and Jeanne Dixons of our time have their false predictions swept under the rug while they are made rich and famous for the *one* which came true.

As a newborn babe in Christ, I was still frightened by the "noises in the night" of the lucky (or educated) guesses Mormons call fulfilled prophecy. But when I researched the false prophecies of Mormon leaders, my fear began to leave and in its place was a new confidence. Now, some years later, I am familiar with more of the false prophecies of Mormonism than with the "fulfilled" ones the average Mormon can quote.

False Prophecies

Much of the prophecy of Joseph Smith's time was centered on Missouri's future as Zion. Almost all these prophecies are easily documented, and most, too, have proven to be false prophecies. In *Doctrine and Covenants* 90:37, for instance, the Mormons were promised that they would not be removed from Missouri, but they of course were driven from that place and most never returned to claim the inheritance they were promised there. Except for the Reorganites and other smaller splinter groups, even their descendants live elsewhere.

Joseph Smith also prophesied in *Doctrine and Covenants* Section 84 that a temple would be reared in Jackson County in his own generation. Even the Temple Lot Church's efforts to make this prophecy come true in the early part of this century were frustrated. Excuses for failure abound, but in *Doctrine and Covenants* 124:49-51, Joseph Smith gave his own: he said the enemy was just too strong. (Since when are opposing forces strong enough to frustrate *any* prophecy of the Living God?)

When the Mormon people were finally ousted from Missouri, Joseph Smith made many foolish and bitter prophecies. Once, when talking to statesman Stephan A. Douglas, he predicted that the United States government would be "utterly overthrown and wasted and there will not be as much as a potscherd *(sic)* left,"[16] unless it redressed the wrongs done to Mormons to their satisfaction.

Oliver Cowdery claimed that Joseph Smith was fond of saying that he (Joseph) would "tarry on the earth" until Christ came in glory at His final advent.[17] In several places in the *History of the Church* we can read of instances where he promised individuals that they would live to see Christ come in His glory.[18] Once Joseph Smith even put a date on when he himself would see Christ, saying that fifty-six years "should wind up this scene."[19] This prophecy was made in 1835.

Though Brigham Young was not as bold as Joseph was in making prophecies, when he did so, they were whoppers. Considering his anti-Negro bent, perhaps it was just his wishful thinking that led him to prophesy that the abolitionist movement would not free the slaves because slavery was "the sentence of the Almighty upon the seed of Ham."[20]

Heber C. Kimball, one of Brigham Young's counselors, had so much faith in Young's powers that he, too, waxed prophetic in proclaiming that Brigham would serve as President of the United States.[21]

The most amazing "revelation" to come out of Mormonism is also the most ludicrous. Though Mormons of today believe that celestialized beings (such as God) live on burning planets, few would agree that there are inhabitants on the moon. But Joseph Smith, as quoted in the journal of one of his most devoted followers, Oliver B. Huntington, not only said that there were moon-dwellers, but went on to describe them as being all about six feet in height, dressing like Quakers, and having a lifespan of one thousand years![22]

A prominent Mormon writer, LeGrand Richards, quoted Giovanni Papini for his definition of what a prophet is: one who must endure insults and abuse from the world.[23] We can certainly see how Joseph Smith could qualify with his descriptions of moon-dwellers. And it is a fact that many true prophets have suffered ill treatment in defending the Word of God. Though that is often the result of being a prophet, it is not necessarily a requirement. The Bible's definition of a prophet reminds us that there is only one way of knowing if a man is a prophet. His words come true!

The Case of King David

Those who criticize Mormon leaders are often taken to task by LDS apologists who say that one cannot condemn a "prophet" because he drank liquor (like Joseph Smith did), or because he was ruthless and ambitious (like Brigham Young).

King David and his ungodly murderous affair with Bathsheba is often cited as proof that a prophet can sin in other than doctrinal teachings. The Bible scholar would agree that prophets, whether of the Bible or of any other "scripture," are human beings of whom we have no right to expect perfection. But let's look at David and see why, even in spite of his sin, he deserves the title of prophet.

First, though he sinned, he repented. It was a sin to covet the wife of another and to have her husband killed. But David saw the grave error he had made, and begged God for forgiveness. He did not rail against God when his first child by Bathsheba was taken from him in death. He reformed his life and spent the rest of it demonstrating to God that he was truly repentant. We might as well take a parallel example from the life of Joseph Smith. How repentant was he when he took wives belonging to other men?

Secondly, whatever David gave to his people as the Word of the Lord harmonized with what the prophets before him had said. No one ever accused David of being an iconoclast. People of God know that He is consistent, and they can judge new revelation by old (see 2 John 9-10, Gal. 1:6-12, and 2 Tim. 3:14-17).

And lastly, David was a prophet because his words came true! He didn't tell the exact date of the birth of Christ, or about dwellers on the stars of his favorite constellation. He listened to what God had to say, and then repeated it to men.

Not all Mormon leaders have been as blatantly confident in their own prophecies as were early leaders like Joseph Smith and Brigham Young. One of the most beloved leaders in the Mormon Church was a crusty old cowpoke who somehow became one of the presidents of the First Council of the Seventy. This man, J. Golden Kimball, was so well loved that when he died, his funeral was more widely attended than that of any other person in Utah's history except Brigham Young.

Some Mormons despised him for his "country" ways and raw language, but most loved him dearly. On one occasion, he was called upon to speak at a meeting in southern Idaho. Since this was a poor mission area in need of encouragement, J. Golden got a little carried away in prophesying about the great wealth that faithful saints would inherit in that place.

But soon after the meeting he disappeared. The local bishop went out to look for him, and found him in a barn. There J. Golden was, alternating between crying and cursing a blue streak. The bishop was stunned, and asked him why he was so upset. "Ah hell," replied J. Golden, "I had to go and prophesy all that about this community and there isn't a damn bit of it will come true!"[24]

At another time someone asked J. Golden if he'd ever had any visions. "Hell, no!" he responded, "but I've had some damn good nightmares!"[25]

I wish I could have met this J. Golden Kimball. I think I would have liked him.

NOTES

[1]Gordon H. Fraser, *A Manual for Christian Workers—A Workshop Outline for the Study of Mormonism* (Hubbard, Oklahoma: Gordon H. Fraser, publisher, 1978), p. 22.

[2]Interview with a polygamist in the *New York Times,* December 27, 1965, p. 18.

[3]Stanley S. Ivins quoted in Tanner, *Mormonism: Shadow or Reality?* p. 237.

[4]Samuel Taylor, *I Have Six Wives* (Greenburgh, N.Y.: 1956), p. 13.

[5]Lowell L. Bennion, *An Introduction to the Gospel* (teacher's supplement) (Salt Lake City: Deseret Sunday School Union Board, 1964), pp. 28-29.

[6]*Doctrine and Covenants* 8:6-8. This was called in the *Book of Commandments* the "rod of nature," and although it was never described fully, Sperry in *Doctrine and Covenants Compendium,* theorized that it was a stick of some sort which could be held in the hand.

[7]Marie Felt, *What It Means To Be A Latter-day Saint* (Salt Lake City: Deseret Sunday School Union Board, 1963), p. 254.

[8]Anonymous, *Jerald and Sandra Tanner's Distorted View of Mormonism: A Response to Mormonism: Shadow or Reality?* (Salt Lake City: 1977), p. 3.

[9]Sperry, *Doctrine and Covenants Compendium,* p. 17.

[10]Joseph Fielding Smith, *Doctrines of Salvation,* I, p. 170.

[11]*Journal of Discourses,* XIII, p. 95.

[12]*Reed Smoot Case,* Vol. I, p. 99, quoted in Tanner, *Mormonism: Shadow or Reality?* p. 184.

[13]"The Place of the Living Prophet, Seer and Revelator," an address to Seminaries and Institutes faculty, BYU, July 8, 1964, p. 14.

[14]Ibid.

[15]Ezra Taft Benson, heir-apparent of the church presidency, stated at a widely-publicized speech at BYU on February 6, 1980 that: *anything* a prophet says should be regarded as coming from the mouth of the Lord, that a living prophet "is more important than any scripture or past prophet," that a prophet can speak for the Lord on temporal and political matters as well as spiritual ones, and that there is no need for a prophet to say, "Thus saith the Lord," for his words to be scripture.

[16]Joseph Smith, Jr., quoted in N. B. Lundwall, comp., *Inspired Prophetic Warnings* (USA: Publishers Press, 6th ed.), p. 59.

[17]Bales, *The Book of Mormon?* p. 134.

[18]Joseph Smith, Jr., *Documentary History of the Church,* I, p. 176: II, p. 188, 191.

[19]Ibid., II, p. 182.

[20]*Journal of Discourses,* X, p. 250.

[21]Ibid., V, p. 219.

[22]Einar Anderson, *Inside Story of Mormonism* (Grand Rapids: Kregel Publications, 1977), pp. 97-98.

[23]Richards, *A Marvelous Work,* p. 52.

[24]Fife, Austin, and Alta, *Saints of Sage and Saddle* (Bloomington: Indiana University Press, 1956), p. 306.

[25]Ibid.

8
The Mormon Pantheon

> How convenient it would be to many of our great men and great families of doubtful origin, could they have the privilege of the heroes of yore, who, whenever their origin was involved in obscurity, modestly announced themselves descended from a god.
>
> —Washington Irving
> *Knickerbocker's History of New York*

Christianity has undergone many attacks through the years. Satan, the wily adversary, has fomented ideas in the mind of man that have shaken the feeble-faithed and alienated the proud and "broadminded" from their God. In 1928, for example, the Scopes Trial brought into focus the conflicts between people who believed in a literal interpretation of the Bible's story of the creation of man, and the Darwinian view of the evolution of all living things from common origins. Many Christians thought then, "What could be more ungodly than the thought that man has evolved from a lower form of life?"

But eighty-one years earlier, in 1844, Joseph Smith introduced a doctrine that Christians have passively ignored for over a century—the idea that our God "evolved" from a lower form of life. This lower form of life, from which the Mormon god evolved, was man.

The Eternality of Man

You cannot understand LDS theology unless you understand what Mormons believe about their own origins and those of their god. Their unique conception of eternity is one that includes the consciousness of every person. In the words of Brigham Young, "There was never a time when man did not exist, and there will never be a time when he will cease to exist."[1] Mormons believe that the essential element of each man's personality, the intelligence, was never created. Each of us has *always* existed, before the creation of the earth, and before our God *was* God. This intelligence had no form, and owed no allegiance to a creator, for it had none. Each intelligence was an individual entity, and was self-existent and coequal with God.[2]

If God did not create man in the way we have always thought, why do we call Him our Creator? Mormons teach that God, an exalted man, had sexual intercourse with His wives, in eternity long before time began, and the bodies which those wives brought forth clothed the "intelligences" He selected from throughout eternity.

The idea of a heavenly Mother is regarded as a logical necessity. The lyrics to a popular Mormon hymn, "O My Father," affirm the existence of this Mother. Brigham Young spoke of God's wife in *Journal of Discourses,* Volume 9, p. 286, and Joseph Smith supposedly once saw her in a vision.[3] But since LDS theology teaches that God is a polygamist, then supposedly an inhabitant of earth could be descended from any one of several "Heavenly Mothers."

Man's spirit, therefore, consists of his inherent *being* or intelligence and the spirit body from his Heavenly Father and Mother. Mormons teach that this spirit body is adult-sized, and looks like we do—thus, Joseph Smith's spirit body looks like his mortal body, and being male, has all the appropriate features. This spirit body is made out of a material so "refined" as to be intangible and invisible to mortals; but it nonetheless exists.

The union or "organization" of intellect and spirit body is also known as an intelligence, in the same way that we might refer to a living man as a soul, though that is only part of his being. The spirits that Abraham supposedly saw before the creation of the world were referred to by him as intelligences (Abraham chapter 3).

The Pre-existence

Thus, man was a fully-functioning, born entity long before his mortal birth. In an attempt to find Bible justification for this point of view, Mormons quote Jeremiah 1:5: "Before I formed thee in the belly I knew thee; and before thou camest forth out of the womb I sanctified thee, and I ordained thee a prophet unto the nations."

Only a part of the entities born to God were designated for this earth. God created many more worlds, and *Doctrine and Covenants* 76:24 tells us that the inhabitants of these other worlds, too, were "begotten sons and daughters unto God."

This time span between the birth of the spirit, its growth and maturing in the spirit world, and its later infusion into a corporeal body on earth is known by Mormons as the pre-existence, or first estate. In this state the spirits of men and women made preparations for earth life. Existing there, too, were the spirits of every plant, fish, bird, and animal that has ever lived or will ever live on earth.⁴ They, too, had spirit bodies, made up of intangible matter.

When God and his wives had finished with the creation of the spirit bodies of all who would eventually live on this earth, He called a great meeting of the spirits. Mormons call this "the council in heaven." He proposed a plan whereby His children could live on earth and be tested, and yet return to Him after death. The spirits divided themselves up into two factions. God's firstborn spirit Son, the pre-mortal Jesus Christ, supported this plan, which was based on the concept of man's "free agency" or ability to choose a lifestyle that would either return him to God or separate him from his Father. Christ's endorsement was no small thing, for if man were given the prerogative of sinning he would surely do so; and Christ's support of this plan required Him to be willing to sacrifice Himself for man's sin, while giving the glory to God.

Another highly-favored son of God, Satan, also proposed a plan that excluded free agency, but *guaranteed* that all God's spirit children would return to Him. One-third of the spirits chose this plan. God, however, rejected it.

When Satan and his followers found they could not have their way, they rebelled against God. Satan had wanted God's glory; now he sought His throne. A great battle in heaven ensued. Satan and his spirits warred against the armies of heaven who were led by Michael, the pre-existent Adam. Satan and his followers were cast down from heaven. But even among the triumphant hosts of glory were some who had been less valiant than the others. These, it was decided, would be sent to earth to inhabit black bodies.

In order to make our "second estate," or experience on earth, a true testing ground, it was necessary that before birth our knowledge of the pre-existence be removed. Mormons of today speak figuratively of this forgetting as a "veil" over our memories. Orson Pratt, however, explained that this loss of memory was due to the traumatic experience of the spirit body entering the physical body of a tiny baby: "When this spirit is compressed, so as to be wholly enclosed in an infant tabernacle, it had a tendency to suspend memory."⁵

Of course all of this is as false to the Bible as it is insulting to the intelligence. Genesis 1:26 and 2:7 clearly show man to be a created being—far from the independent intelligence that was "organized" into a spirit body. Genesis teaches us that man *became* a living soul when God breathed life into him.

Zechariah 12:1 also strikes a blow against the Mormon concept of the pre-existence of the soul. Here the Bible states clearly that man's *Spirit* was *formed within him*. How much more clearly could God say it?

Even the Jeremiah passage, "Before I formed thee in the belly I knew thee; and before thou camest forth out of the womb I sanctified thee, and I ordained thee a prophet unto the nations," when read carefully shows (1) the fore-knowledge of God even before He makes His creations, and (2) His power to fore-ordain His servants to great works—after they are created (even babies *in utero* are normally completely formed before they come "forth out of the womb"). If this passage in Jeremiah were to be used effectively by Mormons to prove pre-existence, it would have to say that *we* knew *God* before birth—not He us.

The Mormons say we are all literal sons and daughters of God, our spirits begotten by Him. But the Bible tells us that we *become* God's children at conversion (John 1:12). In that sense, we are God's sons and daughters, and thanks be to His holy Name that He should adopt any so unworthy as we are into His family.

The Mormon God

Mormons ridicule what the Bible teaches about our God. In a general conference I attended in 1972, LeGrand Richards of the Council of the Twelve Apostles called the Christian world's view of God "the best description of nothing that I have ever heard." Richards, in saying this, was following a long-lived Mormon tradition of reviling the God of the Bible. Joseph Smith once scoffed at the idea of God being three in one by saying,

> I have always declared God to be a distinct personage, Jesus Christ a separate and distinct personage from God the Father, and that the Holy Ghost was a distinct personage and a Spirit, and these three constitute three distinct personages and three Gods . . . Many men say there is one God; the Father, the Son and the Holy Ghost are only one God! I say that is a strange God anyhow—three in one, and one in three! It is a curious organization . . . All are to be crammed into one God, according to sectarianism. It would make the biggest God in the world. He would be a wonderfully big God—he would be a giant or a monster.[6]

The Bible believer is sickened by this sort of discussion of Deity, and would think that surely a direct refutation from the Bible would suffice to show a Mormon where he is wrong. But John 10:30, where Jesus said, "I and the Father are one," is interpreted by Mormons to mean that they are one in purpose only.

In the earliest writings of Joseph Smith, such as the *Book of Mormon*, there is no hint of the concept of many gods that would so preoccupy him later. In his initial written account of his first vision, the so-called "strange account," Joseph did not even mention God appearing to him. The official account, published in the *Pearl of Great Price* as Joseph

Smith Chapter Two, does of course make much of his contention that a corporeal God appeared to him, but this was not written down until years after the supposed experience, and after Joseph Smith had begun formulating his theories of many gods.

The *Book of Mormon* was unabashedly monotheistic and trinitarian, in the strictest sense of the words, as the following quote shows:

> And now, behold, my beloved brethren, this is the way; and there is none other way nor name given under heaven whereby man can be saved in the kingdom of God. And now, behold, this is the doctrine of Christ, and the only and true doctrine of the Father, and of the Son, and of the Holy Ghost, which is one God, without end. Amen.
>
> —2 Nephi 31:21[7]

The *Book of Mormon* also taught that God is a spirit.

> And then Ammon said: Believest thou that there is a Great Spirit? And he said, Yea.
> And Ammon said: This is God. And Ammon said unto him again: Believest thou that this Great Spirit, who is God, created all things which are in heaven and in the earth?
> And he said: Yea.   —Alma 18:26-28

Early sections of the *Doctrine and Covenants,* which now appear as section 5:2 of *Lectures on Faith,* said that the Father was "a personage of spirit," as opposed to the Son, who was a "personage of tabernacle." This was written in 1829.

Doctrine and Covenants 20:17-19, written in 1830, taught that God was unchangeable, the only God; and verse 28 affirms a traditional "trinity" theme. The same is true of section 50 verse 43: "And the Father and I are one. I am in the Father and the Father in me; and inasmuch as ye have received me, ye are in me and I in you" (dated 1831).

But in 1832 Joseph Smith recorded a revelation saying that man could not see God without the priesthood,[8] which conflicted with his later stories about seeing God and Christ in the sacred grove[9] some ten years before the "restoration" of the priesthood.

Even as late as 1833 Joseph Smith was teaching in the "Lectures on Faith" that God was a "personage of spirit, glory, and power," while the Son was a "personage of tabernacle."[10]

It was in Kirtland, Ohio, when Joseph Smith began his study of the Hebrew language, that he realized that one of the Hebrew words for Deity, *Elohim,* was in fact a plural word. In his excitement over this discovery, Joseph ignored the fact that this plural word could be used in the singular (like the English word fish—you can have one fish or twenty fish), and in speaking of God it was always used with a singular verb form.

The thought of plural gods set Joseph Smith off on a tangent which revolutionized his religion. As a result of his teachings and those of his successor, Mormons now believe that the godhead consists of three totally separate persons. The head of this organization is the Father, the one who created our spirit bodies. He was not co-equal with Christ, for He created Him. He is not co-eternal with the Savior, either, for the same reason. But like their Christ, the Mormon God has a body of flesh and bones. Mormons teach that He looks like a man as, indeed, He once was.

When we read in Genesis 1:27 that God created man "in his image," this, Mormons teach, referred to their physical bodies after which our own are patterned. When we read that Christ sits at the right hand of God (Heb. 1:3), it is speaking of God's literal right hand. They say that the voice of God heard at the baptism of Jesus, along with the appearance of the Holy Ghost (Matt. 3:16-17) show that the three members of the godhead are separate and distinct from each other. Joseph Smith chapter 2 verses 18-20, and *Doctrine and Covenants* 76:14 are also used to show that when Joseph Smith saw and talked with Christ, he was not the same as God the Father.

It is hard to talk to a Mormon about God. You can say the same words—but mean entirely different things. You would, in speaking of God, be referring to our Heavenly Creator. A Mormon, on the other hand, uses the word "god" loosely as a title referring more to an attainment of an office than a name of a specific Being. General usage, though, ascribes the title of "God" to that Person who fathered or organized our spirit bodies in the pre-existence. The proper name (though seldom voiced out of respect) for this Being would be Ahman—a word from the "pure Adamic language." It means, "Man of Holiness."

The Mormon God has a real flesh and bones body, like yours and mine in many ways. However, it does not have blood flowing through its veins, for blood is the element of corruption without which man can be immortalized. Another miraculous substance, often referred to as "spirit," runs through the veins of all gods and their wives. The same is true of resurrected personages.

What do the LDS people do with Bible Scriptures like John 4:22-24?

> Ye worship ye know not what: we know what we worship: for salvation is of the Jews. But the hour cometh, and now is, when the true worshippers shall worship the Father in spirit and in truth: for the Father seeketh such to worship him. God is a spirit: and they that worship him must worship him in spirit and in truth.

They say that this passage was mistranslated, and that the end of it should read: "For unto such hath God promised His Spirit: And they that worship him must worship him in spirit and in truth."

Mormons do, however, use other Bible passages to substantiate that

God has a physical body: Proverbs 15:3 which speaks of God's eyes; Isaiah 55:11 which speaks of His mouth; Isaiah 30:27 His lips and tongue; His ear is mentioned in 2 Kings 19:16; etc. *Doctrine and Covenants* 130:22 presses the point, insisting that the Father and Son have bodies "as tangible as man's."

So where did God get this body? This question lies at the heart of the whole Mormon concept of God. The answer is that He gained this body like you gained yours—by birth from two physical parents. This Ahman lived on an earth, like ours; obeyed the commandments of his god; and after his death he was resurrected with the same body he'd had on his earth, only "celestialized," or immortalized. As a reward for his obedience, Ahman was made a God. He took His wives in connubial intercourse and thus created our spirit bodies:

> We were begotten by our Father in Heaven; the person of our Father in Heaven was begotten on a previous heavenly world by His Father; and again, He was begotten by a still more ancient Father and so on, from generation to generation, from one heavenly world to another still more ancient, until our minds are wearied and lost in the multiplicity of generations and successive worlds, and as a last resort, we wonder in our minds, how far back the genealogy extends, and how the first world was formed, and the first father was begotten.[11]

The consummation of Joseph Smith's teachings on the godhead came just a few months before his death. Mormons say that the famous address he gave shortly before his martyrdom, at the funeral of a man named King Follett, was the Prophet's crowning doctrine. In this speech, before two thousand persons, Joseph emphasized that, not only is our God an exalted man, but all men should have as their ultimate goals the attainment of godhood themselves.

Recently when I was speaking to a group of high school students on the subject of Mormonism, I outlined the central points of doctrine covered by Joseph Smith in this King Follett Address. I had explained that it was the last major speech of Joseph Smith before his death, and that the doctrine of an exalted God-man was something that Joseph Smith had been leading up to for about ten years. One of the students raised his hand as I was talking. He seemed a little annoyed. "Yes," he said, "but that was 1844. Mormons don't teach that stuff about becoming a god today, do they?"

You bet they do! There is no doctrine, outside that of continuing revelation, that is more integral to the Mormonism of both the past and the present than that of a progressing God. Their tiny children are taught this from infancy; their adolescents learn "scriptures" to support it; and every faithful adult holds godhood as his ultimate and rightful destiny.

Mormons regard their gaining of knowledge and experience on this earth as a mirroring of the progression that God is even now making. Wilford Woodruff, a prophet of the Church, once said, "God himself is increasing and progressing in knowledge, power, and dominion."[12] But a later prophet, Joseph Fielding Smith, refuted this, saying that God could not increase in knowledge, because that would imply that He was lacking in knowledge in the past.

If God does not progress in knowledge, it doesn't make sense that He could continue progressing in power and dominion. How can the All-Powerful increase in power? As for increasing in dominion—surely that is sticky human desire pressed upon the face of an insufficient deity.

The laws of gravity and other natural principles rule over the Mormon deity. He did not create them any more than he created us. He only "organized" eternal elements which were in existence long before he had a soul, and he combined these elements to form the earth and its inhabitants. In comparing our God to him is seen the difference between Michelangelo painting the ceiling of the Sistine Chapel, and a child who crayons neatly within the lines of the pictures in his coloring book.

Mormons laugh aloud at the idea of our God who can fill the immensity of space and yet still gently touch the heart of man unto repentance. Silly, they say. Their bodily god, whom we should emulate, can only be one place at a time. He sits on a burning sphere called Kolob that revolves once every thousand years. Like an isolated Howard Hughes, he awaits news from his worlds and sends messages via his angels. He is comforted by his wives, and continues the ceaseless reproduction expected of them and him—and us, when we become gods.

I'd rather strum a harp and polish haloes throughout eternity in the sweet rest of my Invisible God, than *be* a Mormon god.

The Adam-God Theory

One of the reasons that Mormons are so critical of Christians' view of God is that they say He is too hard to understand. A god with a body is in some ways easier to visualize than an Invisible One. (But God never commanded us to understand Him. He commanded us to honor, worship, and obey Him!) However, Mormons could never find a more confusing concept of God than the doctrine taught by Brigham Young that has come to be known as the "Adam-God" doctrine. Now, Mormons of today honor "Father" Adam as the greatest figure of the Old Testament. They teach that in the pre-existence he was an archangel and prince.[13]

But in times past, he was believed to be much more than this. Brigham Young said:

> Now hear it, O inhabitants of the earth, Jew and Gentile, Saint and sinner! When our father Adam came into the garden of Eden, he came into it with a *celestial body,* and brought Eve, *one of his wives,*

with him. He helped to make and organize this world. He is MICHAEL, the *archangel,* the ANCIENT OF DAYS! about whom holy men have written and spoken—*HE is our FATHER and our GOD, and the only God with whom WE have to do.* Every man upon the earth, professing Christians or non-professing, must hear it, and *will know it sooner or later.*[14] (Italics and capitalizations appear in original.)

Elaborating upon this, Brigham Young taught that Adam was a part of the Trinity of Elohim (God the Father), Jehovah (Jesus), and Michael. When placed on the earth, Adam-God fulfilled a divine plan by eating of the Tree of the Knowledge of Good and Evil. His body and that of Eve underwent a change because of this, and they were able to conceive children, who were mortal as Adam and Eve now were. Later teachings of Brigham Young indicated that the resurrected Adam was the father of Jesus Christ through sexual intercourse.

This all raises a lot of questions the Mormon Church doesn't want asked. Such as, if Adam were a God before this earth was created, how could he be tested? How could a god "fall"? (—even if it were a "fall upward.") And how could a god die, as Adam did?

As I said before, this is not taught as doctrine in Mormonism today. In fact, President Spencer W. Kimball has openly refuted the Adam-God doctrine, identifying it as false teachings. This has left the LDS scholar with a dilemma. If Brigham Young taught the Adam-God doctrine and it is false (as Christian and Mormon alike would now agree), doesn't that make Brigham Young a false prophet?

Mormon leaders of today fall back on the usage of the word "god" to mean an office attained by the righteous and say that thus, Adam is a god. This explanation will satisfy any Mormon who has neither access to a *Journal of Discourses* nor curiosity to find one; but no one else.

More honest LDS scholars, though, like Rodney Turner, have admitted that an honest examination of church documents "will admit to no other conclusion than that the identification of Adam with God the Father by President Young is an irrefutable fact."[15] And, though Mormons utterly deny the Adam-God theory which has lent so much ammunition to their critics, the secret temple ceremonies of even this day depict the creation of the earth by Elohim, Jehovah, and—who else?—Michael. And all this in spite of abundant scriptural evidence (Gen. 1:27; 2:18, 20-25; 3:19) that Michael, or Adam, was created, not a creator.

Adam was not the only person upon whom Mormons have graciously bestowed godhood. *Doctrine and Covenants* 132:37 teaches that Abraham, Isaac, and Jacob are already gods. They have joined the innumerable gods throughout the ages, as described by Orson Pratt: "If we take a million worlds like this and number their particles, we should find there are more Gods than there are particles of matter in those worlds."[16]

What does the Bible say about becoming a god?

> But the LORD is the true God, he is the living God, and an everlasting king: at his wrath the earth shall tremble, and the nations shall not be able to abide his indignation. Thus shall ye say unto them, The gods that have not made the heavens and the earth, even they shall perish from the earth, and from under these heavens.
>
> —Jeremiah 10:10-11

> Ye are my witnesses, saith the Lord, and my servant whom I have chosen: that ye may know and believe me, and understand that I am he: before me there was no God formed, neither shall there be after me.
>
> —Isaiah 43:10

(See also Isaiah 44:8, 45:21-22.)

The Mormon Christ

Christ, the firstborn Son of God in the pre-existence, somehow managed to attain godhood even before He gained a mortal body (which Mormons say is essential to achieving divinity). While I was a Mormon I never read anything or found anyone who could explain how someone could become a god without a body. Nonetheless, Christ was highly favored of God (the father of His spiritual body) and of all the other pre-existent spirits (who were His brothers and sisters). Up until the time of His resurrection, our "Elder Brother," Jesus, was subordinate to God, but at that time He was exalted to equality with Him.

Even before His mortal life, Son Ahman (Christ's name in the "pure Adamic language") carried out many duties essential to our temporal life and eventual salvation. Under the auspices of His Father, Christ created the world we live on by organizing the existing elements of the universe into this terrestrial ball.[17] Because of this, He is called our Father, too, in the same sense that Euclid could be called the father of geometry. He is also referred to as the Father of our salvation, because of His atonement,[18] and because of a principle known as "divine investiture of authority"—wherein He can speak as if He were the Father in any given situation.[19] Finally, he is known as the Father of all who are born again,[20] and abide in His gospel.[21]

This heavy emphasis on Christ as "the Father" is confusing to non-Mormons, but is essential to LDS theology. They teach that the Father of our spirits, Elohim, never appeared to nor spoke to man after the transgression of Adam. God the Father was seen with Christ only when it was necessary to introduce and bear record of His Son to mankind, as at the baptism of Christ and in the first vision of Joseph Smith. At all other times the Being who appeared as God was Jesus, who through divine investiture of authority was acting as His Father.

As a young Mormon I was very confused by this. I remember asking a missionary, whose knowledge of doctrine I admired, why it was that we prayed to God the Father if Jesus were the one doing all the work, and the only one of the Godhead who would actually communicate back to people. This missionary replied that we prayed to the Father because that was the example Jesus gave us when He offered the Lord's Prayer. That answer satisfied me for a while, but then I was left to wonder why it was that Jesus would say He was the Father, and act as the Father, and then instruct us to pray to a Being we really knew nothing about.

Christ's dealings with humanity before He took on a mortal body were to sharpen His skills, so to speak, at dealing with this unruly race. In fact, I heard it said many times that of all the earths God organized and peopled, ours was the only one wicked enough to kill its own Redeemer. The atonement of Christ on this earth, therefore, applied to all the others of God's earths.

Mormons claim that they have knowledge of certain facts about Christ that people who read only the Bible couldn't know. Though they celebrate Christmas as a religious holiday commemorating the mortal birth of the Savior, Joseph Smith said in *Doctrine and Covenants* section 20 that Christ was actually born exactly 1830 years prior to the organization of the church on April 6, 1830—which would make Christ's birthday April 6, A.D. 1.

Mormons believe in, honor, and teach Christ. They do not, as some suggest, deliberately de-emphasize Him in their teaching. But they have so much extra-Biblical doctrine to deal with that Christ is minimized by everything else that is taught, and crushed by the sheer volume of it. LDS children are taught to follow the examples of their leaders, and they emulate the young Joseph Smith or the youthful David O. McKay. Jesus Christ just lived too long ago to relate to when you have "living prophets," and the Perfect Man drags in a poor second to more contemporary heroes.

Conception and Marriages of Christ

Probably the one Mormon doctrine most offensive to Christians concerns the Mormon idea of the virgin birth of Christ. Fundamentalist Christians say that Jesus Christ would have to have been born of a virgin (that is, a sexually-inexperienced young woman) in order to fulfill Old Testament prophecies. Early Mormon writings, like the *Book of Mormon,* taught the same concept of the virgin birth that Christians believe.[22]

But Brigham Young claimed that the Bible was in error on the "virgin" birth of Christ. "Now remember from this time forth, and for ever, that Jesus Christ was not begotten by the Holy Ghost."[23] What Mormons teach is that God the Father, in His glorified, immortal body, came down to earth and approached the young girl Mary, and had sexual intercourse with her. As a result of this carnal union, Mary became pregnant with a Child who was half divine and half human; and thus the young Christ was truly the *Son* of *God*.

Aside from the sheer blasphemy of this position, it also violates the Mormons' own teachings, for as was previously mentioned, God was never supposed to have appeared on earth after the fall except to witness to the divinity and sonship of Christ, and the only ones who could see Him were those with the priesthood.

By violating a betrothed woman, too, God would have broken one of His own laws—which required the death of any man who had carnal knowledge of a betrothed woman (Deut. 22:23-24). Also, unless God had married Mary, He would have been committing adultery against His other wives. Therefore, Mormons say that Mary had two husbands.[24] One LDS writer speculated that she married Joseph for time (though she was a fornicator against him), and God for eternity.[25] Thus, after the resurrection she will join God as one of His wives—which makes Him guilty of incest, too. Was not Mary His spirit daughter?

Christ, also, was a polygamist according to Orson Hyde, an early Mormon leader. Though the LDS Church of today says it has "no official position" on whether or not Christ married, Hyde implied that Jesus married Mary, Martha, and "the other Mary" at the wedding at Cana.[26] He supposedly also had children by one or more of these women before He died.[27] Jedediah M. Grant, an early LDS leader, identified the Jews' rabid hatred of Jesus and their desire to persecute and crucify Him as the direct result of Christ's advocating polygamy.[28]

There is just too much confusion in the Mormons' conception of Christ for it to be of God. Brigham Young said that Adam begot Christ,[29] Joseph Fielding Smith said God the Father did, but the Bible said what was conceived in Mary was "of the Holy Ghost" (Matt. 1:20).

Mormon doctrine makes Christ a liar, for if He is the Jehovah, the I AM of the Old Testament, the Deity who spoke with all the prophets, then He wasn't very honest with His servants when He let them address Him as eternal God, instead of a created being like themselves (Deut. 33:27; Ps. 90:2).

According to LDS doctrine as seen in Ether chapter 3 of the *Book of Mormon,* the first person to see the pre-mortal Christ in His spirit body was the brother of Jared, Mahonri Moriancumr, who was so full of faith that the Lord Jesus could not withhold Himself from him. This contradicts Mormon scripture which states that the Lord appeared to Adam and his descendants,[30] and talked "face to face" with Enoch.

LDS apologists say that when Christ appeared to Adam and Enoch, perhaps He had part of His body hidden by a cloud or something similar, but He appeared completely to the brother of Jared. The only way you can take that literally is to assume that our Lord was naked when Mahonri Moriancumr saw him!

The Biblical Christ bears no similarity to the Mormon Messiah. Deuteronomy 6:4, the famous rallying cry of the Hebrew people, shows that even then God's people understood that the names Elohim and Jehovah referred to the same Entity: *Sh'mah Yisroel Adonai Elcheinu Adonai Echod* transliterates to "The Lord (Jehovah) our God (Elohim) is one Lord (Jehovah)." Furthermore, the Bible tells us to pray to our Father in the name of Christ (John 16:23-26). The Christ of the *Book of Mormon,* on the other hand, allowed people to pray directly to Him (3 Nephi 19:30).

Because of their preoccupation with the physical bodies that they claim that God and Christ possess, Mormons deny their adherents one of the most precious gifts of God—the indwelling. *Doctrine and Covenants* 130:3 says,

> John 14:23 [Jesus answered and said unto him, If a man love me, he will keep my words: and my Father will love him, and we will come unto him, and make our abode with him"]—The appearing of the Father and the Son, in that verse, is a personal appearance; and the idea that the Father and the Son dwell in a man's heart is an old sectarian notion, and is false.

Besides being a perversion of Scripture, the *Doctrine and Covenants* statement also ignores the Bible's further teachings in Romans 8:9-11, 2 Corinthians 13:5, Ephesians 3:17, and Colossians 1:27.

The Mormon Holy Ghost

The Holy Ghost, the third member of the godhead, is as uniquely characterized by Mormons as are God the Father and Christ. He is the Comforter, the medium through which both spiritual and secular knowledge are conveyed to man. He, like Elohim and Jehovah (and us) has a spirit body (male) that is in appearance like that of a man. *Doctrine and Covenants* 130:22 affirms this by saying: "The Holy Ghost is a personage of spirit." Because this spirit body of intangible yet real matter can only be in one place at a time, he is of limited dimensions, who cannot, himself, be everywhere present.

Just how he, like Christ, got to be a god without a body is another of the great mysteries of Mormonism. Heber C. Kimball once said that the Holy Ghost was "one of the sons of our Father and our God."[31] If that were true, he could be properly referred to as our "brother" in the same way that Mormons call Christ "Elder Brother," though I've never heard the Holy Ghost so described.

Mormons regard the Holy Ghost as the most active member of the godhead in men's affairs. He is responsible, they say, for carrying out most of the godhead's decisions that would not require a personal appearance by the other Gods. Since he is invisible to man, he can work "behind the scenes" in both spiritual affairs of men, and in temporal affairs that would eventually have an effect on the Kingdom.

Since the Holy Ghost is confined to his form as a spirit with a finite spirit body, it follows that he cannot indwell any more than Christ or God can. *Doctrine and Covenants* 130:22 says that the Holy Ghost *can* indwell, but Mormon apologists say that this refers only to his influence.

Poor Mormons! What they are missing by not inviting God in all His manifestations to come inside their hearts! If it is not the Holy Spirit that dwells in them, whose spirit is it?

Mormons emphasize the difference between God and Christ, but not their spirits, which they say are the same. The Spirit of God and the Spirit of Christ are identical. This influence is also known as the "spirit of truth" or the "light of Christ," and is that which lights the way of all men who come into the world,[32] before they are baptized. In contrast, the Holy Ghost influences man through the "gift" of his influence. The Holy Ghost may give a brief, temporary "flash of testimony" to the truth of the Mormon gospel before the baptism of a faithful seeker,[33] but the seeker can only receive the right to enjoy the presence of the Holy Ghost on a more permanent basis by having that gift conferred on him by the laying on of hands by one with Mormon priesthood authority, in a formal ceremony for that purpose.

As in all other matters of doctrine, though, Mormonism betrays its human origins by the confusion that surrounds its precepts. They say that the Holy Ghost is the comforter promised by Christ in John 14:12-27, but Joseph Smith expanded on that passage thus:

> "And I will pray the Father, and he shall give you another Comforter, that he may abide with you for ever;" now what is this other Comforter? It is no more nor less than the Lord Christ himself, and this is the sum and substance of the whole matter.[34]

If ignoring the Holy Ghost as in this passage isn't denying Him, what is? Mormons are caught in a dilemma here—if the "Second Comforter" is the presence of Christ—"forever;'—and Christ has a physical body, does that mean the Savior moves into your house with you? He can't, according to Joseph Smith, dwell in your heart. What about the other people who desire the Comforter?

One of the strangest teachings regarding the Mormon Holy Ghost is his identification with Adam. Brigham Young once stated:

> The world was organized by three distinct characters, namely: Elohim, Yahovah, and Michael, these three forming a quorum as in all heavenly bodies, and in organizing elements, perfectly represented in the Deity as Father, Son, and Holy Ghost.[35]

Why Brigham Young was so hung up on Adam—saying he was God, and then the Holy Ghost—we'll probably never know. The doctrines he bestowed have grown up in a thicket of confusion to snare Christian and Mormon alike. He also taught that the Holy Ghost had nothing to do with the conception of Christ, as the Bible teaches:

> If the Son was begotten by the Holy Ghost, it would be very dangerous to baptize and confirm females, and give the Holy Ghost to them lest he should beget children to be palmed upon the elders by the people, bringing the elders into great difficulties.[36]

To say, then, that the Mormons have a unique concept of the Holy Ghost is no exaggeration. Because of this, Christians cannot communicate with Mormons on the subject of the Holy Ghost any more than they can on the subject of God. Using the same words—Holy Ghost, Comforter, spirit—doesn't guarantee that you are saying the same thing!

The Mormon Satan

As much as any religious group on earth, the Mormons are acutely aware of the reality of the being they refer to as Satan. His prime objective, according to Mormons, is to influence and finally control those souls he didn't win over to his way in the pre-existence.

Doctrine and Covenants section 76 teaches that Satan was once an angel named Lucifer ("Bringer of Light") with a position of authority in the presence of God (v. 25). He led a rebellion against Christ (Moses 4:1-4), and was followed by one-third of God's spirit children. Defeated by the hosts of heaven, Satan became Perdition ("Utter Loss"), and was cast down to the earth (Rev. 12:7-9), with his followers.

Though his counterfeit plan of salvation was rejected in favor of that supported by Christ, Satan still continues to preach his false program through any godless doctrine, no matter how otherwise uplifting.[37] Unlike us, he has retained his memory of the pre-existence and uses it at every opportunity to try to lead us from God. He is wise and cunning, but according to the Mormon definition of intelligence ("light and truth"—*Doctrine and Covenants* 93:36), he is completely devoid of that attribute.

Though they are here upon this earth, we cannot see Satan and his hosts because of their greatest punishment for their rebellion was the denial of the privilege of physical bodies. Many Mormons have wondered, if this were a punishment, why the Holy Ghost has no body either; but LDS leaders consistently refuse to address this issue.

The influence of a devil is necessary, said President John Taylor. "Why is it, in fact, that we should have a devil? Why did not the Lord kill him long ago? Because we could not do without him."[38] Unlike the despicable adversary of Christianity, the Mormon devil is thus a necessary cog in the machinery of God, who *needs* even Satan to carry out his eternal purposes. LaMar Petersen, in his *Problems in Mormon Text,* noted that,

> God tolerates his foe, the Devil, who at times is an unwitting ally, as in the tempting of Eve: the Devil enacted the role requisite to the plan of life and salvation, thus preventing the scuttling of the divine program.[39]

According to Mormon tradition, Satan has his own priesthood, a parody of true priesthood, and he has been seen in Mormon temples.[40] Although God blessed water in the beginning of history, Mormons say He cursed it in the last days, and now the element of water is one that is the dominion of Satan. The day will come, says *Doctrine and Covenants* 61:13-22, that only the upright in heart will be able to travel on the water. The introduction to this same section says that Elder William W. Phelps saw Satan "riding in power upon the face of the waters." That is one of the reasons Mormon missionaries may not swim while on their missions, and why many older Mormons will not get near any body of water greater than that contained in a bathtub.

But Satan's power is only temporary. He is making the best of his influence over men, for at the last resurrection, he and his followers will be cast down to an everlasting hell. Even in eternity he will not have the pre-eminence he has always sought, for the sons of perdition who are placed in hell with him and his angels, though having their progression halted, will be able to rule over Satan by virtue of the fact that they will still have their bodies. Satan and his pre-existent hosts are doomed never to enjoy a body, and thus, never to progress, never to be gods.

Evil Spirits

Many Mormons, in dwelling on the negative forces that they believe surround them on this earth where the devil also abides, have become downright superstitious. Mormon writers Austin and Alta Fife, in their fascinating and well-documented book *Saints of Sage and Saddle,* have found that in places like rural Utah older Mormons believe in witches who can't pass under a steel object, or who can only be banished by having an adolescent urinate in your fireplace.[41]

Young people of even sophisticated LDS parentage are warned not to play with ouija boards or any form of the black arts, even in fun. Missionaries especially are told never to talk of experiences with demons or the occult, among themselves or with non-Mormons.

Heber C. Kimball and Orson Hyde, early leaders in the church, once had an experience with demons that Joseph Smith told them was because they had come so near to the Lord that Satan exhibited his greatest power to inhibit their progress. According to Kimball and Hyde, they were confronted by legions of demons who appeared after Kimball had rebuked an evil spirit that had been tormenting a fellow missionary. The demons seemed to be coming out of the wall of the room where the missionaries were, and looked like the most malevolent and destructive portrayals of wickedness imaginable. Hyde finally "fought them and contended against them face to face, until they began to diminish in number and to retreat from the room."[42]

In another incident, an elder rebuked Satan so severely in London that to this day the adversary is supposed to have no power in that city.[43]

President Wilford Woodruff once estimated that there were one hundred evil spirits roaming the earth to each living person at any given time.[44] These spirits are so jealous of mortals that they will try at any cost to control their bodies. So desperate are they, in fact, that they often settle for the body of a lower animal. Mormons use as an example of this the time when Christ cast a legion of devils out of a man (Mark 5:6-9). The evil spirits then entered into a herd of swine, the only available bodies thereabouts.

Parley P. Pratt said that there was a way to detect if a person was possessed by an evil spirit. The individual would, he said, "produce a shock to the observer and emit an unpleasant odor."[45]

Though Mormons usually will not talk about it to outsiders, exorcisms are not uncommon today. As Mormon writer Bruce R. McConkie cautiously observed, "By the power of faith and the authority of the priesthood, devils are frequently cast out of . . . afflicted persons."[46]

I had two brushes with such experiences while I was a dormitory senior resident in Helaman Halls, Brigham Young University. One night I and other resident assistants were told to be sure to report any strange or inexplicable happenings to our head resident. This instruction was the result of some mysterious occurrences in a nearby hall, where a bishop and other elders were called in to cast evil spirits out of a young girl and to in some way cleanse her dormitory room by rebuking the spirit by the power of the priesthood, forbidding it to return. Though unusual and kept a closely-guarded secret, such an event was accepted almost passively by those Mormons who heard of it. We had been taught that Satan would try most violently to influence the choicest spirits, who were most logically found in the high spiritual atmosphere of an LDS home, dormitory, or missionary apartment.

Even hearing of that experience did not prepare me for what happened a few months later. One evening, as the girls on my floor were just settling down to studies after dinner, two of the most sincere, earnest girls under my responsibility came into my room. Both were pale and frightened. As they began to speak, I could hardly believe my ears. They had been in the dorm room of Carol, the normally vivacious redhead who stood now before me, a shaking mass of fear. Her friend, Vickie, a candid, light-hearted freshman, had stopped by to visit. They were talking—about nothing in particular—in Carol's room with the door closed. According to Vickie, Carol was interrupted in midsentence by an unseen force which picked her up bodily and threw her against the door, then dropped her to the floor. They had stood, stunned, looking at each other for a moment, and then had run down the hall to my room.

I would not ever doubt the integrity of either girl. They were not liars, nor would they joke about or concoct such an experience—faithful Mormon youth like those do not dabble idly in such things. Still, eight years later, I have no explanation for what happened in that room.

In *Doctrine and Covenants* section 129, Joseph Smith perhaps set the mood for such an experience. There he gave a test that Mormons memorize in case they are ever confronted by a supernatural being. Spirits from God, said Joseph Smith, fall into two categories: (1) good angels, who are resurrected personages of flesh and bones and (2) the spirits of "just men made perfect," who have glorious (spirit) bodies, but have not yet been resurrected physically. Mormons know that if they are approached by an unearthly being, they are to offer a hand to that personage. If it is a heavenly angel, he will take the hand and the person will be able to feel the flesh and bone of the angel. A spirit of a just person made perfect, though, will not accept the handshake because the person's spiritual body would not be tangible. A devil, however, in his eagerness to have you mistakenly accept him as an angel from God will extend his unembodied hand. So Mormons believe that if anyone offers you a handshake you can't feel, you've got a problem on your hands. (I often wondered, though, why the devils were so stupid as not to be able to restrain themselves from offering the hand, and thus pass themselves off unsuspected as the spirits of just men made perfect.) Mormon doctrine also teaches that any supernatural visitor with sandy-colored hair is a "bad angel,"[47] as is any being who is afraid of weapons.[48]

Could it be only coincidental that a human being who might masquerade as a heavenly messenger would have a tangible handshake? That would fit in with the (admittedly apocryphal) story told by an early apostate who said that Joseph Smith had Sidney Rigdon pretend to be an angel. Though I've never seen a description of Rigdon's hair color, I'll bet it wasn't "sandy." *Any* mortal would be afraid of a weapon; the only puzzler is why a devil—who has no corporeal body—would be afraid of a gun or bowie knife, as Heber C. Kimball claimed.[49]

All in all, the Mormon conception of Satan doesn't make much sense either. Satan, they say, is the brother of Christ, and of us all; and the son of God. The Bible teaches that a good tree (like God) can only bring forth, or reproduce to make, good fruit. Satan is thus *not* God's progeny.

Men, too, as *created* by God, not sired by Him, are in a natural state of rebellion against their Maker. Only by being born again can we become sons and daughters of God (1 John 4:7; 5:1), and thus logically the good seed from the Good Tree. This is our purpose on earth; not to work our way into being re-accepted as rightful heirs, but to receive the grace of God who would adopt us and make us His children.

Angels

Throughout history, it has been necessary for God to communicate with man by means of heavenly messengers. Mormons call all such messengers angels, and are incensed by the tradition that such beings had wings, haloes, or harps. Parley P. Pratt stated:

> Angels are of the same race as men. They are, in fact, men who have passed from the rudimental state to the higher spheres of progressive being. They have died and risen again to life, and are consequently possessed of a divine, human body of flesh and bones, immortal and eternal.[50]

According to Mormon doctrine, though, Pratt was speaking of those messengers who have appeared in the years since the death of Christ, since there was no resurrection prior to that time. Those who ministered before that time were either (1) unembodied (as-yet unborn) spirits, (2) disembodied spirits (who have lived but are as of yet unresurrected), or (3) translated beings who had a change wrought on their bodies without tasting death (examples of these are the three Nephites, John the Revelator, Enoch and his people, and Moses).

Translated beings dwell in a terrestrial state, with those like them who minister to other of God's planets, and do not dwell directly in God's presence.[51] All other good angels reside "in the presence of God, on a globe like a sea of glass and fire, where all things for their glory are manifest, past, present and future, and are continually before the Lord."[52]

Most Mormons will not claim to have seen an angel, but almost all have heard a "true" anecdote about one from a friend or relative. They claim that the three Nephites, who were translated beings, greeted the sailors on Columbus' ship when he arrived in America, and helped to design the American flag.[53] So much has been ascribed to them that researcher Hector Lee reported:

> The tendency on the part of some members of the Church to attribute any unusual happening to the Three Nephites led to an alleged assertion by Dr. James E. Talmadge, of the Quorum of the Twelve Apostles, to the effect that the Three Nephites "are the most overworked of all individuals."[54]

The Bible shows the fallacy in the Mormons' belief in Nephites or any other of their "angels." In Hebrews 1:13-14 we read that angels are "ministering spirits." Luke 24:39 tells us that spirits do *not* have flesh and bone—which disqualifies all the bodily "angels"—Moroni, John the Baptist, Peter, James, and John—who appeared to Joseph Smith with new revelations and authority to organize his apostate church. In fact, Joseph Smith made the worst possible choice in selecting "angels" to lend credibility to his stories about the *Book of Mormon* and ordinations to the priesthoods. Perhaps Paul, in prophetic warning, was referring directly to Mormonism when he said:

> I marvel that ye are so soon removed from him that called you into the grace of Christ unto another gospel: Which is not another; but there be some that trouble you, and would pervert the gospel of Christ. But though we, or an angel from heaven, preach any other gospel unto you than that which we have preached unto you, let him be accursed.

> —Galatians 1:6-8

The gospel is so precious, so valuable, that not even an angel should dissuade us from it!

A Confusing Deity

Everything about the Mormon godhead is a confused mess if you accept all the teachings of Mormon leaders. Brigham Young said that *God* was *Adam.*[55] *Adam,* according to LDS theology, was *Michael* in the pre-existence.[56] *Michael* was the godhead equivalent of the *Holy Ghost.*[57] The *Holy Ghost,* said Talmadge, is the *Comforter,*[58] and the *Comforter* is the *Spirit of Truth.*[59] *Christ,* though, is also the *Comforter,*[60] and the *Spirit of Truth.*[61] Finally, *Christ* is the *God* of the Old Testament![62]

So it comes full circle—and even through the Mormon perversion of Scripture, truth prevails. There is only *one* God!

In the final view, though, the Mormon god is only a means to an end for his adherents. He did not create man's essential being; he only clothed him with a spirit body. Like children anxious to leave home after school years, Mormons think they owe no more allegiance to their heavenly parents than they do to their earthly ones: each set of parents, by conceiving man, owed him proper upbringing and the necessities of life. Earthly parents were obligated to provide food, clothing, and a home; heavenly parents owe them life, instruction, and salvation (yes, salvation—for was it not the Mormon god's *plan* that man should fall so that he could be redeemed?).

Nothing in LDS theology is as it should be. Each man has two sets of parents: heavenly and earthly. God has many wives, and man should too.

Mary the mother of Christ had two living husbands, without sinning. Their physical god begets spiritual bodied children and infuses them into mortal bodies so they can become gods, too. Meanwhile, his co-partner, the Holy Ghost, has no body at all and is still a god. Other beings are punished with the devil for their sins, and their sentence: No body, ever.

This god is surely the author of confusion. My God, the self-sufficient, holy I AM, is not! Praise His holy Name!

NOTES

[1]*Journal of Discourses,* X, p. 5.

[2]Ibid., VI, p. 6.

[3]Abraham H. Cannon, journal quoted in Tanner, *Mormonism: Shadow or Reality?* p. 165.

[4]Moses 3:1-9; *Doctrines of Salvation,* II, pp. 10-11.

[5]Orson Pratt, *The Seer,* p. 21; see also *Journal of Discourses,* XVI, pp. 333-334.

[6]Joseph F. Smith, comp., *Teachings of the Prophet Joseph Smith,* pp. 370, 372.

[7]See also Alma 11:26-31, 38-39, 44; Mosiah 15:1-5; Mormon 7:7.

[8]*Doctrine and Covenants,* 84.

[9]*Pearl of Great Price,* Joseph Smith 2:14-17.

[10]Joseph Smith, "Lectures on Faith," 1833, Lecture Five. The fact that these lectures did not square with later teachings about God's physical body was the reason that the "Lectures on Faith" were finally dropped from the *Doctrine and Covenants*.

[11]Pratt, *The Seer,* p. 132.

[12]*Journal of Discourses,* VI, p. 120.

[13]*Doctrine and Covenants* 107:53-55.

[14]*Journal of Discourses,* I, p. 50.

[15]Rodney Turner, "The Position of Adam in Latter-day Saint Scriptures and Theology," (unpublished M. A. Thesis, BYU, August 1953), p. 58.

[16]*Journal of Discourses,* II, p. 345.

[17]3 Nephi 9:15; Ether 4:7.

[18]Mosiah 5:7; 15:10-13; Ether 3.

[19]An example of this is found in *Doctrine and Covenants* 29:1, 41-46, where critics of Mormonism see only Joseph Smith's confusion of speakers.

[20]Mosiah 27:24-29.

[21]*Doctrine and Covenants* 25:1.

[22]Alma 7:10; 1 Nephi 11:13-18.

[23]*Journal of Discourses,* I, p. 51.

[24]*Deseret News,* October 10, 1866.

[25]Pratt, *The Seer,* p. 158.

[26]John chapter 2; for the Mormon interpretation of this see *Journal of Discourses* II, pp. 81-82, 210; IV, p. 259; Pratt, *The Seer,* I, pp. 158-159.

[27]*Journal of Discourses,* II, p. 210.

[28]Ibid., I, p. 346.

[29]Ibid., I, p. 50.

[30]*Doctrine and Covenants* 107:53-54; Moses chapter 7.

[31]*Journal of Discourses,* V, p. 179.

[32]*Doctrine and Covenants* 84:44-46.

[33]Moroni 10:4-5.

[34]Joseph Smith Jr., *Documentary History of the Church,* III, p. 380-381.

[35]*Journal of Discourses,* I, p. 51.

[36]Ibid.

[37]James R. Harris, *Ensign,* December 1972, p. 28.

[38]*The Government of God* (Liverpool: S. W. Richards, 1852), p. 81.

[39]Petersen, *Problems in Mormon Text,* p. 20.

[40]Ibid.

[41]Fife, *Saints of Sage and Saddle,* p. 262.

[42]Orson F. Whitney, *Life of Heber C. Kimball* (1888), pp. 144-146.

[43]Fife, *Saints of Sage and Saddle,* p. 138,

[44]Wilford Woodruff, quoted in Whalen, p. 102.

[45]Parley P. Pratt, *Key to Theology* (Liverpool: J. H. Smith, 1883), p. 116.

[46]Bruce R. McConkie, *Mormon Doctrine* (Salt Lake City: Bookcraft, 1966), p. 196.

[47]*Times and Seasons,* III, p. 747.

[48]*Journal of Discourses,* V, p. 164.

[49]Ibid.

[50]Parley P. Pratt, quoted in Layton, *Can the Descendents of Ham Hold the Priesthood?* p. 10.

[51]Joseph Fielding Smith, *Teachings of the Prophet Joseph Smith,* p. 170.

[52]*Doctrine and Covenants* 130:7.

[53]Lee, *The Three Nephites,* p. 36.

[54]Ibid., p. 33.

[55]*Journal of Discourses,* I, p. 50.

[56]*Doctrine and Covenants* 27:11.

[57]Journal of Discourses, I, pp. 50-51.

[58]James E. Talmadge, *A Study of the Articles of Faith* (Salt Lake City: The Church of Jesus Christ of Latter-day Saints, 1968), p. 42.

[59]*Principles of the Gospel,* p. 167.

[60]Joseph Smith Jr., *Documentary History of the Church,* III, pp. 380-381.

[61]McConkie, *Mormon Doctrine,* p. 754.

[62]*Doctrine and Covenants* 136:21-22.

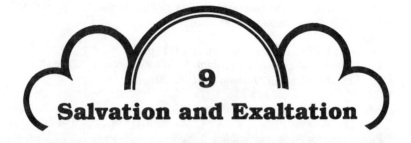

9
Salvation and Exaltation

The straight and narrow way is not an exclusive country club. It is as
wide as infinity . . . it draws our attention to love and truth. It is
confining only in that it marks the peril point.
—Neal Maxwell,
Church Commissioner of Education.
Remarks in a Talmadge Lecture
"Some Dimensions of Disciples"
May 9, 1972

Ask Mormons if they believe in salvation. "Sure!" they'll answer.
Ask them if salvation comes through the sacrifice of Christ. "Certainly,"
they'll reply. Ask them if salvation is a free gift from God. "Of course,"
they'll assure you. But if at this point in your conversation you neglect to
ask your Mormon friends their *definition* of salvation, you'll not understand another thing they'll tell you in regard to the final destiny of mankind.

Salvation Versus Exaltation

When Mormons speak of eternal life, they are referring not just to
living forever, but to the reward that God gives to those who are obedient.
Eternal life as they understand it is based entirely on works.

Immortality, on the other hand, is seen by Mormons to be the free
gift of God. Because of the atonement of Christ, all men will be resurrected, no matter what their deeds. Salvation *equals* resurrection. The
third Article of Faith states: "We believe that through the Atonement of
Christ, all mankind may be saved, by obedience to the laws and ordinances of the Gospel." A close examination of this statement shows what
Mormons believe. The atonement of Christ is a vehicle which sits practically powerless without the fuel of man's good deeds.

Grace, the word of heavenly music to a Christian's ear, has a different interpretation for Mormons. It is a reward, not a gift. "Grace," said Mormon Bruce R. McConkie, "is granted to men porportionately as they conform to the standards of personal righteousness that are part of the Gospel plan."[1] On the other hand, Mormons regard the means of salvation and a resurrection to be "inalienable rights" that God owes them.

Salvation, which Mormons thus equate with resurrection, is supposed to be guaranteed by the atonement. But it does not include happiness, inner peace, or a knowledge that God sees the saved one as justified. To Mormons, these are no free gifts; they must be earned.

"Redemption from personal sin," said James E. Talmadge, "can only be obtained through obedience to the requirements of the Gospel, and a life of good works."[2] The process that leads to this redemption from personal sins is known as exaltation, and is as different from Mormon salvation as a paycheck is from a coin found on the sidewalk.

George Romney, the Mormon former governor of Michigan, once stated, "We believe that everyone will be saved. The question is the degree of exaltation that a man may win for himself in his life on earth."[3]

An adage commonly heard from Mormons is that "salvation without exaltation is damnation." Again, a conflict of definitions is seen. Mormons regard any cessation in their progress to become gods as damnation, and compare "damning" to "damming," or halting, the progress of a mighty stream. This emphasis on exaltation is why you will only irritate a Mormon by asking him if he has been saved. In his mind, even the most ignorant savage and venal criminal has been "saved," that is, guaranteed a resurrection.

As is true with so many other Mormon doctrines, this idea of universal "salvation" evolved gradually in the mind of Joseph Smith. In his early writings, there was no hint that all would be saved. In the *Book of Mormon,* for instance, Joseph Smith penned the story of the wicked preacher Nehor who "testified unto the people that all mankind should be saved at the last day." Nehor was taken to the top of a hill and made to confess that he'd taught false doctrine, then he was killed.[4]

But before his death, Joseph Smith had already begun to teach that not only would all men be saved, but in order to be pleasing to God, they must be exalted. He advocated that men literally "work out their own salvation." In *Doctrine and Covenants* 132:32 his god told the Mormon people, "Go ye, therefore, and do the works of Abraham; enter ye into my law and ye shall be saved." Here he was referring specifically to polygamy, but the fact that anyone could teach people both to be Christian and to do the works of an Old Testament prophet suspends belief.

In contrast, we know that Christ's atoning sacrifice did away with the old law under which Moses and other Old Testament prophets lived.

Because it was so demanding a schoolmaster, Christians rejoice that we have been released from its strictures into the liberty of Christ, for as the apostle James pointed out, "Whosoever shall keep the whole law, and yet offend in one point, he is guilty of all" (James 2:10).

All Christians, though, are promised eternal life by God: "For God so loved the world, that he gave his only begotten Son, that whosoever believeth in him should not perish, but have everlasting life" (John 3:16). This Scripture verse, Mormons should note, does not say that one must be married in the temple, or research your genealogy, or keep the Word of Wisdom. In fact, it doesn't say anything about works at all!

Christians do work out their own salvation, as Philippians 2:12 tells us to do. But we don't work *for* our salvation, we work *because* of it. Because we are saved by God's grace, our grateful hearts are pleased to do good works to honor our Father. But poor Mormons—though they take the resurrection of their bodies for granted, they are continually admonished to work for anything else. They are compelled to do more, and more, and more.

Christians, on the other hand, feel the sweet peace of knowing that, even though all their righteousnesses are as filthy rags before God, He accepts them! (Isa. 64:6).

The Bible does teach that all human beings will be resurrected.

> Marvel not at this: for the hour is coming, in the which all that are in the graves shall hear his voice, And shall come forth; they that have done good, unto the resurrection of life; and they that have done evil, unto the resurrection of damnation.
>
> —John 5:28-29

And the Christian knows that not everyone will be "saved," in the correct Bible sense of the word.

> For the time is come that judgment must begin at the house of God: and if it first begin at us, what shall the end be of them that obey not the gospel of God? And if the righteous scarcely be saved, where shall the ungodly and the sinner appear?
>
> —1 Peter 4:17-18

But do works matter? Of course they do! We are known by our fruits, and works are a fruit. But we're not dependent upon them for our salvation, for no one knows better than each of us knows, in our heart of hearts, how feeble and selfishly-motivated many of our "good" deeds are. Christians, rejoice! We are free! God will give us every good thing we need, and only because He loves us. But pity the poor Mormons, who through Wallace Bennett affirm that "once we have been resurrected, it will be our own efforts, not Christ's sacrifice, that will be the deciding factor."[5]

Baptism

The fourth Article of Faith states:

> We believe that the first principles and ordinances of the Gospel are: first, Faith in the Lord Jesus Christ; second, Repentance; third, Baptism by immersion for the remission of sins; fourth, Laying on of hands for the gift of the Holy Ghost.

This Article of Faith forms a framework of the first duties of a prospective Mormon who would earn his exaltation. By "joining" the Mormon Church, a person makes himself eligible for eternal life. Without this church membership, he would only have the right to resurrection, along with all the rest of the "Gentile" world.

When a person becomes a Mormon, his new brethren believe it is due to the fact that the convert has the "believing blood" of Jacob. All Mormons are pronounced to be of Jacob's lineage, not because of any genealogical findings, but because they believe that God sent His special spirits to earth to be born into the bodies of Jacob's descendants.

These spirits in the pre-existence supposedly had the special intellectual and spiritual gift of being able to know truth when they saw it. The fact that a person accepts Mormonism is seen as proof positive that he has this ability to recognize truth; and therefore the conclusion is that he *must* be of Israelite descent.

If this were not enough, Joseph Smith taught that after baptism, the blood of a convert was actually changed to make him of this lineage. "The effect of the Holy Ghost upon a Gentile is to purge out the old blood and make him actually of the seed of Abraham."[6]

All Mormons therefore consider themselves to be of triply Jewish descent: they are first born into Jacob's line; then at baptism any Gentile blood is flushed out; and finally they are adopted spiritually into the lineage of Abraham, who was promised multitudes of righteous progeny. No wonder they can call the rest of the world (including Jews) Gentiles!

They teach that at birth, a child is born in an innocent state, in spite of what the *Pearl of Great Price* says about children being "conceived in sin."[7] But the world being as wicked as it is, a child soon becomes "natural," an enemy to God,[8] and by the age of eight when he becomes accountable, this child already needs to have the effects of Adam's sin nullified.

We Christians know that when we first come to Christ, we come repenting of our sinful nature which has alienated us from our Maker, as well as for specific sins we have committed. We realize that until conversion we are in a state of rebellion (Eph. 2:3) that does not allow us to enter God's kingdom until we repent of our natures, as well as our sins.

Mormons, on the other hand, believe that they are inherently good, even before conversion, because they are children of God. They repent of the things they have done which they know to be wrong, but their belief that they are by nature noble prevents them from seeing that when they lay hold on God's saving promises they are doing no more than simply putting themselves in line for exaltation. Baptism, according to Mormons, has a fourfold purpose: (1) to remit the sins that hinder a person's progress toward godly perfection, (2) to establish membership in the Church and Kingdom, (3) to provide access to the Celestial Kingdom, and (4) to form the foundation for personal sanctification.

Mormons are only baptized once in life for themselves. If by chance all records of baptism become destroyed or lost (an unlikely eventuality with today's information retrieval systems), then a second baptism is performed. Or, if a person is excommunicated from the Church and then repents fully, that person may be rebaptized.

New Mormons are usually overwhelmed by what is expected of them as far as church work is concerned. But they see others around them pressing sometimes frantically, sometimes complacently, toward the goal of exaltation, and they soon conclude that this must be the right way to reach that goal.

"Saviors on Mount Zion"

Joseph Smith once stated that a person's greatest responsibility on this earth was to "seek after his dead." A Mormon's hair might still be damp with baptismal water when he may be reminded that now, since he can be exalted, his dead relatives need the same ordinance. Not only do Mormons believe that their ancestors cannot receive exaltation without vicarious baptisms done for them in a Mormon temple, but also that they themselves cannot be exalted if they ignore their responsibility to research their genealogy.

Mormons emphasize that the family succession of baptized persons must form an unbroken chain back to Adam. I have heard several Mormons claim proudly that a certain line of their ancestry was traced back that far. This is usually because in their research they were able to find a distant relative who was a king or a nobleman who claimed descent from a Biblical character whose genealogy is found in the Bible.

Since 1965 all members of the Mormon Church have been asked to fill out a four-generation sheet, a legal-sized sheet with blanks for family members' names, dates of birth, death, and other pertinent information. These are bound in what is called a "Book of Remembrance," a heavy notebook binder. When completed with verified information, duplicates of the "pedigree sheets" are sent to the church's genealogy headquarters where they are recorded and microfilmed.

The negatives are stored along with millions like them in great vaults deep in the granite cliffs of Cottonwood Canyon, outside Salt Lake City.

Built at a cost of two and one-half million dollars, these vaults make the records stored therein impervious to damage from humidity, dryness, earthquakes, and atomic disasters. Pedigree sheets to be microfilmed pour in daily, the result of millions of hours of work from church members who believe that their ancestors will be lost without their help.

Mormons believe that all the names which were never written down or which would in some other way be impossible for them to obtain will be revealed during the millennial reign of Christ. Referring to this, Jerald and Sandra Tanner asked: "Since the Mormon leaders believe that the Lord will have to provide many of the names anyway, would it not be better to spend this time and money helping the living instead of searching for the names of the dead?"[9]

Genealogy has become big business with the Mormon Church. Many of its members have become fanatical about their duties to their dead. It is hard for a genealogist of any (or no) religion to do research without bumping elbows with research done on his relatives by some distant Mormon kin he didn't know he had.

Mormons believe that through their genealogical efforts, they are saviors of the world.[10] John Taylor once boasted the same thing, saying, "We are the only people that know how to save our posterity in the celestial kingdom of God . . . we in fact are the Saviors of the world!"[11]

In an effort to secure some favorable publicity, Mormons have given personal genealogies to public figures like Johnny Carson and President Jimmy Carter in publicized presentations. In one case, though, this backfired—when the governor of Washington was presented with her pedigree, she refused to have the press attend the presentation. Christian people like Jimmy Carter, however, probably would not be as thrilled at the Mormons' work at searching out their dead if they knew that all their deceased relatives have already had proxy baptisms performed for them in Mormon temples. There is no such thing as a free lunch.

Doing genealogy work has not always brought the peace and satisfaction to Mormons that they often claim. Many Mormons who feel obligated to search out their ancestors and yet hate sitting in front of microfilm readers or poring over dusty legal records often take the easier route. If they can possibly afford it, they have their genealogy researched by a professional. The story is told of a man who paid a genealogist a thousand pounds to trace his pedigree—and then later paid the researcher ten thousand more not to tell anyone what he'd found.[12]

Baptisms for the Dead

The doctrine of vicarious baptism as a way to save someone who has already died was introduced in August of 1840 by Joseph Smith. At first, it was apparently just for relatives of Latter-day Saints.[13] By September of

1842, when Joseph Smith penned the letters that appear now as sections 127 and 128 of the *Doctrine and Covenants,* he had worked out the details of this practice well enough to present them to his people.

The principles behind vicarious baptisms are carefully orchestrated so as not to conflict with the Mormon emphasis on the free agency of a person. Mormons do not claim that every person for whom a proxy baptism is performed will be exalted. But they assume that most will be, because there are other Mormons who have died who are teaching prospective Mormons in the spirit world. Once a spirit decides to become a Mormon, he merely accepts the baptism which was done in his name on earth, and the end result is the same as if he had been himself baptized while alive. If no proxy baptism has been done, the person must wait for it. If this spirit person, though, led an evil life while on earth, he must suffer in the spirit world until he has paid for his sins—"the uttermost farthing"—and then when he has atoned sufficiently, he can accept a proxy baptism.

Mormons use several Bible references to justify their practice of vicarious baptism. Some of these references have such an obscure supposed connection to the idea of a spirit prison and baptism for the dead that non-Mormons may have trouble seeing it; such as in Zechariah 9:11; 1 Peter 3:18-19; 4:6; and John 5:25-28. Their favorite is: "Else what shall they do which are baptized for the dead, if the dead rise not at all? why are they then baptized for the dead?" (1 Cor. 15:29).

All of these Scriptures lose a lot of their Mormon punch, however, when read in a more modern version than King James, and are practically defused when read in context, keeping in mind the purpose and audience for which they were written. The Corinthian passage, it is valuable to note, speaks of people who are not Christians ("they") doing baptisms for the dead—not Paul or his followers.

No matter how Mormons stretch Bible Scripture, they can find no Biblical precedents for actually baptizing one person to bring to pass the salvation of another. Mormons say there is a precedent in principle, if not in deed, of such a practice. They cite the case of Levite priests who acted on behalf of the people in ancient ordinances. Mormons who are anxious to take on responsibility for others should be reminded that even Christ shuddered to do so (Mark 14:36; *Doctrine and Covenants* 19:18-19). But he did take responsibility for our salvation, and is now the only intercessor we need, as John noted:

> My little children, these things write I unto you, that ye sin not. And if any man sin, we have an advocate with the Father, Jesus Christ the righteous: And he is the propitiation for our sins: and not for ours only, but also for the sins of the whole world.
>
> 1 John 2:1-2

Proxy Baptism

I participated two times in proxy baptisms. The first was in the old temple at Manti, Utah. I was taken with a group of other young people by bus from our home ward in Albuquerque. Before going, each of us had gone through an extensive interview with our bishop who asked us some of the following questions:

Are you morally clean and worthy to enter the temple?
Will you and do you sustain the General Authorities of the Church, and will you live in accordance with the accepted rules and doctrines of the Church?
Do you have any connection, in sympathy or otherwise, with any of the apostate groups or individuals who are running counter to the accepted rules and doctrines of the Church?
Are you a full tithe payer?
Are you exempt from paying tithes?
Do you keep the Word of Wisdom?
Do you always wear the regulation [temple] garments?
Will you earnestly strive to do your duty in the Church, to attend your sacrament, priesthood, and other meetings, and to obey the rules, laws, and commandments of the Gospel?
Have you ever been denied a recommend to any temple?
Have you ever been divorced?

When the appropriate questions were properly answered, the bishop gave a few instructions on what to wear on the "temple excursion," and then gave the applicant a signed "temple recommend" which was to be countersigned by the stake president. This was the same basic procedure followed by my bishop in Provo before I obtained a recommend to do baptisms there.

The Manti Temple had been running behind schedule on baptisms, and I had been baptized thirty times there for deceased women. The Provo Temple, though, had several modern conveniences to help keep things running more smoothly. After presenting our recommends, girls and boys were sent to separate dressing rooms where we were given amorphous white baptismal garments made of terrycloth.

Our street clothing was put into lockers and we went into the underground baptismal room, which held an immense bowl-like metallic font which was supported on the backs of statues of twelve life-sized brass oxen, symbolic of the twelve tribes of Israel. A platform extended along one side of the great bowl, where we all waited, wide-eyed and silent, for the baptisms to begin.

One by one we were called by name to descend into the font. A recorder sat on a high stool, not unlike a lifeguard's stand, at one side of the font, and witnesses watched. An elder stood in the font in garments like ours, and beckoned for each participant as his or her turn came. He spoke the baptismal prayer in a hurried, monotonous voice, stopping only to lower a proxy into the water.

I sat on the platform, looking furtively for the angels I had heard often appeared in temples. When my name was called, I went down into the water. The baptizing elder turned me around so that he could see a large screen, something like an electronic football scoreboard, which he looked at over my shoulder. On top of the screen was my name, and below it a name I don't remember, but which I'll say was Elizabeth Anderson.

"Sister Celeste Latayne Colvett," he said, looking at the screen, "having been commissioned of Jesus Christ, I baptize you, for and in behalf of Elizabeth Anderson, who is dead, in the name of the Father, and of the Son, and of the Holy Ghost. Amen." Then he quickly dropped his right arm from the square and lowered me beneath the water. As I was regaining my footing (you learn after the third or fourth time to put one foot slightly behind the other to help you get back out of the water) he had already begun the same prayer, inserting this time the name of another dead woman which had flashed onto the screen behind me. Fifteen consecutive baptisms were performed with me as proxy in a matter of about three minutes. As I left the font, another proxy was preparing to be baptized.

Then I was led into a "confirmation room" where a man sat on a high stool with a chair near his knees. I sat on the chair, my back to him, and he and several other elders placed their hands heavily upon my head while he pronounced this prayer: "Sister Celeste Latayne Colvett, in the name of Jesus Christ, we lay our hands upon your head for and in behalf of Elizabeth Anderson, who is dead, and confirm you a member of the Church of Jesus Christ of Latter-day Saints, and say unto you: Receive the Holy Ghost. Amen."

As soon as he had finished, he lifted his hands off my head for no more than a fraction of a second and then replaced them, beginning the same prayer again, this time with the name of the second person for whom I had been baptized. This continued, and took only a minute or so, because he spoke very quickly.

This sort of mechanical processing of proxies goes on daily in the twenty or so temples around the world. Literally millions of dead persons have had proxy baptisms done for them in this assembly-line fashion. The more converts made to the church, the more names submitted, and the more proxy ordinances done.

So far, most of the deceased presidents of the United States, and other prominent persons of the past including Catholic popes and saints, have had vicarious ordinances performed in their behalf in Mormon temples. Wilford Woodruff, a president of the Mormon Church during the turn of the century, said that on April 10, 1898, all the signers of the Declaration of Independence, along with George Washington, appeared to him in the St. George Temple two nights in a row, begging that vicarious ordinances be done for them. Woodruff obliged, and also did the proxy work for Christopher Columbus, John Wesley, and other prominent men of the past, one hundred in all.[14]

A Christian in looking at this doctrine that a person can accept Christ after death will want to know how Mormons explain the story of the rich man and Lazarus as found in Luke 16:19-26. The late President Joseph Fielding Smith, in his book, *Way To Perfection,* explained around the great truth of the Bible's teachings on repenting after death by saying that the "great gulf" was only fixed before the death of Christ. After the Savior's resurrection, it no longer existed. Thus the righteous dead can intermingle with and teach those who have not received the Gospel in mortal life.

With such official rationalizations, it is no wonder that Mormons continue researching their genealogies at a record-breaking pace. In 1975, more than three million proxy baptisms were performed in the sixteen Mormon temples. That year, too, the LDS Church spent over 125 million dollars on genealogical and proxy work, employing over eighty camera crews just to keep up with microfilming the bales of documents which pour in daily.[15]

In all this, Mormons see themselves as saviors, and Christians as bloodthirsty hypocrites who would condemn to hell any who died without law, adults and children alike. When asked why there is no Biblical endorsement of ordinances for the dead, Mormons claim that New Testament saints were too scattered to understand the necessity for temples and the need for such practices.[16]

I have never read of an authenticated ancient record which clearly documented the practice of baptism for the dead as Mormons understand it, and which identified such ordinances as anything but a presumptuous heresy. Even the *Book of Mormon* (which is far from an authenticated ancient document, but the Mormons accept it as such) teaches that if you reject their gospel after hearing it here on earth, there is no second chance,[17] and says that if you die without ever hearing it, you'll be blessed anyway, "for the power of redemption cometh on all them that have no law."[18]

Einar Anderson, in trying to analyze why Mormons work so hard in "saving" their dead, concluded that it is because such work salves the

195

consciences of those who didn't effectively witness to others while they were alive. I remember thinking, when I was a Mormon, that it would be better not to tell a hostile Gentile anything about the Gospel and wait until he or she died and could hear it preached in the spirit world.

Endowments for Exaltation

Proxy baptisms are not the only ordinances performed in the Mormon temples. They are, however, the most available—any Church member who is an adolescent or older and can pass the temple recommend questions may participate in baptisms for the dead. A young man, though, will usually receive his own endowments—a higher temple ordinance—just before going on a mission, at about age nineteen. A young woman receives the endowments when she goes on a mission (at age twenty or twenty-one), or (as is more common) just before her marriage—whichever comes first. Converts to the church who are already married, and thus would not soon be going on missions, are usually required to wait six months to a year after their baptisms to ascertain their worthiness to participate in the secret temple ordinances.

There are basically three kinds of temple ordinances other than vicarious baptism. First, there are the washings and anointings. This particular ceremony is for the living only. The second type of ordinance is the endowment of the priesthood, wherein those who show themselves to be worthy and humble can symbolically pass through the veil to the highest level of heaven. The term "endowment," though, is often used to refer to these ceremonies as well as the washings and anointings. The third type of ordinance is eternal marriage. It, like the endowment, can be done in proxy for dead persons who have already had vicarious baptisms and endowments done in their behalf. An appendage to this ordinance is a sealing ceremony where children born to parents who were not LDS at the time of their children's birth can be sealed to them after all are proven worthy.

These ordinances were not practiced in the first Mormon temple which was built in Kirtland, Ohio. In fact, there were no secret rites conducted behind its doors—all its meetings were open to the public. Its main floor was used for regular worship services, while its upper story served as a classroom for missionaries. Built at great expense, it was reluctantly abandoned when the Mormons were forced to leave Ohio. It was later used as a barn, an auditorium, and a school. The Reorganized Church now owns it and, as in the past, holds public meetings there.

The church's second temple, in Nauvoo, was the first for vicarious rites. Though it was never completed, proxy baptisms were performed there, and endowment ceremonies took place in its attic. It, too, was abandoned under pressure, and was burned in 1848 by enemies of the church who were incensed by the secrecy that accompanied what went on inside its walls. In 1850, a tornado struck down the remaining walls of the building. All that remains today is the pump and well which once supplied water for the baptismal font.

It was not for another nine years that Latter-day Saints had a place in which to receive their endowments, when the Old Endowment House in Salt Lake City was dedicated. Since then many more temples have been built throughout the world. All these have the same purpose, and the ordinances performed in them are uniform except as to the languages spoken.

The number of temples now in operation or planned for the near future approaches fifty worldwide, including several in Utah and across the United States and a number of temples in Europe and around the world. In places like Salt Lake City and Hawaii, temples and their visitor centers are big tourist attractions. The construction of some temples, however, like the one in Denver, Colorado, has been delayed repeatedly because of strong community opposition.

Mormons look forward to the day when they will be able to build the temple in Independence, Missouri, as Joseph Smith prophesied. However, a splinter group tenaciously owns the site Joseph Smith said was revealed by revelation. Also revealed to him, he said, were the temple's dimensions (with a capacity of up to fifteen thousand people), including twenty-four rooms whose names were given to Joseph Smith by God. It will be the temple of temples—when and if it is ever built.

Today's temples, even the older ones, are a strange mixture of old traditions and ultra-modern conveniences. The newer ones are self-contained units that contain cafeterias for the workers and industrial-type laundry facilities so that garments used therein never have to be seen by outsiders.

Since many young Mormons go on temples excursion for vicarious baptisms, as I did, this experience usually serves as a whet for their curiosity to see the other parts of the temple. Every faithful youth looks forward to the day he or she can receive the endowments.

Usually, though, after a first trip to a temple to receive endowments, a young Mormon is confused. He has been told all his life about how sacred and uplifting the endowment ceremony is, and if it hasn't seemed that way to him, he is told that it is only because he didn't understand it. That the proceedings there are disorienting, there can be no doubt; but Mormons who have already received their endowments are not allowed to talk about that experience to anyone, even to prepare someone for it.

A trip to a temple may either be a hurried once-a-week affair sandwiched between appointments for someone who lives near a temple and does vicarious work often; or it may be a once-in-a-lifetime event preceded by much planning and expense, as is the case with many Mormons who live in foreign countries where there is no temple.

Going for one's own endowments is a milestone in the life of every Mormon, a sort of coming-of-age where young people are introduced to the secrets their parents have kept all their lives, and which they themselves are expected to honor and guard with their lives. The endowment experience has many parallels with initiation ceremonies of primitive cultures. It is secret; the newly-initiated is tested to prove worthiness; he is given a badge or token to prove he has passed (in this case, temple garments); and finally (before temple marriage) it signals sexual maturity and encourages virility and fertility.

Since I never went through a temple for endowments or for celestial marriage, I do not know from experience the details of these ceremonies. However, many former Mormons, some of whom worked regularly in the temples, have written about them. These ceremonies (which last upwards to several hours) are often boring, even to Mormons. Christians would probably find them boring, too, if they weren't so blasphemous, and in places, ludicrous. That they are usually tiring would be agreed to by all.

Temple Ceremonies

A temple session begins when a Mormon presents his recommend for verification at the office-like annex of a temple. He has registered in advance, and he has submitted earlier the completed pedigree sheets on persons for whom he will do vicarious work, if that is his purpose. Before leaving the annex, he usually leaves a cash contribution in a receptacle prominently displayed for that purpose.

He is shown into a chapel, where he waits until enough others, men and women like himself, have assembled to form a group. A few songs are sung, a prayer offered, and a short talk on the solemnity of the occasion is presented by a temple worker.

Men doing vicarious work are taken aside at this point and ordained elders in behalf of the deceased for whom they are taking out endowments. When they return to the group, men and women are separated into dressing rooms where each removes all clothing except for a tunic-like "shield" which is open at the sides like a Catholic priest's chasuble. He is then washed with a spray nozzle by a temple worker of his own sex who says a rote formula, blessing all the parts of the body as he touches them. The washing is then "confirmed" by a temple worker who places his hands on the head of the endowee.

He then moves to another part of the little booth where the washing took place, and sits on a stool as a temple worker anoints the various parts of his body with oil. The anointing is then confirmed and sealed in the same manner as the washing was.

The endowee then dons a temple garment. Prior to 1975 this temple garment was similar to what most people would describe as a union suit, that is, a garment that covers the entire body from neck to ankles to wrists. It had a collar and embroidered "marks" on it. Nowadays, however, a regular abbreviated "everyday" garment is put on at this point.

A "new name" is given to the endowee by the temple worker. He is cautioned never to reveal this name to anyone except later in the temple ceremony. The name is usually taken from the Bible or *Book of Mormon*, and it is common for all men in a session group to have the same name, and all the women another. A man is to remember his name and that of his wife, but a woman is not allowed to know any name but her own.

After the presentation of the garment, which is supposed to represent the clothing God gave to Adam in the Garden of Eden, men put on a white shirt, trousers, belt, socks, and moccasins. Women put on white clothing also: a blouse, skirt, stockings, slip, and soft shoes. If receiving vicarious endowments, the endowee receives the "new name" for the deceased. He leaves the washing and anointing room carrying a bundle which contains a green apron embroidered with nine fig leaves, a cloth cap (which for women has a veil attached), a white "robe," and a "girdle."

Much of the temple ceremony from this point on is watched, as well as participated in, by the endowees. They are led by a temple worker to a large unornamented room and seated in theater-type seats, men on one side, women on the other. In more modern temples they stay in this room and watch scenes projected on the walls by movie projectors. But in the past and in older temples this first room was representative of the chaos or unorganized state of affairs before the world was created.

In this room a temple worker dressed in white addresses the endowees in front of a curtained doorway. He tells them that they have been washed clean of the blood of their generation, anointed in expectation of becoming kings and priestesses, and given a new name and a garment. He retires behind the curtain, and voices are heard, indicating a conversation between Elohim, Jehovah, and Michael. Jehovah and Michael appear and pretend to act out the six-day creation process. The dimmed room is illuminated by the lighting of a chandelier after Elohim commands light. Then, Michael pretends to go to sleep in a chair while Elohim and Jehovah make passes with their hands over him. He awakens to be Adam, devoid of remembrance of the recent events. A woman temple worker appears—Eve—and is given to Adam.

Endowees and actors now go into another room that is painted with peaceful animal life and vegetation intended to portray the Garden of

Eden. A tree with a shelf attached to its back stands at one end of the room, and on the shelf is an apple, or strawberries, or other fruit. Adam is instructed not to eat that particular fruit, but to enjoy his new home and any other products of it. Then Elohim and Jehovah leave.

The next person to enter the room is dressed in black, carrying a cane and wearing a black silk hat and an embroidered apron. This is Lucifer, and he persuades Eve to eat the forbidden fruit after she is reassured that "there is no other way." Adam, when he learns of this, is stubbornly opposed to partaking also until Eve reminds him that she will be cast out of the Garden, and without her, Adam cannot replenish the earth. He, too, then eats.

When Elohim and Jehovah return, they curse Lucifer, who slinks out of the room, shaking his fist at the gods. The endowees rise and put on the clothing they have brought with them. Women then covenant to obey their husbands, and all swear to be willing to sacrifice life and goods for the Kingdom. They are then taught the "First Token of the Aaronic Priesthood." Its name is the "new name" given to them earlier. Its sign is demonstrated by holding the left arm up to the square, palm forward, while the right hand is placed at the neck with the thumb under the left ear, palm downward. Its penalty is that those who betray this secret agree to have their lives taken. (In the past the oath was to have their tongues torn out by the roots, and their throats cut from ear to ear.) The penalty is demonstrated by forming the "sign," quickly drawing the right thumb across the throat, then dropping both hands to the sides. Its grip or handshake is given when hands are clasped, and the knuckle of the index finger is pressed with the thumb. The endowees all practice these signs and tokens until everyone can do them properly.

In the older temples, the endowees are at this point led into another room, whose wall murals depicting wild animals and tangled vegetation identify it as a representation of the Lone and Desolate World. Adam stands at an altar in front of the audience and, lifting his arms above his head, then to the square, then dropping them to the side, he recites three times a prayer in the "pure Adamic language," which sounds like "Pay Lay Ale." It is supposed to mean, "Oh God, hear the words of my mouth!"

Lucifer enters the room and is joined there by a preacher, whom he hires to teach Adam. The preacher declares that no one can preach without knowing the dead languages and then claims belief in such things as a God who sits on the top of a topless throne. The endowees find this part humorous, but Adam refuses to listen to him. Elohim then sends down Peter, James, and John to instruct Adam. When the preacher sees them, he says that they couldn't be apostles, for Lucifer had taught him that apostles could cut off an arm or leg and then restore it. After rebuking the preacher, Peter, James, and John persuade him to become a preacher of the truth, which he resolves to do—to the great disgust of Lucifer.

Peter then proves his divine authority to Adam by giving him the First Token of the Aaronic Priesthood. The endowees rise and take oaths to keep "the Law of the Gospel," which includes prohibitions against disparaging the prophet, and behavior which is not sober and befitting. They put their robes on their left shoulders, put on their hats, girdles, and moccasins, and replace their fig leaf aprons. They are now ready to receive the Second Token of the Aaronic Priesthood. Its name is the given name of the endowee. Its sign is like that of the First Token, except that the right hand is placed across the chest instead of the neck. Its penalty is an agreement to give one's life rather than reveal its secrets. (The old penalty was an agreement to have one's heart and vitals cut out and given to wild animals.) The penalty is demonstrated by a cutting motion across the chest with the right hand. Its grip is given by pressing the thumb in the hollow between the first and second knuckles of the hand.

After putting their robes on their right shoulders, the endowees are led into the Terrestrial or Blue Room. After taking a vow to have sexual intercourse with their spouses only, they are given the First Token of the Melchizidek Priesthood. Its name is the Son (of God). Its sign is demonstrated by first putting the left hand cupped in front of the body, the arm to the square. The right hand is drawn quickly from left to right across the stomach. Its penalty, like the others, is an agreement to have one's life taken if the secret is revealed. (The old penalty was to have one's body cut asunder so that the bowels would gush out.) The grip for this token is given by placing the thumb on the back of another's hand, and the forefinger on his palm, indicating the piercing of the hand by a nail.

The Second Token has no penalty, but still may not be revealed. It follows a vow to consecrate time, energy, talents, and material possessions to the church. The sign is made while reciting the phrase PAY (raise both hands over the head), LAY (gradually drop hands to shoulders with palms facing front), ALE (lower hands to sides, palms to the rear). Its handshake, the Patriarchal Grip, or Sure Sign of the Nail, is based on the belief that nails had to be driven through the wrists of Christ. The little fingers are locked, and the index fingers are extended up the other's wrist.

After a review of the signs, tokens, penalties, and grips, the endowees a dozen or so at a time form a prayer circle around the altar at the end of this room, while the temple worker who represents John offers a prayer. Then the endowees seat themselves in front of a very wide curtain. Behind it is a wide archway held up by five pillars. When the curtain is drawn, it shows that between each pillar is hung an embroidered veil which has on it the same marks as on the garments: compass (representing the bounds established by God), square (a reminder of the endowment oaths), navel mark (representing spiritual and physical health), and the knee mark ("every knee shall bow"). Each veil also has several other larger holes, known as "marks of convenience." Through some of these holes, a worker representing the Lord gives the grips and asks each endowee in turn their meanings. Through another hole the endowee gives his answers. Through two other holes the arms of the temple worker and the endowee are thrust so that they can embrace in the "Five Points of Fellowship"—foot to foot, knee to knee, hand to back, and mouth to ear.

Those who are receiving their endowments for the first time usually need some promptings to help them answer all the questions asked before the veil. A woman is always accompanied to the veil by a man who may be her husband, or if she has none, a perfect stranger—but she cannot pass through the veil without a man.

After all the questions are answered, the endowee passes through the veil to a luxuriously-furnished Celestial Room. If this was his first endowment, he will probably sit there and rest for a while. Others who came through the ceremony bearing the name of a dead person are probably old hands at this and usually hurry downstairs to get dressed and go about other business.

Couples who received their endowments prior to marriage that same day are led into a small "sealing" room which has two opposing mirrors and a small kneeling altar in the middle. Here a couple is joined in "eternal" marriage and encouraged to multiply. They are told to look at the infinity of reflections in the mirrors and told that that is a representation of their progeny when they become gods. The ceremony is usually considerably abbreviated if it is just a proxy wedding for the dead.

Here, too, children are sealed to parents in a very brief ceremony that guarantees the children the same blessings as if they had been born into an eternal marriage covenant.

The temple ceremonies have changed considerably over the years. Around the middle of the last century, oaths were sworn by endowees to avenge themselves against the government of the United States which neglected to protect the Mormons in Illinois and Missouri. Many old oaths, too, referred to polygamy, but were dropped when that practice was discontinued.

I had a married friend at Brigham Young University whose children I often kept as she went to the Provo Temple for vicarious endowments. Though she never revealed to me any of the oaths or signs (nor did I, being ignorant of them, ask any questions), I remember her reaction once when I asked her if she looked forward to temple work. "Why, of course!" she said, and then a bittersweet look of mixed emotions passed over her face, and she sighed almost inaudibly. She was obedient and willing to do what she was told to do; but I know now that she, and thousands of other Mormons must go to their graves confused at the relationship of playacting and handshakes to eternal salvation.

Any Mason who reads even such an abbreviated account of the temple ceremony as I have outlined will be amazed at the similarities between temple ordinances and Masonic lodge ordinances. Joseph Smith claimed that he got much of the substance of the temple ceremony from the Book of Abraham papyri. The truth is that Joseph Smith was himself a Mason of "the Sublimest degree."[19] He joined, he said, just to find out how far Masonry had "degenerated" from the original temple ceremony he said was first practiced in Solomon's temple.

Responsible Masonic apologists don't claim any direct connection with Old Testament rites that Joseph Smith claimed were the source of both Mormon and Masonic rites. Masonic ceremonies do of course refer to Biblical personages and Scriptures, but no Masonic authority would say that they are descended from the Israelite rituals. The Grand Lodge of Utah has refused initiation to known Mormons, and denied admission to any Mormon Mason who was initiated in any other state.[20]

Traditional Masonic symbols are rampant in Mormon temples. Representations of beehives, heavenly bodies, clasped hands, the All-Seeing Eye, the square, the compass, and cloud-painted ceilings are easily seen. Mormon initiates, like their Masonic counterparts, wear special garments and soft shoes, hats, and aprons. They give grips, signs, and penalties; approach altars, holding a Bible, by means of three steps; and see an individual who wears a silk hat and apron. Over both rites hangs a heavy atmosphere of secrecy and fear of retribution for exposing that secrecy.

Mormons say that temples exist as a reward for the faithful, who are privileged to learn what they call the "mystery of God." They could save themselves much of the priceless time God has given us here on earth by reading God's Word. The Bible teaches us two important things about the "mystery of God" in Colossians 1:26-27:

> Even the mystery which hath been hid from ages and from generations, but now is made manifest to his saints: To whom God would make known what is the riches of the glory of this mystery among the Gentiles; which is Christ in you, the hope of glory.

First, this mystery is manifested to every man—not just in secret temple ceremonies. The mystery is for the poor, the abused, the sick of soul, not just for those who need no Physician. And *what* is this mystery? It is the greatest miracle of all! It is Christ *in* us! Christians can't afford to put this Light under the bushel of a temple roof—it is for all men.

The claim that Mormon temple ceremonies are patterned after Old Testament temple practices is opposed by reason. First, the ancient ceremonies were not for all faithful, like the Mormon ones are. Secondly, they were not secret. They are described in minute detail in Deuteronomy and Leviticus—and they don't even faintly resemble the endowments. The only ordinances performed in the Jerusalem temple were (1) the sacrifices offered for the sins of the nation, and (2) a vicarious offering of worship, by one priest, in behalf of all Israel. A quick study of the design of the temple itself as described in the Bible also shows the difference of function as compared to the Mormon temple.

And finally, First Corinthians 3:16 indicates where the temples of Christ are located from New Testament times on: "Know ye not that ye are the temple of God, and that the Spirit of God dwelleth in you?"

Sins Which Prevent Exaltation

Today the endowment blessings of future godhood are contingent upon faithfulness for the rest of the life of the endowee. All the endowment ceremonies have as their ultimate realization the assurance of exaltation. However, the receipt of endowments puts a person in an all-or-nothing situation, for he has thus gained enough knowledge to hang himself, so to speak. One cannot be exalted to godhood without endowments, but neither can one go to hell without them; a non-endowed person simply can't be held accountable for enough knowledge to go to hell.

By receiving endowments, a person gains enough knowledge and independence that the Atonement of Christ actually becomes lessened. Joseph Smith so taught his people, and added that certain sins would actually put an offender outside the pale of the Atonement.

What are these sins? LDS theologian Sidney Sperry said, "The atonement of our Savior will not apply to a man who deliberately refuses to repent of his sins."[21] Another "unpardonable" sin is the sin against the Holy Ghost. This is defined as (1) denying the Holy Spirit after having received it, and denying Christ,[22] and (2) blasphemy against the Holy Ghost, which is identified as the "sin unto death" of shedding innocent blood after having been sealed unto eternal life and married for eternity.[23] Bruce R. McConkie, in *Mormon Doctrine,* stated that any man who accepted Mormonism, and received from the Holy Ghost absolute testimony of the divinity of Christ, and then denied the Church, would be committing the unpardonable sin of murder, because by his actions he assented unto the death of Christ.[24]

For persons who have committed the unpardonable sin, the result would be as if there had been no Atonement, except that the bodies of such sinners would be resurrected along with everyone else, but never to enter the kingdom of God. Joseph Smith taught that the only way that a person might have atonement for such sins would be through the doctrine of blood atonement, wherein the sinner's blood could be shed to cover the sins which Christ's blood could not.

This doctrine expanded after the death of Joseph Smith, and before long the following were the other crimes which Mormon leaders said deserved the shedding of the offender's blood: adultery,[25] stealing, [26] marrying or sexual intercourse with an African,[27] apostasy,[28] taking the Lord's name in vain,[29] and breaking covenants.[30] Murder was of course the most serious, because of the impossibility of restitution. Adultery was next in seriousness, and though it could be forgiven once, it was unforgivable on the second offense.[31]

The actual practice of shedding the blood of someone who had committed one or more of these grievous sins was never, admittedly, a widespread practice in early Utah. But Brigham Young taught that the doctrine had two purposes: (1) to allow a sinner to atone for his own sins and (2) to put fear into the hearts of any who might contemplate such a sin.[32] He taught, too, that shedding a sinner's blood for him was a way of showing your love for him.[33]

Mormons have gone so far as to say that blood atonement was *never* practiced, but Gustive O. Larsen documented a case where a man, Rosmos Anderson, who was guilty of fornication, allowed his throat to be slit so that his blood ran into an open grave in which he was subsequently buried. This was done by his bishop and two counselors, who hoped thereby to save his soul.[34] This example could hardly, I grant, be termed proof of a common practice, though its very occurrence is indicative of their values. But blood atonement is taught and believed in today, too; for Joseph Fielding Smith once stated that the only hope of a person who committed the unpardonable sin was to have his blood shed. The Mormon Church no longer serves as executor in such cases, but it heartily approves capital punishment of murderers.

As evidence of this, Utah is the only state in the union that gives a condemned killer a choice of his death method. He is allowed to choose death by firing squad if he believes that the shedding of blood is necessary. Not many years ago criminal Gary Gilmore exercised this option in a Utah prison.

Mormons today believe that one's blood must be shed to atone for murder. A few months after I left the LDS Church, a Mormon girl friend called me long distance to tell me some very distressing news. The younger brother of a mutual friend, she said, had stabbed to death his teen-aged wife in the woods near Provo. My girl friend was very upset about this (as I was also), but she became even more agitated when she told me that he had also been accused of stabbing to death his premature newborn son.

"He can atone for killing one person by facing a firing squad," she sobbed, "but not two! There's no forgiveness for that!"

I would never disparage the reality of my friend's grief. But as I look back, I feel sadness, too, for such Mormons who are more concerned about what their own blood *can't* atone for, rather than focusing on what Christ's blood *can* cleanse.

Blood atonement is denied in the *Book of Mormon,* which shows that man's blood is of no efficacy in atonement. "Now there is not any man that can sacrifice his own blood which will atone for the sins of another. Now, if a man murdereth, behold will our law, which is just, take the life of his brother? I say unto you, Nay" (Alma 34:11).

Moses murdered an Egyptian (Exod. 2:11-12), and yet he appeared in glory on the Mount of Transfiguration (Luke 9:30-31). King David murdered, too; but God put away his sin (2 Sam. 12:13). Saul consented unto the death of Stephen (Acts 8:1) and "persecuted unto the death" of many others (Acts 22:4). Were these men forgiven?

> But if we walk in the light, as he is in the light, we have fellowship one with another, and the blood of Jesus Christ his Son cleanseth us from all sin. If we say that we have no sin, we deceive ourselves, and the truth is not in us. If we confess our sins, he is faithful and just to forgive us our sins, and to cleanse us from all unrighteousness.
>
> —1 John 1:7-9

The doctrine of blood atonement is wrong. The teaching that Christ's blood cannot atone for sins that man's blood *can* atone for makes mockery of Christ's sacrifice of Himself as the unspotted Lamb. And finally, the honoring of men who would teach such doctrine is itself blasphemy against the gentle voice of the Holy Spirit.

The Mormon Hereafter

Christians believe that after death a person either goes to heaven or hell. The precarious choreography of Mormon theologians on matters of which sins are forgivable and which are not, though, is based on the many possible destinies they believe a man may have.

By Mormon definition, death is the separation of the spirit body from the physical body. When this happens, the spirit body stays upon this earth, where the spirit world is. When a spirit body is released from the strictures of the physical body through death, it joins the spirits of all the other persons who have died but who have not yet been resurrected.

The spirits of the dead, Mormons teach, are all around us, but we cannot discern them because of the refined substance of which the spirit body is made. The spirit world has two great divisions: prison and paradise.

In the spirit prison are those who rejected the gospel while on earth, and sinned greatly. These spirits suffer what Mormons call eternal punishment, or endless punishment. This is not to be confused with punishment which will go on forever, or which will never end. Mormons teach that two of the names of God are Eternal and Endless,[35] and that when Mormon scripture refers to endless or eternal punishment, it is referring only to the fact that God is doing the punishing, and has nothing to do with the *duration* of the punishment. These spirits in the spirit prison who are suffering endless or eternal punishment, then, are in a temporary state where they are paying the price of their own transgressions. When this price is paid in full, they are given the opportunity to hear the Gospel preached and to accept it.

They may then migrate to the other part of the spirit world, which is paradise. Those who have lived honorable lives on earth, whether or not they knew Christ, dwell in this part. They are intermingled with Mormons who are as actively propagating their doctrine there as they did in life.

Here, say Mormons, is where the efficacy of vicarious baptisms, endowments, and sealings is seen. Those spirits who accept the Mormon gospel in the spirit world can accept the vicarious work done in their names on earth. The average Mormon's conception of the spirit paradise—that of a great multitude of people impatiently waiting for temple ordinances to be done for them—is undoubtedly an effective goad to their efforts at researching their own genealogies.

Those in the spirit world who had fair and ample opportunity to accept Mormonism in mortal life, but who rejected it, are given a second chance in the spirit world. According to the Mormon point of view, they'd be crazy not to accept it this second time, after waking up in a strange shadowy place that looks exactly as the Mormons on earth had described it, and where vicarious baptisms are the only way to be saved. However, there is a price attached to the first rejection: such a second-chancer cannot receive exaltation in the highest level of heaven, as might his more ignorant brethren on earth.

The Resurrections

This spirit world is where all the spirits wait for the resurrections, the first of which will occur just before the Millennium. This resurrection, believe Mormons, will be heralded by a great blast on a horn blown by Michael, or Adam. The proceedings will then be directed by Joseph Smith (which implies he will be resurrected first). According to Brigham Young, the prophet Joseph will hold the keys of the resurrection, and will pass this authority on to other holders of the priesthood as they are resurrected. They will in turn resurrect their wives (as prefigured by the veil ceremony in the temple), and others who had vicarious ordinances done for them.[36]

At this time the righteous Mormons who are living on earth will be "translated" into a resurrected state without tasting death. They will join the resurrected Mormons and all the animals, fish, birds, and other creatures which have lived on earth, which will also be resurrected.[37]

After the Millennium begins, the second phase of this first resurrection will occur. Whereas the "morning" of the first resurrection saw the arising of those who would soon become gods, this "afternoon" of the same resurrection involves those who lived disreputably on earth but paid the price for it in the spirit prison.[38]

After the one-thousand-year reign of Christ on earth comes to an end the second resurrection will come, or the resurrection of the unjust. Two classes of people will be resurrected at that time: people who were so wicked on earth that the entire one thousand years of punishment was necessary, and the sons of perdition, those former temple-endowed Mormon men who rejected their covenants, and who will be filthy still.

Thus, every person will be resurrected, even the most wicked. The resurrections will also be indicative of a judgment, for the time when one is resurrected determines one's final fate.

Mormons say that the Bible teaches that there are three heavens, and a paradise, because of what Paul said in Second Corinthians 12:2-4 about "the third heaven" and "paradise." According to LDS doctrine, these three heavens are named the Celestial (highest), the terrestrial (middle), and telestial (lowest). If you have trouble remembering the order of these, use the learning hook employed by Mormon children who think of them as a sandwich where the slices of bread—Celestial and Telestial—rhyme.

Brigham Young said that the Celestial Kingdom was closed to anyone who did not have the consent of Joseph Smith to enter it.[39] This kingdom is identified as the "administrative" section of heaven, a sort of higher training ground for gods-to-be.

To be able to enter the Celestial Kingdom is in the Mormon mind the enjoyment of exaltation in the most finite sense. The ultimate fate of all Celestial Kingdomites is continued progression toward godhood, at which point they would be given dominion over worlds and people of their own. In order to begin this progression, a celestial being must have been married in the temple. They will, according to *Doctrine and Covenants* section 76, receive all the things of the Father, and become kings and priests, queens and priestesses.

The Celestial Kingdom will be located on the sanctified earth, which will serve as a great Urim and Thummim for its inhabitants. The result of this will be that it will seem to all celestial beings that they are in the presence of God, even though He will be on His own planet, Kolob. Each celestial being, in addition, will receive a white stone as described in Revelation 2:17. This will serve as an individual Urim and Thummim to each owner, revealing things pertaining to the higher priesthood.

The glory of the inhabitants of the Celestial Kingdom will be like the sun's glory, and one of the manifestations of this glory will be their ability, and desire, to procreate and reproduce themselves endlessly. However, there will be people in the Celestial Kingdom who will not have this power. They are those who fulfilled all the necessary entry requirements *except* "the new and everlasting covenant of marriage." In other words, either they refused to be married on earth or to accept proxy marriage in the spirit world; or if married on earth, they refused to accept plural marriage after death. These unlucky souls are designated to be servants to those who did marry and accept plural marriage. They are referred to as "ministering angels."

The middle, or Terrestrial Kingdom, will differ as much from the Celestial, teach Mormons, as the moon does from the sun. One analogy would give the Celestial Kingdom an "A" grade, and the Terrestrial a "B." This kingdom will be the final destiny of those who "died without law" and did not accept Mormonism in the spirit world. There, too, will be the people who rejected the LDS gospel on earth, but later embraced it in the spirit world. Honorable men, who were blinded by the teachings of other men which prevented their conversion, will also be in this kingdom, as will lukewarm Mormons who weren't valiant in their testimonies.

Unlike the people in the Celestial Kingdom, the inhabitants of this middle kingdom will not be able to enjoy the presence of God, but they will be ministered to by Jesus Christ.

The inhabitants of the lowest kingdom of heaven, the Telestial Kingdom, will arise in the resurrection of the unjust, after the Millennium of suffering required to cleanse them of their sins. Their sins on earth were such that the atonement of Christ extended to them only as far as the resurrection of their bodies. The glory of the Telestial Kingdom, though as different from the Celestial and Terrestrial as the stars are from the sun and moon, is nonetheless so wonderful that I often heard it said that anyone who could conceive of such glory would kill himself immediately so as to sooner partake of it.

The word "telestial" does not appear in First Corinthians 15:40, which was the source of the names of the other two kingdoms. This word was added by Joseph Smith to that verse in his Inspired Revision of the Bible. He said that it referred to the lesser glory of this kingdom.

The inhabitants of the Telestial Kingdom will be the dregs of humanity—liars, sorcerers, adulterers, pimps, and prostitutes. Also in this "hell" will be those who swore falsely, those who mistreated servants, and those who did wickedness;[40] sex sinners;[41] persecutors of the church;[42] those who taught infant baptism and other false doctrines;[43] the rich who refuse to share with others;[44] and those who cursed.[45]

Even murderers like King David, and others who atoned personally for committing the unforgivable sin, will be in the Telestial Kingdom. People who rejected Mormonism on earth and in the spirit world, but who never denied the Holy Ghost will be there too, as will ex-Mormons who never repented of their apostasy.

Apparently the bulk of the human race will end up in this kingdom. Neither God nor Christ will commune with these people throughout eternity, but they will have the presence of the Holy Spirit. They will also be visited by emissaries from the higher kingdoms. Unlike the other inhabitants of heaven, Telestialites may not progress to higher kingdoms, and their greatest punishment will be anguish at the thought of their former potential.

Who then will go to the Mormon hell? Very few. Those who go to the Telestial Kingdom will already have suffered from the time of their deaths until the end of the Millennium in the hell of the spirit prison. Mormons say that their suffering, or self-atonement, in the Millennium, will have been as exquisite as the passion of Christ.

The final hell, though, will have a sparse human population. Its inhabitants will be resurrected in the second resurrection, along with the inhabitants of the Telestial Kingdom. At that time, the hell of the spirit prison will be cast into the "lake of fire" (Rev. 20:14). It was, after all, only "eternal" and "everlasting" in the sense that God instituted it. The lake of fire is the final hell, and the home forever of Satan, his angels, and the sons of perdition—who remained filthy even after a thousand years of detention.

These sons of perdition (literally, "sons of Satan," who is Perdition) will have their bodies restored, but they will not be glorious bodies, they will be shameful. They alone of all mankind will not be released from the control of Satan, but because of their bodies they will have certain powers over Satan. Their eternity will be one of struggle and contention, forever.

Mormons teach that these sons of peridition were those who sought to be a law unto themselves.[46] Very few persons are qualified to be sons of perdition. These were holders of the Melchizidek Priesthood, and had personal knowledge of the power of God. They had made the sacred temple covenants, and had partaken of God's power. Some shed innocent blood; others sinned in other ways against the Holy Ghost. In this final hell, said Joseph Smith, man will be his own tormentor.

Most Mormon authorities teach that this hell will have no end. But others, like John A. Widstoe, taught that the sons of perdition will finally have their spirit bodies disintegrated, and they will revert back to their original condition as intelligences. They would await new spirit bodies from another god, and a chance to start all over again.[47]

The Bible View

The Bible does not teach two hells, nor a temporary state of suffering which can be terminated through self-atonement. Nor does it teach three degrees of heavenly glory. First Corinthians 15:40 does teach two degrees of glory, but they refer to our resurrected and earthly bodies, not to states of residence. According to Ira T. Ransom, the Bible *does,* though, teach three heavens.[48] There is the atmospheric heaven where birds fly, rain falls, and clouds float (Gen. 7:23; 8:2; Dan. 2:38; 7:13). The second heaven is where the sun, moon, and stars are (Gen. 1:14-17; 22:17; Mark 13:25; Rev. 6:13; 12:4). Finally, there is the heaven of God's residence (Matt. 6:9), where angels dwell and where the saved finally go (Mark 12:25; 1 Peter 1:4).

Mormons say that Christ referred to their three-tiered heaven when he told His apostles of the many mansions awaiting them (John 14:2). Is three "many"? If Christ meant three, why didn't he say so?

What Mormonism teaches about a resurrected body is proven to be false by the Bible, too. If it has flesh and bones (Luke 24:36-43), it will not be a densely physical body like the one we now wear, because Christ in his resurrected body could pass through a closed door (John 20:19). The Bible tells us that Christians don't *know* what Christ will be like, but we are given assurance that we will be like Him (1 John 3:2). Who could want more?

The Scriptures do put a great deal of emphasis on the body—but not Christ's physical body, and not ours either, here or in eternity. The body Christ is concerned about is *His church.* A careful reading of First Corinthians chapter 12 underscores this.

Mormons teach that those who go to hell are burned forever with unquenchable fire.[49] But their heaven isn't much better, for the saved of Mormonism are promised a home with their God who dwells in "everlasting burnings."[50]

The only conclusion I could offer is that Mormons had better reject their gospel—and soon—or be burned forever!

NOTES

[1]McConkie, *Mormon Doctrine,* p. 339.

[2]As quoted in *Will the "Saints" Go Marching In?* by Floyd McElveen. (Regal Books Division, G/L Publications, Glendale, CA., 1977), p. 132-133.

[3]George Romney quoted by Wallace Turner, *The Mormon Establishment* (Boston: Houghton Mifflin Company, 1966), p. 72.

[4]Alma chapter 1.

[5]Wallace Bennett, *Why I Am a Mormon* (New York: 1958), p. 191.

[6]Joseph Smith Jr., *Documentary History of the Church,* III, p. 380.

[7]Moses 6:55.

[8]Mosiah 3:19.

[9]Tanner, *Mormonism: Shadow or Reality?* p. 453.

[10]*Doctrine and Covenants* 103:9-10.

[11]*Journal of Discourses,* VI, p. 163.

[12]Fife, *Saints of Sage and Saddle,* p. 226.

[13]Joseph Smith Jr., *Documentary History of the Church,* IV, p. 231.

[14]*Journal of Discourses,* XIX, p. 229.

[15]McElveen, *Will the "Saints" Go Marching In?* p. 86.

[16]*Principles of the Gospel,* p. 47-48.

[17]Alma 34:33-35.

[18]Moroni 8:22.

[19]Joseph Smith Jr., *Documentary History of the Church,* IV, p. 552.

[20]Whalen, *The Latter-day Saints in the Modern-day World,* p. 204.

[21]Sperry, *Doctrine and Covenants Compendium,* p. 101.

[22]*Doctrine and Covenants* 76:31-37.

[23]*Doctrine and Covenants* 42:18; 64:7; 132:27.

[24]McConkie, *Mormon Doctrine,* p. 817.

[25]*Journal of Discourses,* III, p. 247.

[26]Ibid., I, pp. 108-109.

[27]Ibid., X, p. 110.

[28]Ibid., IV, pp. 219-220.

[29]*Journal of Hosea Stout,* Vol. II, p. 71. (p. 56 of typed copy at Utah State Historical Society).

[30]*Journal of Discourses,* IV, pp. 49-51.

[31]*Doctrine and Covenants* 42:25-26.

[32]*Journal of Discourses,* IV, p. 51.

[33]*Journal of Discourses,* IV, p. 219.

[34]Article in *Utah Historical Quarterly,* January, 1958, p. 62, footnote #39.

[35]Moses 7:35.

[36]Quoted in Richards, *A Marvelous Work and A Wonder,* p. 334.

[37]*Doctrine and Covenants* 29:23-25.

[38]Ibid., 88:99.

[39]*Journal of Discourses,* VII, p. 289.

[40]*Doctrine and Covenants* 76:103; 2 Nephi 9:27-39; 26:10.

[41]2 Nephi 9:36.

[42]*Doctrine and Covenants* 121:23.

[43]2 Nephi 28:15; Moroni 8:14, 21.

[44]*Doctrine and Covenants* 104:18.

[45]3 Nephi 12:22.

[46]*Doctrine and Covenants* 88:33-35.

[47]Widstoe, *Evidences and Reconciliations,* pp. 213-214.

[48]Ira T. Ransom, "Pillars of Mormonism," Utah Christian Tract Society, p. 15.

[49]*Doctrine and Covenants* 63:32-34.

[50]Joseph Fielding Smith, *Teachings of the Prophet Joseph Smith,* p. 347.

10
Priesthood, Purse Strings, and Proselyting

The Church of Jesus Christ of Latter-day Saints must be the most elaborately organized and disciplined religious structure of modern times.

—*New York Times*
August 1, 1962, p. 17

Many unwary church-goers have become Mormons after accepting the lie told them by Mormons: that the Latter-day Saint church is organized just like Christ's church as described in Ephesians 4:11. Since this verse mentions apostles, prophets, and, in some versions, patriarchs, many have falsely concluded that such offices are necessary in a New Testament-type church, not just in its foundation. However, the Mormon church does not have only these offices, but has also added "stake presidents," "Relief Society presidents," "visiting teachers," "ward clerks," "high counselors," and a host of other "callings" that never existed in the Bible.

All these officers are held together by the cementing influence of Mormon priesthood, which they define as "the authority to act for God." This priesthood has two divisions, the Aaronic or preparatory; and the Melchizidek, or higher priesthood. It is regarded as exclusive Mormon property. According to them, all the prophets from Adam on down were priesthood holders, and it was only because of a great apostasy that this authority was taken from the earth at the death of the last apostle.

All worthy Mormon males above the age of eleven hold a priesthood office. This privilege can only be conferred by someone who himself holds it. A person is "ordained" to the priesthood in a formal ceremony, by the laying on of hands.

Mormons say that when Jesus ordained his apostles in John 15:16, He laid His hands on them. This, though, is without scriptural foundation. The only Bible-documented cases where Jesus laid hands on anyone were when He healed or blessed, and when He drove the money-changers out of the temple.

Of course the Bible contains examples of hands laid on persons to send them out to do particular tasks, or to impart a spiritual gift, but no evidence exists that priesthood was ever conferred in this way.

Exodus chapter 29 gives a graphic description of how Jewish priests were ordained to the Aaronic priesthood—through sacrifices, the burning of flesh and fat, the sprinkling of blood, offering up of bread, and other rituals. No hands were laid on them for ordination. As for the Melchizidek Priesthood, the only two holders of this priesthood mentioned in the Bible were Melchizidek and Christ, so no one else was "ordained" to that order, by the laying on of hands, or by any other method.

Mormons teach that priesthood is essential for anyone wishing to baptize or perform any religious ordinance. Any such ordinances performed without priesthood is, in their eyes, useless. But they believe that a priesthood holder can lose his authority through unrighteousness. Such a man could still appear outwardly to be worthy, but all the ordinances he performs would be invalid. Thus God would permit an unsuspecting convert's baptism to be nullified because the power of the priesthood was not operating in the unrighteous, hypocritical elder who baptized him. This would set up a chain reaction—any ordinances performed by the convert would also be invalid, and so on. One person's salvation in Mormonism is dependent upon the inner righteousness of many other persons.

The Aaronic Priesthood

The Aaronic, or lesser priesthood, was introduced in 1829, when, as you will remember, John the Baptist supposedly conferred it upon Joseph Smith and Oliver Cowdery. John had come, Joseph Smith claimed, under the direction of Peter, James, and John the Revelator. He put his hands upon the heads of Joseph and Oliver and gave them the Aaronic Priesthood, the power and authority to baptize. After the two men baptized each other, they ordained each other to the priesthood. Many Christians have wondered why it was that they conferred priesthood on each other after John had already conferred it upon them; and why it was that John *the Baptist* could ordain them by the physical act of laying on of hands but could not baptize them.

The Aaronic Priesthood is known as the "preparatory priesthood." Mormons believe that they, through the changing of their blood and through adoption,[1] become the sons of Levi when they are ordained. It matters little to them that their patriarchal blessings designate them as members of the tribes of Ephraim or Manasseh.

One of the prerequisites for LDS priesthood is that one be "called, as was Aaron" (Heb. 5:4). Mormons often quote Exodus chapter 28, verses 1 and 41, to try to show that Aaron was called, but leave out the thirty-nine verses between, and the entire chapter following which show *how* Aaronic priests were commissioned. Aaron was called by God, not another priesthood holder, and all those who followed in his priestly office were by God's command of his direct lineage only, and could prove it. Any one else pretending to priesthood was an imposter, and was severely punished (Num. 16:1-35; 2 Chron. 26:1-3, 16-21; 1 Kings 13:33-34). Besides lineage, though, the Bible also gives some very specific qualifications for holders of the Aaronic Priesthood in Leviticus 21:1-23 which would disqualify many Mormon priesthood holders, among them Joseph Smith (who had part of a legbone surgically removed when he was a youth), and Brigham Young (who cut his beard), and many modern-day General Authorities who married widows.

Choosing the story of John the Baptist as the one who restored the Aaronic Priesthood was certainly an imprudent decision on the part of Joseph Smith. Aside from the fact that this John never held the priesthood he supposedly conferred, Mormons believe that there were others living on earth in 1829 who held this priesthood (the Three Nephites, and John the Revelator).

The Melchizidek Priesthood

Hebrews 7:11-12 shows that the Aaronic Priesthood was "changed," or discontinued, after Christ. It was replaced by *a* priest after the order of Melchizidek. This priest was, of course, Christ. He, aside from Melchizidek, was the only one ever to stand in this priesthood office.

Mormons say that, while the sons of Aaron held the Aaronic Priesthood, the sons of Moses held that of Melchizidek. According to *Doctrine and Covenants* 107:4, this priesthood is called after Melchizidek to avoid the repetition of its true name, "Priesthood after the Order of the Son of God."

When John the Baptist appeared in 1829 to Joseph and Oliver, he promised a greater priesthood would come. Between that time and the organization of the church on April 6, 1830, Peter, James, and John supposedly gave this Melchizidek Priesthood to Joseph Smith. However, this ordination was *never* mentioned in Joseph Smith's detailed daily journal accounts of that period.[2] Records, like the *Doctrine and Covenants*, which tell of this ordination were written years later and deliberately falsified to make it seem that the Melchizidek Priesthood had been given in 1829.[3]

Petersen noted, "There seems to be no support for the historicity of the restoration of the Priesthood in journals, diaries, letters, nor printed matter prior to October 1834.''[4] Could such a momentous event have gone unnoticed by *all* Mormons?

This priesthood, like the Aaronic, can only be conferred by the laying on of hands of one who already holds it. The Bible, however, teaches that the only one who holds it is Christ. Other men had to give up their priesthood at the time of death, so they had to pass it along to others to guarantee its continuity. But Christ, who lives forever, holds this priesthood forever, according to Hebrews 7:23-24.

The whole Book of Hebrews, in fact, was written to those who insisted upon a continuance of the now-dead Aaronic Priesthood. It teaches that the Old Law came to an end at the death of Christ (10:1-10), and that at that time the old priesthood was taken, too (7:11-12). Other Bible verses (1 Peter 2; Rev. 1:5-6) show that we are all priests of a *new* kind of priesthood.

Christians don't need the Aaronic or Melchizidek Priesthoods to do God's work. Hal Hougey pointed out that when Peter healed a lame man and was questioned about *his* authority (Acts 4:7-12), he didn't say that he had been ordained to do so, or that it was the power of priesthood working in him. Peter set the example for Christians everywhere when he put himself and his powers in the background, and *Christ* in the foreground.

What has this insistence on Old Testament practices done to Mormonism? Floyd McElveen responded:

> The Mormons have done exactly what Jesus Christ said *not* to do. They have put 'new wine into old bottles.' They have wed grace to law and made Christianity into a Jewish sect. They have resurrected what Christ buried. They have figuratively 'sewn up' the veil that Christ, as our High Priest, rent forever to provide for us free access in to the Holy of Holies . . . Only those who would out-Hebrew the Hebrews would cling to a system long set aside by God.[5]

The Mechanics of the Priesthood

The membership of the Mormon Church is currently between five and six million, and about 200,000 people a year are converted because of the LDS missionary program. The priesthood holders have become the network holding this vast religious empire together, and the means of communication between leaders and members.

In any community where Mormons worship together, they meet in congregations of 250 to 500 people, known as wards. Up to ten wards in a given geographical area form a stake (name taken from Isaiah 54:2). Usually two or three wards will share a meetinghouse, and attend worship services in shifts.

In areas of sparse Mormon population, the congregations may be weak, and widely separated. They are referred to as branches instead of wards, and are organized together into mission districts.

All authority in the Mormon Church comes directly from the top; that is, the prophet who expects (and generally gets) obedience to his edicts. Much of the high leadership of the church has for its 150 years of existence been in the hands of about twenty families—the Smiths, Romneys, Kimballs, Cannons, Richards, Bensons, and others.[6]

These leaders, along with all other priesthood authorities in the church, are regularly "sustained" by their followers. Several times a year Mormons are called on to show a vote of confidence in their leaders by raising their hands in public worship. In ten years as a Mormon, I never saw a hand raised to oppose a single one of my leaders.

However, the story is told of President John Taylor, who once sent Heber J. Grant to a stake which was having problems with its stake president. When Grant asked the stake members to sustain their unpopular stake president, most refused to raise their hands. Grant went back to Taylor, explaining that the people had no confidence in their leader. President Taylor would not take "no" for an answer. He sent Grant back. At their next meeting Grant kept all the stake members in the church building until they finally agreed to sustain the stake president. Then, as per Taylor's instructions, Grant asked the stake president to publicly resign. This he did gladly, for he realized himself that he was unfit for the job. The moral of this story for Mormons is that church leaders must be sustained, and supported, no matter how unworthy they might be.

Stephen L. Richards clarified the role of the common member in Mormon decision-making when he said, "This church is not democratic. This church is a kingdom . . . We have a democratic method in that we sustain those who are appointed."[7]

General conferences of the church are held twice a year, in April and October, in Salt Lake City. Here the top leaders are sustained and new ones appointed to fill vacancies left, usually by death. These conferences are televised through much of the United States and broadcast by radio to much of the world. On the mornings that conference is held, members are expected to watch the proceedings as they are received by the hundreds of satellite dishes installed outside stake centers. Many Mormons and non-Mormons view these pompous assemblies as political conventions where officials vie for favor from leaders. These conferences are always solemn and didactic. Once in the early 1970s Apostle Le Grand Richards gave a speech that ridiculed the traditional Christian view of a bodiless God. He was rebuked afterwards, not for his irreverent caricature of the Deity of Christians, but because he made members laugh in the "solemn assembly."

The control of Mormon church leaders over their people has changed since the days when all Mormons lived in Utah. In the past, the "general authorities" could dictate morals, dress, even politics—at one time the church had its own "Peoples Party," which it officially dissolved in 1891. Most high-ranking Mormons today are Republicans. Ezra Taft Benson, next in line for the office of Prophet, has repeatedly brought unwelcome attention to the church with his extremely conservative positions, and was once "exiled" by Joseph Fielding Smith to Great Britain to "purify his blood."[8]

The Hierarchy

The head of the Mormon Church is its prophet.[9] He, with two other high priests (also called "president") he chooses to be his counselors, form what is called "the First Presidency." Mormons admit there was no mention of such an organization in the Bible, but assume that since Jesus was transfigured before Peter, James, and John, they must have been the First Presidency of the New Testament.

It is not correct to say that the LDS Church has twelve apostles, as in the New Testament. Since the president and his counselors are also apostles, at any given time the church has fifteen apostles. And though I was told when I was a Mormon that it was miraculous that the apostles were always unanimous in their choice of a new prophet when an old one dies, I have since learned that the senior member of the Council of the Twelve Apostles always becomes the new prophet. Both this number of apostles and the method of choosing a new prophet are foreign to the Bible pattern Mormons claim to follow. Revelation 21:14 speaks of *twelve* apostles who will form the foundation of the city of God. Which twelve—the Jerusalem twelve, the Nephite twelve, or any of the scores of modern-day "apostles" of 150 years of Mormondom? And as for voting on a new prophet, such an idea is much closer to Catholicism than to early Christianity.

The leader of Christ's church is of course Christ. And the Bible teaches only one qualification for apostles. When the eleven apostles chose one to replace Judas, they required that he have seen and been with Christ (Acts 1:21-22). Paul showed that he, by the same yardstick, measured up as an apostle also (1 Cor. 9:1). No apostle was above his brethren in the New Testament—even Peter was given no more authority than the others (see Matt. 16:19 with 18:18). The Bible is adamant about *false* apostles, and their "authority" (2 Cor. 11:12-15; Rev. 2:2).

Prophets, apostles, seventies, patriarchs, and presiding bishops all hold the Melchizidek Priesthood office of high priest. In 1982 there were 170,000 high priests in the Mormon Church, though most served in lower offices such as in stake presidencies, as high councilmen, and ward bishops. However, the office of high priest was in the Old Testament a part of the Aaronic, not the Melchizidek Priesthood. The duties of high priests in the Bible were to offer gifts and sacrifices for sins (Heb. 5:1), which makes the office obsolete after the supreme Sacrifice of Christ (Heb. 10:2, 17-18). Also in the Bible, only *one* high priest served at a time. (The only exception to this was when the Romans deposed the rightful high priest and put in Caiphas, so the Jews were forced to recognize both—see Luke 3:2.) However, the Bible tells us that we have only one high priest now, Christ, who is both our "apostle and High Priest" (Heb. 3:1).

Of particular interest to Christians is the fact that Mormon elders aren't very elderly—they are ordained at age 19, and the 12-year-old deacons couldn't possibly fulfill the requirements for that office as outlined in First Timothy 3:8-12.

According to Mormon teaching, the line of priesthood communication from prophet to individual goes like this: prophet to counselors, to Council of the Twelve, to Stake President, to bishop, to quorum leader, to family head, to individual.

The Organization of the Church

Mormons teach that Christ's church must bear His name. The term "Mormon" is not offensive to them, though they do not use it in official pronouncements of doctrine, or on their buildings, preferring the full title of "Church of Jesus Christ of Latter-day Saints."

Wherever Mormons worship together in wards or branches, they subdivide themselves for the tasks at hand. There are committees to take care of the aged, to do genealogical and welfare work, and even to determine musical selections for worship services. The Sunday school has a superintendent, greeters, organists and pianists, choristers, a secretary, teachers, teacher trainers, media aids supervisors, and more. The Relief Society—the women's organization—has a presidency of three women, visiting teachers, class teachers, and numerous project committeeheads.

The Primary Association, which teaches children from four to twelve years of age, has an array of leaders and teachers and organizers. The same is true for what was formerly called the Mutual Improvement Association, but which is now referred to as "Young Men." The church also sponsors many Boy Scout troops for boys, and "Beehives," "MIA Maids," and "Laurels" for girls.

Workers and leaders in all these ward organizations serve without monetary compensation. They are proud of saying that Mormons do not resign from church jobs; they must be released by their leaders.

The Church also maintains over 75,000 students in church-supported schools and universities (most notably Brigham Young University), and 290,000 high school and college students in seminaries and institutes (similar to Bible Chairs).

The Welfare Program

One of the showcase programs of Mormonism is its welfare plan. The church sees it as a way to help members help themselves. Every ward has its own welfare project. Some grow food crops or maintain dairy or egg farms, using volunteers from the ward. One ward I attended had an apple orchard and picked and packed apples each season. Another staffed a woodlot. Some wards grow animal fodder, and large silos in Utah store these as well as tithes-in-kind that farmers donate for welfare use. The church has a large factory that manufactures rugs, blankets, and clothing. It also operates large canneries which are staffed, like the other industries, by volunteers.

A needy Mormon in Utah is given a slip of paper by his bishop or home teachers which is marked "Bishop's Orders." This enables him to enter the large church-owned supermarket where he can choose produce, meat, dairy products, and canned goods packaged under the Mormon "Deseret" label. If he or his family needs clothing, shoes and other dry goods, these are also available. The only currency used in these welfare stores is the Bishop's Orders.

Recipients in good health are expected, though, to donate their time working on welfare projects and church building programs. But what of those in poor health? John L. Smith visited a young Mormon who was a victim of cerebral palsy, unable to walk or talk. Smith related,

> I called the church (LDS) officials and asked why he could not be a recipient for the famed Mormon welfare program. All my efforts were to no avail. I was told, "That kid may live to be 70 years old. Do you know what it would cost to provide for him over an expected lifetime? $250,000.00! We can't use our welfare funds on one like him!"[10]

Mormons and Money

In 1899, fifty-two years after the pioneers entered the Salt Lake Valley, the Mormon Church was two million dollars in debt. In the midst of a three-year drought, President Lorenzo Snow told his people that if they would covenant ten percent of their goods to the church, "the windows of heaven" would open to them. The Mormon people in their poverty tithed. The rains came, and the church soon was out of debt.

When I was receiving the missionary lessons, I was told that an agreement to tithe was necessary even before baptism. Tithing today is used by the church as a primary indicator of one's faithfulness. Originally, tithing meant giving all of one's "surplus" to the bishop, *plus* ten percent of one's increase.[11]

Now Mormons are expected to give one-tenth of their clear profits after doing business, or ten percent of salary before deducting taxes or living expenses, plus one-tenth of any interest earned on funds or investments. A rough estimate of the amount that a faithful Mormon will give annually, including tithe, ward quotas, contributions to welfare projects, and the cost of sending children on missions would average about twenty-six percent of his income. Wallace Turner quoted a faithful Mormon who held an administrative position as saying that the actual demand on his yearly salary was thirty-five percent.[12]

However, it is estimated that only one in four Mormons pays a full tithe.[13] Their leaders prod them, telling them that they should have more spendable money since they, unlike Gentiles, do not buy coffee, tea, liquor, or tobacco. Mormons who work for church-owned industries like ZCMI or Deseret Industries can even have tithe and ward budget (two percent of salary) deducted automatically from their paychecks, along with state and federal taxes. Those who refuse to tithe, though, are branded as robbers and told that they'll go no higher than the Telestial Kingdom unless they change their ways.

The Mormon Church has become as much a business as a religious organization. The church's annual income, according to one source, is over a billion dollars.[14] Much of this is spent on their advertising—expensive radio and television spots, as well as multi-page spreads in national magazines. Much, too, goes for sumptuously-furnished temples and for meetinghouses (Mormons boast that they dedicate a new one each day). A large chunk goes to pay for sophisticated educational materials.

Church leaders a quite active in encouraging members to economize for the church. Three wards share the facilities of each chapel. In order to accommodate all the various functions of each ward, meeting times are staggered and coordinated activities are carefully scheduled. Although these chapels are usually paid for when construction begins on each, local members no longer have to raise the entire amount—only 4 percent or less of the total figure needed.

Mormons don't raise money for church projects through bingo, raffles, lotteries, or anything else faintly resembling gambling.

The Twelve Apostles manage the Church's enormous financial empire, as Whalen noted:

> Most of the apostles have distinguished themselves in the business world. Indeed, only shrewd business men could manage the worldwide investments of the church, and only committed believers would undertake this management for the pittance offered by the church in lieu of salaries.[15]

The "pittance" mentioned by Whalen contradicts the popular Mormon claim that their leaders are all unpaid. Though local bishops and missionaries receive no salaries, many of the higher-ranking officials of the church do. Some also receive salaries for the positions on boards as directors of the various Mormon-owned companies, which include Beneficial Life Insurance and U and I Sugar.

The Mormon Church does now or has recently owned hotels, department stores, newspapers, bookstores, publishing companies, a funeral home, farms, canneries, mills, factories, salvage stores, food-producing industries, cattle grazing land, banks, mines, and much of the land and buildings in downtown Salt Lake City. It finances supermarket chains and food processors, and controls the copper and sugar beet industries. Mormons own automobile factories, and control paper mills and newspaper chains. According to Gordon Fraser, "they have built a financial enclave second only to the Bank of America."[16] Fraser also surmised that Mormons control the vice industry of Las Vegas, reasoning that almost all the industry of that city is vice-related, and one-half of its population is Mormon.

Though the Mormon Church won't give out the information, it is estimated that nearly two million dollars a day comes into church coffers in the form of tithing alone. Without this tithing, the Mormon Church would soon cease to function. But they also receive extensive tax privileges—paying taxes on corporate holdings, but not on welfare farms and other philanthropic-type projects.[17] The United States government, though, has begun to clamp down, denying many requested tax exemptions because the church has of recent years refused to disclose its total financial standing.

The *Salt Lake Tribune* in its July 1, 1971, issue noted that the Idaho State Board of Tax Appeals upon investigation of Mormon welfare projects found that in many cases the produce and products were sold—not given to the needy. The proceeds were then used to pay off loans on church farmland and equipment, and what was *left* was put into a general welfare fund for the needy.

The Mormon empire grows daily, and because it has increasingly more to lose, the church will do anything to protect its monetary holdings. It has refused disclosure, operated tax-free welfare projects for its own profit, issued new revelations (blacks and the priesthood), and denied old ones (polygamy).

But it is now losing the great independence from Gentiles that Brigham Young fought so vigorously to protect. he threatened excommunication for Mormons who traded with Gentiles;[18] now outside revenue mingles with tithing as the church's lifeblood.

The Missionary System

One reason that the LDS Church can be so very wealthy and yet so successful at winning converts is that it expends comparatively little money on mission work. None of its missionaries are salaried.

In 1978 there were over 26,000 missionaries serving the Mormon Church.[19] However Mormons may boast of such a figure as an indicator of faith, it tarnishes their image somewhat to have it revealed that this represents only a small fraction of those young Mormons who are eligible, and thus expected to serve in missionary service.

Mormon elders serving on missions are considered to be ordained ministers who may baptize, confirm, perform marriages, conduct funerals, bless and name newborns, and heal the sick. Their primary duty, though, is to teach. But the *Doctrine and Covenants* warns them, "Ye are not sent forth to be taught, but to teach" (43:15). They believe they are the only ones in the world authorized by God to preach the gospel.

There are several kinds of missions a Mormon can serve. *Temple missions* are served by couples who for six-month periods pay their own expenses while living near a temple. Once or twice a day they go to the temple and take out vicarious endowments for the dead. Many Mormons serve as *stake missionaries*. This part-time missionary work was begun in 1936 as a way for Mormons to maintain their regular jobs, but work several nights a week trying to convert non-Mormons and bring backsliders into the fold again. Sometimes whole Mormon families have been "set aside," or chosen to be stake missionary families. *Health missionaries*, professional medical personnel, pay their own expenses, usually in foreign countries, and provide medical aid and instruction on nutrition.

Many Mormons have worked as *labor missionaries* when temples, chapels, and Mormon schools were being built. When the Hawaii temple was under construction, for example, thirty-one young Tongan men left wives and families for two and one-half years to work on the temple. Their families were meanwhile supported by the Church. Every year, too, successful businessmen are called to leave home and profession for three or more years to serve as *mission presidents* supervising young missionaries. The father of a college roommate of mine left his medical practice, rented his home, and moved his family across Canada to serve as a mission president.

It has only been in recent years that Mormons have made any effort to minister among prisoners. Perhaps this is because they believe that murderers are beyond the grace of God, and cannot be baptized for that unforgivable sin. Gordon Fraser has also noted that Mormon missionary efforts have shunned "skid row" type areas, saying, "They have consistently avoided preaching to the poor and destitute and have confined their ministry to middle-class whites."[20]

Preparing for a Mission

Many Mormon children have little cardboard banks given to them with their first allowance. These banks have three slots, one marked "tithing," one marked "savings," and the third, "mission." Mormon parents often start saving along with their young sons for their future missions. When I was about fifteen, I and other Mormon friends received additional preparation—we were taken in pairs to the area around our church building where we witnessed in the neighborhood homes. In this already heavily-tracted area, some people were rude, others baiting. Our leaders apparently thought this was a good way to thicken our spiritual skins. They were right.

Young men are encouraged to go on missions before completing their college education. Many graduate from high school and work a year to earn money for their coming missions, while waiting for "the call." They have never been exempt from the draft, though; military service was just deferred until after their ministerial service.

All young women over twenty-one with no immediate prospects of marriage are considered for missions. Some go on missions to escape for a year and a half from weight problems, conflicts with parents, or to wait out their boyfriends' missions. Others desire sincerely to serve God. Older couples, too, whose children are grown, are often called to serve together as full-time missionaries.

A potential missionary is interviewed by his bishop to see if he is worthy to serve a mission and if he (or his family) can support him for eighteen months. (On rare occasions a needy missionary will be supported by his home ward during his mission.) The bishop forwards the results of this interview to the stake president, who sends it to the president of the church. A "call" comes by mail, signed by the prophet himself. It contains encouragement, an area assignment, and a date for the missionary to report to the mission home in Provo, Utah.

A missionary must put all his financial dealings in order, get a Wasserman test, and assemble a white-shirt-dark-suit wardrobe before entering the mission home. (Women are allowed a limited number of modest street dresses.) Once a missionary leaves for Provo, Utah, he or she is allowed no more contact with family, friends, or sweetheart other than through letters and an occasional phone call. He stays in the mission home for about two weeks. He hears lectures, receives orientation, takes tests, meets General Authorities, and goes to the temple for his endowments.

If he has been chosen to serve in a foreign mission whose language he does not know, he is sent to the Language Training Mission in Provo, Utah. Here missionaries learn the elementals of one of twenty foreign languages taught by the "immersion" method. At the end of a six-week stay, a missionary can speak (at least about Mormonism!) fairly competently in a new tongue. The logic of who should be sent to what foreign country is often puzzling, though. A man I knew of at Brigham Young University was taught Japanese and sent to Japan even though he spoke Spanish fluently.

Their training completed, missionaries are flown to various parts of the world. Upon arriving at his mission headquarters, a missionary is introduced to his new "senior companion," usually a seasoned missionary near the end of his two-year service. This young man will be the one with whom the new missionary will eat, work, and live for the next few months. A missionary is not allowed to get out of sight or hearing of his companion for the entire time they are assigned to each other.

The Missionary Lessons

A "greenie" or new missionary is introduced to the various proselyting methods. He is taught tracting, where he and his companion go door to door leaving tracts and trying to set up appointments to teach. He learns to work with the referrals of church members who give names of friends for the missionaries to visit. Other members have "share the gospel" evenings where they invite non-members and the missionaries to meet in their homes so the missionaries can teach. Many missionaries also set up neighborhood volleyball or basketball competitions to attract young people, whom they try to teach, and whose parents they also contact. Missionaries often ask strangers on buses or subways the "Golden Question" ("What do you know about the Mormons? Would you like to know more?") to start conversations they hope will lead to teaching appointments.

Once an appointment is obtained, the missionaries encourage the entire family to be present (why convert one when you could get a houseful?). The lessons they present are designed to last about forty-five minutes and are illustrated by slick flip-charts. These lessons (in use since 1973) start with emphasis on the family unit, to prepare for future discussion of temple work and genealogy. The first lesson deals with the story of Joseph Smith's search for truth. Other lessons (presented in the order deemed appropriate by the missionaries) cover eternal progression, continuing revelation, individual responsibility, truth versus error, the baptismal challenge, obedience, our relationship to Christ, and membership in the kingdom. These "canned" lessons require much more memorization on the part of the missionary than the previous lessons did.

Missionaries call their contacts "Brother" or "Sister" if they think there is the slightest chance of baptizing them. They will ask the prospects to pray vocally, too, unless they strenuously object. This atmosphere, along with the carefully phrased, leading questions soon have the prospects concluding that their own church is apostate, their baptism or conversion unrecognized by God, and their souls lost without Joseph Smith, the Word of Wisdom, the *Book of Mormon,* and a modern-day prophet. However, missionaries never appeal to a prospect's concept of himself or herself as a sinner. Instead, they stress a person's inherent nobility, and future status as a god. Christ is not seen as Savior, but as a trailblazer to godhood.

Mormonism attracts many who just will not see themselves as sinners in need of help. Many more are intrigued by the concept of priesthood, the idealized family life, or the secrecy of temple rites. In the final analysis, the foundation of Mormon membership is built upon selfishness and a sketchy knowledge of the Scriptures.

The missionary's best tool is his "testimony." Usually a young elder will say to a balking prospect, "Well, Brother Doe, I'd like to bear you my testimony that the Mormon Church is true, and the *Book of Mormon* is true, and there is a prophet leading the Church today. I know these things as surely as I am standing here. I say these words humbly in the name of Jesus Christ. Amen." The all-important truth which Christ spent his whole life demonstrating is ignored in most Mormon "testimonies"—that Christ is the Son of God, and the Savior of our souls.

One former Mormon missionary noted,

> It puzzled me that the church, while saying that the Holy Ghost convinced their converts, relied instead on techniques of salesmanship and psychology . . . Mormon missionaries promise people that the Holy Ghost will bear witness of the *Book of Mormon.* They ask contacts to pray for that witness. None whom I asked ever got any witness except one. That lady said that the Holy Ghost revealed to her that the *Book of Mormon* was false. We simply denied her witness and left.[21]

When spurned, Mormon missionaries have been seen stamping the dirt off their feet outside the door of those who reject their message. Though this isn't an everyday practice, the *Doctrine and Covenants* tells missionaries to do so to "be filled with joy and gladness; and know this; that in the day of judgment you shall be judges of that house, and condemn them" (75:21).

The Life of a Missionary

Missionaries serve under a mission president and his two counselors. A missionary who watches over several of his peers is known as a district leader. Several districts are the responsibility of a zone leader, who reports to the mission president. Missionaries have a system in which mission districts compete with each other—a certain number of points are given to an elder for a baptism, and sometimes points are deducted for such things as sleeping in when there is tracting to be done.

Partly, this is to liven the tedious day-to-day work of the missionaries. John L. Smith estimated that for each one thousand doors knocked on by a missionary pair, they make only one convert. Many become discouraged. For this reason, a strong, dedicated missionary is usually paired with a weaker one.

The many rules and regulations governing missionary life sometimes become burdensome. Except for half a day a week, missionaries are expected to wear conservative suits, white shirts, and dark ties. They address each other, even their own companions, as "Elder Smith" or Jones or whatever, while women missionaries call each other "Sister." In fact, they do not address any adult by the first name.

Rules vary from mission to mission, but in many cases missionaries rise at 5:00 A.M. and study until 7:00. Typically they eat and dress between 7:00 and 8:00; then study again until 10:00. Tracting fills up the two hours before lunch. From 1:00 until 5:00 they tract and make calls. If they're lucky some kind church member invites them to dinner. If not, sometimes all their budget, time schedule, and culinary skills allow is a peanut butter and jelly sandwich. Evenings are spent at meetings, and setting up and teaching cottage meetings with nonmembers.

Missionaries are only allowed a certain modest amount of money, out of which they must pay rent, groceries, and car rental fees and gasoline. (Many prefer bicycles because when the car runs out of gas and there's no more money, there's only footpower until the first of the next month.) "Free time" is only one-half day a week. During this "Diversion Day," as it is called, they must clean house, do laundry, write letters home, and if there's time, play basketball or attend a mission-approved movie. At the stroke of five o'clock that day, though, they turn back into missionaries. During their entire missions they are admonished not to watch television, play any contact sports, or swim. Most regard radios, too, as an unnecessary distraction.

Another distraction that hinders the work of a missionary is the girl friend back home. Few teen-aged girls, though, can wait two and one-half years without seeing or hearing the voice of the object of their affections, so "Dear John" letters are as common as tracts. Their recipients finally admit that such letters tended to make them more single-minded towards missionary work.

Other letters, too, mold a missionary's life. Those that come in brown envelopes from the mission president signal the coming transfer of a missionary to another spot in the mission. Usually two men will be missionary companions for about three months; then one or the other is transferred.

227

Many missionaries undoubtedly spend their missions trying sincerely to serve God. Others, though, serve only because of parental or peer pressure, regarding a mission as a necessary requirement for advancement in the Mormon community. Lewis Price noted that the most successful missionaries (in terms of numbers of baptisms) were "those with good looks and pleasant voices. Those with an attractive manner or sex appeal thrived."[22] Many see mission life as a challenge of hierarchal offices to be ascended, and "glory sheets" of accumulated points to be boasted about. The pressure of the regimented life has caused a few young men, though, to go "AWOL," or to indulge in fornication, and has driven others to suicide. Scarcely a missionary alive finishes his mission without a sigh of relief that the "best two years of his life" are finally over.

The returned missionary ("R.M.") is encouraged to go back to school and to marry as soon as possible. Most do get married quickly, and replace the constant companionship of the missionary buddies with a more permanent companion who can cook a whole lot better and who is prettier, besides.

Many R.M.'s put their foreign language training to lucrative use and become teachers. Many others, because of their knowledge of a foreign tongue and their unquestioning obedience to authority, have been successfully recruited to CIA work.[23]

Missionaries at Your Door

John L. Smith noted that, in twenty-five years of teaching Mormons, he knew of no authenticated case of a missionary who was won to Christianity while serving a mission.[24] There are several reasons for this. First, he is called on constantly to "bear testimony" of his church. Many missionaries will admit frankly that they had no real "testimony" of their religion before going on a mission. Lewis Price noted, "Testimonies exercise a kind of thought control, sometimes even a hypnosis over him. He is a victim of his own propaganda."[25] Even if a missionary were to begin to doubt Mormonism, his companion would surely notice, and duty-bound, report it to his leaders. If such a doubter were being profitably influenced by a Christian, it wouldn't last long. The wavering missionary would be transferred to another district before he knew what was happening to him.

With chances so slim of converting a missionary, what should a Christian do with the fresh-faced young men who knock at his door? The Bible tells us that we are under no obligation to receive any person who does not teach true doctrine (2 John 10; 1 Tim. 1:3). Don't feel guilty for not opening the door if you are unprepared! Many church-goers have done so, and are now sitting in Mormon pews each Sunday, singing, "All is well.'' If, though, you feel prepared to witness to them, Gordon Fraser says to make your doctrinal points and witnessing to them forceful the first time, for whether or not you touch their hearts, they probably will not come again. If they question your ''authority,'' question theirs. But for goodness sake, don't challenge them to perform a miracle for you—remember what the devil told the preacher to do in the temple ceremony? Missionaries are just waiting to tell Christians what a wicked and adulterous generation they belong to.

John L. Smith suggests in *Witnessing Effectively to Mormons* that the best tack is to question a missionary (or any Mormon) about his concept of God. He will respond that God is anthropomorphic, eternally progressing; he was once a man, etc. Then ask this Mormon to find substantiation for these concepts in the *Book of Mormon.* (There is none.) Bob Witte's book, *Witnessing to Mormons,* is a good tool, too, and has an excellent handbook of original documents that can be used to show doctrinal inconsistencies.

All these men, and many others, are experienced at teaching Mormons, and their words carry much weight. They know that dedicated Mormons are not won to Christ in one sitting. It just does not happen. First Corinthians 1:18 tells us to expect this, for ''the preaching of the cross is to them that perish foolishness.''

As familiar as I am with Mormonism, I will not argue with missionaries. They, by their own admission, are out to teach and *not* to be taught. I don't see much danger of their converting me back to Mormonism, but neither do I feel obligated to waste my time sowing the Gospel of Christ on such unreceptive ground.

Mormons like to say that every one of their members is a missionary. Indeed, if you live near a college or university that has a Mormon Institute of Religion nearby, Mormons are actively proselyting in your area—even if they never tract in your neighborhood. Their prime target is lukewarm church members, but their prize is the child of a faithful Christian.

Up until this year my black Christian brethren have been safe from Mormon proselyting. Now even they must tread with caution, and warn their children about the deceiving glitter of false godhood.

Many communities, especially in the South and the Northeastern United States, have seen few Mormon missionaries in the past. But as the LDS Church grows, so does its missionary force. How can you know if your area is about to be canvassed by Mormons? While I was a Mormon, I interviewed the Church Commissioner of Education, Neal Maxwell. He outlined a proposed system that is sometimes used by the Mormon Church. A ''virgin'' area is selected to be inundated with radio and billboard propaganda. Printed advertising in local papers, and public-relations-type television spots and features (usually emphasizing family relationships) are aired. All stress love, caring, and other virtues no reasonable person could object to. A few weeks later, the missionaries arrive. The first words to Mrs. Housewife: "Hi, we're Mormon missionaries. You've heard of our family program, haven't you?"

Who could turn away these clean-cut young men who are sacrificing two and one-half years of their lives to tell you how to show love for your family?

You can!

> As we said before, so say I now again, If any man preach any other gospel unto you than that ye have received, let him be accursed.

> —Galatians 1:9

NOTES

[1]*Doctrine and Covenants* 84:33-34.

[2]B. H. Roberts, *Comprehensive History of the Church,* I, p. 40, footnote.

[3]For a detailed discussion of this matter see Hal Hougey's "Latter-day Saints—Where Did You Get Your Authority?" and La Mar Petersen's "Problems in Mormon Text." Both are available through Modern Microfilm.

[4]Petersen, "Problems in Mormon Text," p. 8.

[5]McElveen, *Will the "Saints" Go Marching In?* pp. 83, 89.

[6]Whalen, *The Latter-day Saints in the Modern-day World,* p. 149.

[7]Stephen L. Richards, *Church News,* November 21, 1951, p. 2.

[8]Turner, *The Mormon Establishment,* pp. 279, 287.

[9]*Doctrine and Covenants* 28:6.

[10]An atypical case documented by John L. Smith in *Witnessing Effectively to Mormons* (Marlowe, OK: Utah Missions, Inc., n.d.), p. 50.

[11]*Doctrine and Covenants* 119.

[12]Turner, *The Mormon Establishment,* p. 48.

[13]Ibid., p. 141.

[14]Associated Press quoted in Cowdrey, Davis, Scales, *Who Really Wrote the Book of Mormon?* p. 7.

[15]Whalen, *The Latter-day Saints,* p. 156.

[16]Gordon Fraser, *Is Mormonism Christian?* (Chicago: Moody Press, 1977), p. 19.

[17]*Deseret News,* Church Section, January 9, 1971, p. 7.

[18]Tanner, *Mormonism: Shadow or Reality?* p. 418.

[19]*Church News,* July 29, 1978.

[20]Fraser, *Is Mormonism Christian?* p. 18.

[21]Lewis Price, "The Testimony of a Former Mormon Missionary," Utah Christian Tract Society.

[22]Ibid.

[23]*Salt Lake City Messenger,* April, 1976.

[24]John L. Smith, *Witnessing Effectively to Mormons,* p. 19.

[25]Price, "The Testimony of a Former Mormon Missionary."

11

From Mirage to Reality:

The Legacy, the Tragedy,
and the Hope of Mormonism

But whosoever drinketh of the water that I shall give him shall never thirst; but the water that I shall give him shall be in him a well of water springing up into everlasting life.

—John 4:14

This book began over two years ago when I met Joyce Landorf, that beautiful example of Christian womanhood, at an autograph party given on her behalf. We were speaking of her new book and her others which had influenced my life. Then I mentioned that before becoming a Christian, I, too, had published. "But that was when I was a Mormon," I said apologetically.

"You were once a Mormon?" she exclaimed, clasping my arm. "Why don't you write about that? I know many people would be interested in reading about why you left Mormonism!"

I was not so sure. After I had found out the truth about Mormonism, I wasn't so proud to admit my connection with it. Many other people had told me before that I "ought to write a book" about my experiences, but I first thought that my reasons for leaving Mormonism wouldn't fill a book. A large pamphlet, maybe, but not a book. But the more I meditated on it, the more I realized that though I had a limited number of reasons for knowing Mormonism to be false, each of these reasons had many facets.

I examined the life of Joseph Smith and found him to be the antithesis of all that Mormons claim he was. Not only was his account of the First Vision unlikely and out of harmony with God's Word, he himself couldn't relate the stories the same way from one telling to another. Because of his reckless merchandizing of men's souls, the legacy he left his people has been one of persecution, broken promises, and rash, unfulfilled prophecies.

The *Book of Mormon*, too, has done more harm to the Mormon

people than good. While archaeological findings almost daily reaffirm the truth of the Bible, the *Book of Mormon* stands unaccompanied by even a single non-Mormon archaeological advocate. Its stumbling rhetoric, its pretentious heroes, and its brazen twistings of God's Word shame its claim of superiority to the Bible.

The *Doctrine and Covenants* I see as the boldest (and most effective) attempt at the manipulation of the human spirit since Machiavelli. No man could live its complicated precepts and be acceptable to God. Paul warned of such in Second Corinthians 11:3: "But I fear, lest by any means, as the serpent beguiled Eve through his subtilty, so your minds should be corrupted from the simplicity that is in Christ."

Mormons derive their leadership from their prophets, past and present, and their claim to divine inspiration. That they receive powerful promptings, there can be no doubt; but the nature of their utterances shows the origin to be their own darkened hearts (Rom. 1:18-23, 25). Their claim that God will do nothing without revealing His secrets to prophets (Amos 3:7) is their own death-knell, for no prophet of the Bible foretold Mormonism in approval. What they have "restored" simply never existed.

The remnant of Christians who through two thousand years have remained faithful to truth are seen by Mormons as heretics. But as Hal Hougey is fond of saying, just because we don't know the names and addresses of Christians throughout the ages, that doesn't mean they didn't exist. Martyrs who died with the name of Christ on their lips and forgiveness for their tormentors in their hearts are seen by Mormons as only misguided souls who will be anxious to accept the Mormon counterfeit of gospel in the spirit world.

The *Pearl of Great Price* self-consciously presses doctrine upon the Mormon people in the guise of antiquity, while all around the world archaeologists and linguists laugh politely behind their hands at it. Part of the pressure on this book was relieved when Spencer W. Kimball magnanimously gave his priesthood to blacks. This satisfied the world but raised unanswerable questions in the minds of Mormons who tried to sort out just what their variable god expected of human beings.

The god of Mormonism, that self-glorified man, the polygamous Christ of Mormonism, and the Holy Man-Ghost of Mormonism are not the eternal God of the Bible. The baptisms and ordinances done in the name of this unholy trio are as impotent and invalid as that deity. So also is the promise of salvation for almost all in a three-tiered heaven where even the rebellious and ungodly live parasitically on the riches of God.

The earthly church has become an overwhelmingly wealthy entity totally dissimilar to the independent servants of God of the first century. Unlike early apostles who took no thought for words in defending the truth of the Gospel, knowing that the Holy Ghost would speak through them, Mormon missionaries memorize word by word the testimonies of other men.

What happens when a faithful Mormon is confronted with such a different attitude towards the church he loves? I cannot speak for all Mormons, but I can look into my past and tell what happened to me. When I had been a Mormon for about three years, someone gave me a booklet called "Mormon Claims Examined" by Larry Jonas. What I read there upset me so much that I gave the booklet back and resolved to forget what it said. And I *did* forget it. I managed to avoid or throw away unread all other anti-Mormon literature that came my way for seven years.

Wallace Turner noted that "to be a Mormon is to be born with a second nationality. The duties to maintain this connection are at least as demanding as those of the American citizen, and perhaps more demanding."[1] For a faithful Mormon, leaving this way of life is as hard as trying to accustom oneself to life in a foreign country. One man who lived and worked among Mormons much of his life noted that this pressure is best analyzed in the cases where Christians marry Mormon spouses. Thirty-nine times out of forty, he estimated, the Christian partner will become a Mormon.[2] From social, economic, and emotional viewpoints, it is infinitely easier to become a Mormon than to become an ex-Mormon.

For one thing, Mormons who show signs of "losing their testimonies" are usually assigned extra jobs by their leaders. The thought behind this apparently is that the busier a man is, the less he will think of who and where else he could be worshiping. Those wavering in the faith who sneak furtively off to a public library to check out a book critical of Mormonism will find many such listed in the card catalogues but few, if any, on the shelves. One Mormon missionary explained this phenomenon by saying that in his area it was common practice for missionaries to keep anti-Mormon books checked out of the libraries continuously until the books got "lost."[3]

Harold B. Lee, the former president of the church, exemplified another common tool used by Mormon leaders to discourage apostasy. Lee once stated that no one who left Mormonism ever had any influence in his or her community thereafter.[4] This is paralleled in the statement of my BYU branch president who told me that if I left Mormonism I would never be happy again. (Am I happy? I am at peace with God, but I am scared to death for the souls of the Mormon people.)

In the past, God's "direct revelations" to the prophet guided the lives of most Mormons, who followed without question. But as many of these revelations, like the *Book of Mormon* and the Book of Abraham have proven to be less than what was originally claimed for them, many of the church have begun to doubt the authority of these prophets.

Latter-day Saint leaders tell their members that complete obedience is essential, and that individual thinking is not necessary. As one Mormon publication put it, "When our leaders speak, the thinking has been done. When they propose a plan, it is God's plan . . . Satan wins a great victory when he can get members of the Church to do their own thinking."[5] Romans chapter 13 teaches that subjection to civil authorities is a true principle. But it is dangerous in spiritual matters! Where our salvation is concerned, we alone are responsible for doctrinal discernment by using our guidebook, the Bible.

Many Mormons have in conscience "left" Mormonism while still remaining on church rolls. Some do not want to hurt relatives with the public scandal of excommunication. Others, especially in Utah, want to preserve business connections. Still others who no longer recognize the authority of Mormon leaders over them have seen no need to instigate formal excommunication procedures, which in itself could be a frustrating and harrowing experience.

It is interesting to note that almost every vocal ex-Mormon of today started out by trying to disprove the claims of those who wrote or spoke against Mormonism. One of the founders of Ex-Mormons for Jesus, Melaine Layton, looked into Mormonism's past to investigate charges against her church and found more questions than answers. Jerald Tanner, too, tried to defend the LDS Church against charges made by one of its first apostates and now is himself perhaps one of the most influential apostates of all time.

Apostasy from Mormonism is no new thing, but most Mormons believe it is a rarity. Most don't know that of the eleven "witnesses" to the *Book of Mormon,* over half apostatized permanently. Some even received their own revelations—telling them that Mormonism was false.

One of the twenty-one sons of prominent LDS leader George Q. Cannon in 1911 angered the Mormon church by publishing a book relating how Mormon leaders persisted in the practice of polygamy for years while publicly repudiating the doctrine.[6] Charles A. Shook, once a member of the Reorganized Church, was also vocal and influential in his apostasy.

Arthur Budvarson, a powerful writer against the Mormon myths, left the church in 1944 and has continued tirelessly to teach Mormons and non-Mormons alike the saving truth of Jesus Christ.

In 1945 the niece of prophet-to-be David O. McKay published the most authoritative work on the life of Joseph Smith ever assembled: her *No Man Knows My History* led to Fawn Brodie's excommunication in 1946, and the repercussions shook Mormondom for years afterwards. Jerald and Sandra Tanner were both excommunicated from the Mormon Church in 1960. Ironically, many faithful Mormon scholars have had to come to them for copies of original documents which their own church suppresses.

The former president of the Mormon "New World Archaeological Foundation," Thomas Stuart Ferguson, wrote much in support of *Book of Mormon* claims. His *One Fold and One Shepherd* was widely read by Mormons, but he, too, left Mormonism. Another influential Mormon, Dr. John William Fitzgerald, served twenty years as LDS chaplain in the Utah National Guard. He wrote his master's thesis at Brigham Young University on the *Doctrine and Covenants,* but even in spite of such ties and indoctrination, he left Mormonism.

A young man by the name of Marvin Cowan left Mormonism to serve as a powerful minister for Christ. Grant Heward, who served four local missions for the Mormon Church, tried to reconcile the Egyptian Alphabet and Grammar to the *Pearl of Great Price.* What he found disturbed him so much that he distributed a paper entitled, "Why Would Anyone Want To Fight The Truth?" at the April, 1967, general conference. He was excommunicated—for telling the truth.

About that same time, the controversial Mormon Egyptologist Dee Jay Nelson began translating the *Pearl of Great Price* papyri. Though his educational credentials were later shown to be shoddy, his nonetheless valid discoveries about the papyri led him and others to request excommunication from the Mormon Church.

Doug Wallace, the young man who ordained a black friend to the priesthood before the "revelation" authorized it, was excommunicated. He followed Byron Marchant, the Mormon Scoutmaster whose Salt Lake City Boy Scout troop drew national attention to the Mormon church. A suit was brought against scouting and the LDS Church to force the Marchant troop to allow two Negro scouts to become patrol leaders. In the ensuing battle Marchant was excommunicated.

Many of the active ex-Mormons around the country belong to an organization called "Ex-Mormons for Jesus" which apostates Roger and Melaine Layton and Bob Witte spearhead.[7] It publishes a monthly newsletter for anyone interested in the work of reaching Mormons. There are many, many ex-Mormons who are serving Christ. Unfortunately, there are also many ex-Mormons who have been so disillusioned by Mormonism that they have vowed never to be tricked again by "religion." These live without God, preferring no salvation at all to the lies of Mormonism.

When I was a Mormon, I thought that godlessness was the fate of all who left the Mormon Church. I had almost begun to believe the old Mormon story that all apostates fail at everything when they leave Mormonism. I had been a Christian for three years before I met an ex-Mormon Christian in person.

While researching for this book I sent out inquiries to ex-Mormons to find out their reasons for leaving the church. In addition to hearing from some of those apostates already mentioned, I received many beautiful letters from others. I heard from a young man named Jay Banks, who left Mormonism after serving a mission where he chafed under the burden of telling others that he *knew* the Mormon Church to be true when in reality he had no such conviction. Alan Cheney was another young man who wrote me and told of his experiences on a church mission in northern California and Nevada. While there, he began investigating claims made by Christians against the LDS Church. He prayed sincerely that God would vindicate Mormonism, but he says that "it was only after I stopped asking God to prove Mormonism to me and began asking Him to show me the truth and to help me cope with it, that I finally came to peace within myself."

Another ex-Mormon, Patricia Blaziek, told of how she was "brainwashed" into Mormonism while never being brought into *Christ*. Richard Driscoll stressed the mechanical and overbearing emphasis of his fellow Mormons on works, and their ostracism of those who did not fit into the Mormon social mold.

What these letters, and others I received from ex-Mormons, show is that there are many ex-Mormons who are finding peace for the first time in their lives through knowledge of Jesus Christ as Lord and Savior. Without a single exception, every ex-Mormon I've ever asked about church denominational preference has stated strongly that though he or she might attend a certain church, each is first and foremost a member of the body of Christ. I myself attend the Church of Christ because I believe the teachings of Christians there to be in harmony with the Bible. But I am a follower of and a believer in Christ—a Christian—above all.

This is the common bond I have found among all who have left Mormonism—we will never again give allegiance to any creed but the Bible, nor any name but Christ's. Though my interpretation of certain Bible principles may differ from those of another ex-Mormon, our similarities bind us overwhelmingly together in the love and service of our Master.

Though leaving Mormonism for Christianity is an exhilarating emancipation, it is not without its disadvantages. As a Mormon once wryly observed, "It's the banana that leaves the bunch that gets skinned." Only in Mormonism, though, do the other bananas do the skinning. One faithful Mormon man who became disenchanted with the church for doctrinal reasons was harassed by anonymous phone calls to his place of employment and recurrent rumors that he was a polygamist.[8] Jerald and Sandra Tanner have received some ugly and threatening letters which try to keep them from publishing the truth about Mormonism. One critic even burned their book and sent them the ashes in a box!

Baptist minister John L. Smith, though never a Mormon, was for years pressured by Mormons in local government in the Utah towns where he preached. Once a Mormon who was renting from him admitted spying on Reverend Smith and turning in reports to Mormon leaders on him and other Protestant ministers in an attempt to uncover "secrets." (Sorry, Mormons—the only old documents we Christians have are our Bibles, and we don't suppress those!)

At the other end of the extreme, a young woman on a recent "Tomorrow Show" told Tom Snyder of being terrorized by Mormon "hit men" because of her opposition to the LDS Church in England.

Christians know that to live is Christ, and to die is gain (Phil. 1:21). Every ex-Mormon Christian feels deeply the burden of knowing that his former associates do not have truth. Floyd McElveen noted,

> It is true that we should not major on minors. It may be unnecessary to tell our neighbor that he has bad breath, or that a shingle on his roof is loose. However, it is criminal not to wake him up if he is inside his house and his house is on fire. No excuse, and no empty professions of love will ever satisfy God in such cases.[9]

Each Sunday morning my Mormon friends and yours sit in Sunday school singing, "Oh Say What Is Truth" while they allow their leaders to lull them into false security with false doctrine. But no faithful Mormon will be won to Christ in a single sitting, as anyone who has taught Mormons will tell you. You must first make Mormons feel a need for salvation—"get them lost"—before the Atonement of Christ will have any meaning in their lives. There can be no satisfaction in showing a Mormon how his religion is like a sieve without giving him another Vessel into which to pour his soul.

I haven't written this book just to antagonize Mormons. I hope, though, that it will disturb all who read it. I pray in agony of heart often for Mormons who do not know Christ, and are searching for him. The Bible tells believers to test all things (1 Thess. 5:21; 1 John 4:1). By every Bible standard, Mormonism has failed the test of God.

A few years ago a Mormon magazine, the *Ensign,* published a letter from a young Mormon, Stephen D. McKasson. In reflecting on what Mormonism had done for him, he noted, "It seems that hardly a day goes by that I'm not placed in a situation where I don't stop and ask myself, "What would Joseph Smith have done?"[10]

This is the tragedy of Mormonism. It has substituted man for God and cheated its people out of confidence in the Savior. It has denied the free gifts of God and made its people work like Sisyphus at the impossible task of saving themselves.

I can say again that I do not regret my years as a Mormon. I pray that my experience can lead others to Christ. I am grateful that God has forgiven me for the wrong things I believed and taught, and that those ten years of my life have been wiped clean by the scarred hand of Christ. If God forgets when He forgives, then those years are a great blank on the record of my soul. For this I am ever thankful.

But oh, Mormons—how much better to have had rich and beautiful experiences with my Savior there, instead of a blank space! God will cleanse you, too—but don't continue in sin just so grace may abound later!

This is the hope of Mormonism. For two thousand years, *now* has always been the hour of salvation. May you find the peace I know. Truth, and truth only, will make you free.

Latayne Colvett Scott

NOTES

[1]Turner, *The Mormon Establishment,* p. 4.

[2]John L. Smith, *Witnessing Effectively to Mormons,* p. 10.

[3]Bailey, *Inside a Mormon Mission,* p. 113.

[4]*Conference Reports,* October 1947, p. 67.

[5]*Improvement Era,* June 1945, p. 354.

[6]Frank J. Cannon, *Under the Prophet in Utah.*

[7]"Ex-Mormons For Jesus" chapters number over fifty, and are growing at the rate of one new chapter a week nationwide. Each non-denominational chapter can provide counseling, speakers, films, etc. to groups and to individuals. Write for a catalog containing an extensive listing of books, tapes, tracts, and other sources on the subject of Mormonism. Address: EMFJ Ministries, P.O. Box 3947, Santa Fe Springs, CA 90670-1947.

[8]Turner, *The Mormon Establishment,* p. 148.

[9]McElveen, *Will the "Saints" Go Marching In?* p. 10.

[10]Stephen D. McKasson quoted in the *Ensign,* December 1972, p. 81.

Appendix

Whenever a new acquaintance finds out that I used to be a Mormon, it seems he or she will always have a question to ask. "Can they ever take temple garments off?" "What is a Family Home Evening?" "Why can't Mormons play cards?" This appendix is a collection of those questions I'm most frequently asked, and is presented in the hopes that Christians will be able to better understand their LDS friends.

Can a non-Mormon ever go into a Mormon temple?

Sometimes non-LDS people boast that they toured the Salt Lake Temple. This is because they have confused the temple with the Tabernacle. The temple, the six-spired, three-story building, is closed to all but Mormons with temple recommends. Other non-Mormons say they have several Mormon temples in their hometown. Here they have mistaken meetinghouses for temples.

However, many non-Mormons have been able to tour the insides of new temples before they are dedicated. Before the Provo temple was dedicated in 1972, thousands of people walked through it. Between the time that an older temple is redecorated and then rededicated, non-Mormons can also tour the building. Only faithful Mormons, however, may witness the actual dedication ceremonies of temples. The dedication of the Provo temple was broadcast by closed-circuit TV to the 25,000 seat Marriot Activity Center on the BYU campus. All participants, at one point, waved white handkerchiefs in the air and gave a "Hosannah shout." It was an impressive sight.

There are many interesting traditions connected with Mormon temples. Supposedly a light appears around each temple as it is dedicated. Twenty people are said to have spoken in tongues at the dedication of the Kirtland Temple, and some said a halo appeared around the head of

239

Joseph F. Smith at the Salt Lake Temple's dedication. Brigham Young, John Taylor, and others who were dead reportedly appeared at the dedication of the Manti Temple.

Some Mormons believe that you can't get an infection in a temple baptismal font. Others, like J. A. Widtsoe, who graduated summa cum laude from Harvard in just three years, claimed that he had received a revelation on agrarian chemistry while in the temple.

Why don't Mormons play bridge?

A tradition has it that one of the requirements made of soldiers in the Mormon Battalion was that they abstain from playing cards. Today, face cards are a forbidden item in the dorms of Mormon colleges and in homes of faithful Mormons. Mormon leaders reason that face cards encourage gambling. They permit playing with other kinds of cards (like Authors or Old Maid) but caution that they are generally a waste of time.

Where do Mormons believe the Ten Lost Tribes are?

Shalmaneser and Sargon carried away the ten tribes of Samaria in about 724 B.C. Mormons believe that those ten tribes weren't "lost" by being absorbed into other cultures (and so lost their national identity) as Christians and historians claim. Mormon doctrine teaches that God led them away and hid them "in the land northward."[1]

Since almost all the world's land surface has been explored, the traditional LDS explanation that they are in the North Pole region[2] has been rejected by many Mormons. They have hearkened back to an old theory that a part of the earth was taken to form a planet for them.[3]

They will supposedly return to earth before the Millennium, their planet colliding with our earth with such force that a great highway will be cast up as their orb plows through the northern waters. They will bring copies of their own writings, which will join the ranks of the *Book of Mormon* and the *Pearl of Great Price* as scripture.

Do the Mormons believe in Transubstantiation?

No. The partaking of the elements of the Lord's Supper—which they call "the sacrament"—is only done in remembrance of Christ's bodily sufferings. However, it has few ties with the meal of which Christ partook. Whereas our Savior ate the Passover feast of unleavened bread and the fruit of the vine, Mormons serve regular white sandwich bread and water in their communion service.

Though the Mormon Church claims to abhor rituals, the sacrament service is very ritualistic. Young deacons dressed in white dress shirts serve the communion after it is blessed by a young priest who says exactly these words:

O God, the Eternal Father, we ask thee in the name of thy Son, Jesus Christ, to bless and sanctify this bread to the souls of all those who partake of it; that they may eat in remembrance of the body of thy Son, and witness unto thee, O God, the Eternal Father, that they are willing to take upon them the name of thy Son, and always remember him, and keep his commandments which he has given them; that they may always have his Spirit to be with them. Amen.[4]

O God, the Eternal Father, we ask thee, in the name of thy Son, Jesus Christ, to bless and sanctify this water to the souls of all those who drink of it, that they may do it in remembrance of the blood of thy Son, which was shed for them; that they may witness unto thee, O God, the Eternal Father, that they do always remember him, that they may have his Spirit to be with them. Amen.[5]

If he misses so much as a pronoun, the bishop shakes his head and the prayer must be repeated. I once sat in a sacrament service where a hapless and humiliated young priest repeated the prayer over the bread five times before he got it right. (For this reason a small card with the prayers written on it is usually stashed behind the communion table.) The communion is given to the highest officials present before it is passed to the congregation. Traditionally Mormons hold the tray containing the sacrament in the left hand and pick up the bread or cup with the right. They also offer it to their young unbaptized children. However, it is considered harmful to partake of the sacrament unworthily—i.e., if you have sinned and not yet repented.

What is a Family Home Evening?

A Family Home Evening is a commanded, not optional, meeting held weekly in the home of each member of the Mormon Church. A new Family Home Evening manual providing lesson suggestions, visual aids, games, etc., is printed each year and distributed to members. No church meetings whatsoever are held on Monday evenings so all members will be free to attend their individual Family Home Evening.

Sometimes if a family member's work schedule interferes, the Family Home Evening night is changed. This is rare, though allowable. Family Home Evening activities vary from family outings (like ice skating) to popping corn and hearing a spiritual lesson presented by a family member.

I heard it said many times that sporting events televised on Monday nights were the devil's way of trying to prevent Family Home Evenings. However, many LDS families compromise and hold an episodic Family Home Evening during time-outs and half time.

Or if the male-female family member ratio permits a voting bloc, often Monday Night Football *is* Family Home Evening—and Mom and sisters cook goodies for the entranced male spectators of the family.

Part of the purpose of family home evenings, though, is to counteract the influence of such things as television. Family solidarity is certainly increased when even one night a week is reserved for loved ones, and a family council is held to iron out problems. Though Family Home Evenings should not be exclusive Mormon property, nor are they the cure-all claimed by Mormons, they are undoubtedly an excellent way to reaffirm paternal authority and cement family ties.

Are Mormon worship services open to the public?

Yes. According to *Doctrine and Covenants* 46:3, no one is to be cast out of a public meeting or sacrament meeting of the Mormon church.

Mormons are only commanded to attend two meetings a week—their own Family Home Evenings and the sacrament meeting held late Sunday afternoon or early that evening. The men are also required to attend priesthood meeting, which is held early each Sunday morning.

In priesthood meeting, the young men and boys divide up into quorums according to priesthood office (i.e., deacon, priest, etc.). Women meet concurrently in Relief Society, while youth attend Young Men and Young Women meetings. They are joined at church by the rest of their families for Sunday school services. This consists of announcements, a few songs and prayers, two short talks, and a memory verse recited by the congregation. Then the sacrament is administered. It is interesting to note that women and girls often lead the songs and give sermonettes. Young boys do these as well as leading prayers and blessing and passing the sacrament.

The ward then divides up into classes for instruction. The lessons presented there are standardized: all three-year-olds in the Mormon Church, for example, would on a particular day be having the same lesson, which was prepared by the Deseret Sunday School Board. There is a special class for "investigators" and new converts.

Mormons say jokingly that sacrament meetings start on "MST"—Mormon Standard Time—almost always a few minutes late. It is supposed to last about seventy minutes. The bishop and his counselors preside over this meeting, usually sitting with the speakers and the ward clerk (who takes notes on the proceedings) on a raised platform facing the congregation.

Sometimes the bishop or a stake authority will address them. Since Mormons don't have preachers, the speakers at a sacrament meeting are usually ward members. They present lessons of about twenty minutes apiece, sometimes on a scriptural theme. More often, though, the talks consist of missionary reminiscences (complete with travelogues), or talks on food storage, self-improvement, or events from the life of a General

Authority. Often charts, photographs, slides, and other visual aids are used. Sometimes the talks are serious. Others are not—once a speaker started his address at a meeting I attended by saying, "Whoopdedoo! The gospel's true!"

There is no invitation offered, no mourner's bench, no collection plate passed, and no baptismal font in sight. The speech usually ends with the phrase, "I say these things in the name of Jesus Christ. Amen"— even though such may be the only mention of the Savior's name during the entire meeting.

Mormons attend other meetings during the week. About once a month youth and young adults attend an informal "fireside" on Sunday evening, which features refreshments and a speaker. There are church-sponsored "roadshows" (short musical plays), concerts, chaparoned dances, sports events, banquets, and other youth activities. Mutual Improvement Association (MIA) is held on a weekday evening, providing doctrinal classroom instruction. Women of all ages attend Relief Society, usually on Tuesday mornings, where during the month they have lessons on the four themes of Social Relations, Cultural Refinement, Spiritual Living, and Homemaking. Also during the week (usually late on a schoolday afternoon), children under twelve years of age attend a "Primary" class similar to a Catholic catechism class.

Do Mormons seek persecution?

Many religious groups, like Jehovah's Witnesses, consider persecution by Christians to be a sign that they are doing God's will. Though Mormons do not as consciously affirm this, they also recognize the foreign nature of most of their doctrine, and are not surprised to have it vehemently rejected much of the time.

In the past, Mormons moved house and home to escape physical persecution (as in the exodus from Nauvoo). Today, though, they seek the support and approval of the public in general and try to circumvent questions about their strange doctrines and practices.

I don't think it's too presumptive to say, however, that the greatest threat to Mormonism is not from outsiders, but from those who once embraced its tenets and then found the "more excellent way" of Christ.

Do Mormons regard wealth as a help or a hinderance to spirituality?

Obviously the great wealth of the church itself should indicate something of its attitude toward wealth. Orson Pratt once said, "Riches are not a curse, but they are a great blessing: it is the inequality in riches that is a great curse."[6] In other words, Mormons want all to be rich—all Mormons, that is. Money for Mormons in need comes from the "fast offerings" of his brethren, so that all help each other. Surely the pressure from finances is burdensome to a Mormon family, for not only are Mormon families large in this day of zero population growth, but Mormon children must be sent on missions as well as fed, housed, and educated.

Many Mormon leaders, especially the late J. Reuben Clark, have continually counselled their people to stay away from installment buying and debt at all costs. For this reason, many Mormon families may appear less affluent than their mortgaged neighbors, while in fact being more solvent.

Wealth is vitally important to the Mormon dream. Their god promises them not only salvation but an inheritance of land and earth,[7] so that they might have the advantage over the world,[8] if they give over their own "treasures."[9] Joseph Smith and Brigham Young lived sumptuously much of their lives, supported by the church. Many other Mormons have sought to use their "spiritual gifts" to obtain riches—like the Mormon bishop who started a "dream mine" in the Utah Valley, and the many other Mormons who even today follow the example of Joseph Smith by using divining rods to search for hidden treasure.[10]

Do faithful Mormons ever take off their temple garments?

The ankle-to-knee-to-neck garments once worn in the temple prior to 1975 are no longer used. The shorter garments are what the average Mormon wears at all times unless he is taking a bath, or participating in a sport (like basketball) whose uniform would expose the garment. They are regarded as a "protective" article. Some women wear them even during childbirth, and LDS soldiers claim the garments have saved lives during battle.

Military men can dye the garments green, or when prevented by regulations from wearing the garments, are allowed to pin white pieces of cloth resembling the garment markings onto the issued service underwear. They must remove these markings when sending the underwear to the laundry and replace them on the cleaned underwear.

Up until the early sixties one could buy the LDS garments in any department store in Salt Lake City. Now, though, they are sold through Mormon outlets so as to protect them from curious Gentile eyes. Most Mormons will dry them indoors for the same reason.

The garments are made out of nylon, silk, cotton, or just about any fabric commonly used for regular undergarments. They are always white, however. The legs come to the knee, and the sleeves cover the upper arm. They come in a variety of necklines (round, V-neck, etc.) and in one- or two-piece versions. The constant wearing of a garment, thus, precludes the wearing of shorts, tank tops, strapless dresses, or sleeveless shirts. In the days of the mini-skirt some women rolled up or cut the legs on the garments, for which they were chastised.

The garments are worn next to the skin: regular underwear and hosiery are worn on top of them. They are underwear, and for this reason I think it is tasteless for non-Mormons to display them—even for the purposes of instruction. Since garments are only worn by those who've been through the temple for their endowments, they are like a status symbol of faithfulness. On the BYU campus some freshmen boys who have not yet been on missions wear white T-shirts under their regular shirts (even when it's sweltering) if they want a girl to think they're a returned missionary (and thus eligible!).

Is it true that Jack Anderson is a Mormon?

Yes. Jack Anderson, named "one of five most influential men in America" is a Mormon. If you're one of the fifty million persons who read his column and didn't know that, it's because he doesn't publicize the fact.

Other famous Mormons include: the late Ernest L. Wilkinson, a lawyer who obtained the largest judgment ever levied against the U. S. government in a U. S. Court of Claims, in favor of the Ute Indian tribe, and who served as president of BYU; Dr. Harvey Fletcher, former director of research for Bell Telephone and the first Mormon to be named to the National Academy of Science; financeer Marriner S. Eccles; former Congressman Richard J. Hanna; former Senator Wallace Bennett; Stewart Udall, Secretary of the Interior in the Kennedy and Johnson cabinets; David Kermedy, former Secretary of the Treasury; George Romney of American Motors and former governor of Michigan and Secretary of HUD; J. Willard Marriot who owns food chains like Roy Roger's, Farrell's Ice Cream Parlours, Hot Shoppes, Bob's Big Boy's, as well as fifty hotels, sixty-two flight kitchens for airlines, and 210 other food service outlets;[11] Ezra Taft Benson, former Secretary of Agriculture and next in line to be Mormon prophet; former U. S. Treasurer Ivy Baker Priest; Rosel Hyde, formerly of the Federal Communications Commission; E. Cardon Walker, president of Walt Disney Productions; Philo T. Farnsworth who is credited with inventing the television; Dr. Henry Eyring, one of the top scientists of the U. S.; President O. Meredith Wilson of the University of Minnesota; Dr. Dallin Oaks, President of BYU; poet Max Golightly; the late Richard L. Evans, radio speaker; actor Johnny Whittaker ("Family Affair" and "Tom Sawyer"); sports figures Billy Casper, Harmon Killebrew, Kresmir Kosich, Todd Christensen, and Golden Richards; and innumerable mothers of the year.

And unless you've been in a cave for several years, you well know that Donny, Marie, and the other Osmonds are Mormon. They have documented 25,000 converts, and their family tithe reportedly tops one million dollars a year.[12]

Do Mormons cremate their dead?

According to Mormon leaders, cremation is not to be practiced since it is destructive to the body. At a Mormon funeral the casket is usually closed. Mormons who have been through the temple for endowments are buried in the full temple regalia, including the green apron.

If the deceased was a woman, after the funeral and just before interment, a high priest puts the temple veil over the face of the corpse. They believe it will remain there until her husband calls her from the grave to resurrection.

Mormons are buried in gravesites which were "dedicated" in a simple ceremony before the interment.

Why do Mormons often have such large families?

Because Mormon authorities teach that birth control is "tampering with the font of life." Joseph Fielding Smith, in fact, stated: "Birth control is wickedness . . . iniquity which must be punished."[13] Abortion is even worse, for it ranks with murder as the "shedding of innocent blood."

Faithful Mormons believe in having as many children as they can possibly support and raise, because they believe that there are only a limited number of spirits still in heaven waiting for bodies. Why not, they reason, have them come into Mormon homes? It is thus a sin against your spirit mothers and sisters to deprive them of Mormonism. A speaker at a sacrament meeting I once attended quipped, "Where would I be/And what would you do/If Adam and Eve/Had stopped at just two?"

Mormons believe that sexual activity in marriage is a God-given (and godly) attribute. While Mormon leaders do not condemn the rhythm method of birth control, they do not approve of it, either, except for health reasons; any other conscious limiting of the marriage act weakens the union. I have known Mormon families with stairstep children to live in utter poverty because of their refusal to practice birth control. This belief wedges a socially-conscious woman between a too-crowded world and her desire to obey her leaders.

When an LDS couple decides not to have another child, they are reminded that the child which could have been theirs will probably be born into a non-Mormon home.

Why don't Mormons eat out on Sundays?

Mormons believe that Sunday is the Sabbath.[14] Of course Hosea 2:11 indicated that the Jewish Sabbath would be done away with for the new "Lord's Day," but Mormons believe Sunday is both Sabbath and Lord's Day.

Their Sunday activities are, therefore, limited in keeping with the idea of a Sabbath. They are not to participate in sports activities or recreation, travel unnecessarily, go hunting or fishing, or watch T.V. They are not to patronize any business establishment except in the case of an emergency (to buy medicine, for example), because their patronage might prevent an employee from being able to attend worship services.

Acceptable Sabbath activities include attending Sunday school and Sacrament meetings and firesides, visiting friends and relatives, reading uplifting books, listening to restful or inspiring music, going for a quiet walk, and reading scriptures.[15] While I was a Mormon I never studied (except scriptures) or watched T.V. on Sunday and found that it truly was a refreshing day of rest.

What is Fast Sunday?

Many a Mormon child has been heard to observe that Fast Sunday is the slowest day of the month. The day before the first Sunday of the month faithful Mormons do not eat anything after the evening meal. They continue fasting until the next afternoon. Pregnant and lactating women, the aged, the infirm, and young children are exempt from fasting.

There is only one worship service held on Fast Sunday—a Sunday school service which is followed by a "Fast and Testimony" meeting. Here Mormons get a chance to stand up and give a spontaneous account of their feelings about the church. Even the youngest children often participate. Sometimes, though, many long minutes of uncomfortable silence tick away between testimonies until the end of the meeting.

After the family returns home, young deacons make the rounds of the homes in the ward, collecting from each family head the amount that would have been spent on the missed meals. This is used to feed the poor. The story is told of a young deacon, too lazy to collect fast offerings, who was taken to the homes of the needy who had to do without food and fuel that week because of his negligence.

Mormons often fast on other days, too. I regularly fasted five times a month for guidance when I served as a resident assistant in the BYU dorms. The spiritual and physical benefits of fasting shouldn't be underestimated by Christians.

What do Mormons think of the "New Morality"?

Milton R. Hunter, a General Authority, once stated flatly that the new morality is really the teachings of the devil. One reason that many Mormon youth can stay so morally clean is not only that they are expected to, but they are *told* to. When I was a teen-ager, I lived by the rules set forth by church leaders in a little pamphlet called, "For the Strength of Youth." Here were found rules that left little question about what was allowable and what was not. We weren't told, for instance, "dress modestly and neatly"—we were told to wear dresses and shorts to the knee, to wear street clothing over a bathing suit when en route to the pool, never to wear curlers in public, and so on. Guidelines for dating, too, were strict—double dates at fifteen, no single dates until sixteen. Acceptable date activities included sports, clean movies, and church dances.

The Mormon Church has always been concerned about the actions and appearances of its members. Brigham Young, in the 1850s, once designed a "Deseret Costume" which he required all LDS women to wear—bloomers, a full skirt, a cape, and a high bonnet—and forbade hoops because he said whores wore them. He condemned men's trousers that buttoned in the front, too, calling them "fornication pants."[16]

Nonetheless, Mormon youth are taught that chastity is their most treasured asset—more valuable even than life. Fornication ranks in Mormon minds with adultery and prostitution. I am sure that even centers of Mormon youth such as BYU have their share of immoral sex. But it is also true that a common sight around dormitories there is that of a young man and young woman standing with hands clasped and heads bowed, beginning their date with a prayer.

Morality to the conscientious Mormon doesn't just mean sexual morality. Integrity is also a treasured virtue. Most young Mormons know the story of Karl Maeser, former president of BYU. He once said that his enemies could build prison walls around him higher and thicker than any in existence, and somehow he would find a way to escape. But they could draw a circle with chalk around his feet and if he gave his word of honor not to cross that line, he would be their prisoner forever.

I am often asked if it is harder to be an LDS youth than a Christian youth. It seems to me it would be harder growing up in Mormonism if one had difficulty in accepting and living by specific rules of conduct and dress. But it is harder to be a Christian youth if one has difficulty discerning, on your own, what is good and what is not. Becoming a Christian didn't necessitate any great changes in my *behavior*—but I sure had to learn to think on my own!

What do Mormons mean when they speak of "Zion"?

The term "Zion" is one of the most overworked in Mormondom. Here are some of its definitions: (1) The city of Jerusalem, (2) the city of Enoch which was taken to heaven with him,[17] (3) any group of people who are "pure in heart," as were Enoch's people, (4) a city to be built in America by the descendants of Joseph,[18] and (5) any center of Mormon population, especially Utah.

How is public prayer offered?

Mormons in public worship do not kneel to pray, nor do they fold their hands. Rather, they teach their children to fold their arms in front of them.

Several specific rules govern public prayer. It is to be extemporaneous, unless it is a dedicatory prayer or a sacrament prayer. Deity is to be addressed as Father, but the repetition of the names of God or Christ is to be avoided. The sacred pronouns ("Thee," "Thine," "Thou") are used, never "You" or "Your." At the end of a public prayer, all listeners repeat aloud the "Amen."

What is the role of women in Mormon thought?

I was once sitting in a Relief Society meeting when the speaker made an attention-getting remark. In explaining the relationship of husband and wife she said, "Women are the doormats upon which men wipe their feet before going in to God."

I was stunned. I looked open-mouthed at my friends in the room. Surely someone else was as outraged about this as I! But all around me young women were nodding in contemplation and agreement.

This is an extreme example of an extreme attitude. But it is reflected in the Mormon beliefs that a woman can't be resurrected without a man to call her temple name to raise her from the dead, and that she can't be "exalted" without a husband. The supreme role of men and their priesthood in Mormonism is underlined by the continued emphasis on woman's dependence on man.

Naturally there are Mormon women who perhaps through Bible study have realized that this chauvinism is not God's way at all. Naturally, too, many groups outside Mormonism have begun to pressure the church because of these views. In response to these influences BYU has established a new Women's Research Institute. The church also dedicated a monument to women at Nauvoo, Illinois, where they honored prominent women of Mormonism by erecting statues of them. But it will take a lot more than classrooms and statues to bring LDS women into the freedom given us by Christ Jesus.

Do Mormons consider homosexuality to be a sin?

Yes, a serious sin of fornication. However, as Boyd K. Packer pointed out at a fireside I attended in April of 1972, the thought that homosexuals can't repent is a lie perpetrated by the devil. The sin is grievous but not unforgivable.

I never knew a Mormon homosexual.

Have the Mormon people created any great works of art?

Brigham Young encouraged dancing, the theater, music, and education in the arts. Mormons encourage their children to learn to play a musical instrument. Once a month in Relief Society Mormon women study in depth one great painting, or symphony, or work of art by a famous artist or musician. Each year original plays, as well as road shows, music festivals, and dance festivals take place in local Mormon cultural halls. It is true that Mormons are a very culturally aware people.

In an effort to bring together Mormon writers, dramatists, artists, dancers, sculptors, and composers, BYU first sponsored a Mormon Arts Ball in Provo in 1973. Here creative spirits of all genres congregated and exhibited their talents. The aim of many of them was and is to create art forms that are uniquely Mormon.

Have they succeeded? Probably the only artist whose work Mormons would recognize as exclusively Mormon would be Arnold Friberg, who illustrated the *Book of Mormon* with barrel-chested heroes in dramatic poses. Sculptor Mahonri Young and lyricist Eliza R. Snow are part of Mormon cultural heritage—but nonetheless of the past. If we exclude doctrinal writers, then poet and dramatist Carol Lynn Pearson, playwright Orson Scott Card, and poets Max Golightly and Clinton F. Larson would be the only contemporary names recognizable by even educated Mormons. Only a few non-Mormons have heard of any of them.

In my journal on April 3, 1972, I noted, "I talked at length with Sister Tate [a friend] on the role of the Mormon artist. I contend that most art (literary art, especially) came out of despair and misery of the creator's soul. Sister Tate and I concluded that reasons for no great Mormon art are the facts that we (1) are so darned happy, (2) are *told* to be happy ("The Gospel has all the answers" attitude), and (3) we have so little time left over from meetings, etc., for the production of great art." Though I wrote this when I was a Mormon, I would still agree with the conclusions I made.

Do Mormons operate Theological Institutes?

In the sense that all graduates of BYU must have a certain number of Mormon religion course credits, it could be said that BYU is a school of religion. But its educational offerings are far more varied. *Doctrine and Covenants* 88 tells Mormons to learn about astronomy, agronomy, geology, mineralogy, history, current events, prophecy, domestic and foreign affairs, warfare, signs of the Second Coming, geography, languages, and many other fields, and BYU provides training in all.

The LDS church does not operate theological seminaries to train their clergy. The youngsters receive their training in the home, church service, and in seminary classes. These are high school classes taught by accredited teachers offered at a building near the public high school. In Utah a student may leave the high school campus to attend seminary classes and receive elective credits for his grades earned there. In areas of sparse Mormon population, seminary classes are offered early in the morning—usually around 6:30 A.M.—at the church building. Though no high school credit hours are earned, a surprisingly large number of high school students attend.

Young men on missions are further educated in the catechism of Mormonism; and of course, service in the various church jobs is in itself an education.

Do you have to be a Mormon to attend BYU?

No matter how excellent the quality of education available at BYU, I wouldn't recommend anyone sending a son or daughter to a Mormon university just because of the moral atmosphere—unless you want a Mormon in the family. Mormon schools don't have sororities or fraternities, just service clubs and church-related activities. Non-Mormons are either pressured constantly to convert or excluded from the social life.[19]

What was the Deseret Alphabet?

This was a short-lived try by Mormons in the 1850s to formulate a phonetic alphabet using new letter characters. A few copies of the *Book of Mormon* and other documents were printed in this script.

Are Mormons patriotic?

If that question were asked eighty years ago, the answer would have been a resounding "No!" Before the turn of the century, Mormon leaders resented the influence and interference of the U.S. government, and made many bitter comments about it.

Now, however, Mormons pride themselves on their love of country. *Doctrine and Covenants* Sections 98 and 101 tell Mormons to uphold the constitutional government of the U.S., and to take an active part in its workings and maintenance.[20] They believe that the U.S. government was fostered by God to be the cradle of Mormonism, and that the U.S. Constitution was inspired by God.

Brigham Young University's new law school specializes in constitutional law. This emphasis can be traced to a speech given by Brigham Young in 1885 when he stated that at some future time the Constitution of the United States would "hang as it were, upon a single thread" and the Mormon elders would be summoned to save it from utter destruction.[21]

One of the arch enemies of constitutional government and thus Mormonism is Communism. They regard it not only as an evil political force but also as an empty pseudo-religion.

There are few Mormon conscientious objectors in wartime. In the words of Mormon Paul Dunn, "I hate war. But I would fight to the death anything that would take from me my God-given rights."

Though Mormons advocate the separation of church and state, they look forward to the Millennium when they believe Christ will reign politically as well as spiritually over the whole world.

How can Mormons remember everything said in their Patriarchal Blessing?

When a patriarch gives a blessing, his words are recorded and transcribed. The recipient of the blessing receives a copy of what was said. Mine was a legal sheet, single spaced on both sides of the page.

Often LDS women embroider or crochet fancy envelopes for the blessing. Members are encouraged to read them often.

The sudden death of a young person whose blessing promised a spouse and children is usually rationalized by the thought that these promises will be fulfilled in the hereafter.[22]

What is the connection between Boy Scouting and Mormonism?

The LDS Church was the first religious organization in the world to sponsor Scouting, and today it sponsors more units than any other church. In 1975 there were 224,027 LDS Boy Scouts, and 74,000 adult leaders in 14,344 units.

Mormon girls, however, are not sponsored in Girl Scouts but rather in the similar Mormon organizations of "Beehives" (like Brownies) and "Gleaner Girls."

Are Mormons Charismatics?

If the definition of a charismatic is that of one who believes in and seeks after the supernatural gifts of the New Testament apostles, then Mormons would definitely qualify.

Doctrine and Covenants 46:11-27 teaches that all Mormons are given a gift. These include supernatural gifts, as well as the gift of knowing Jesus is the Christ, which this passage says is not available to all men. *Doctrine and Covenants* 24 teaches that only certain miracles require the Lord's permission. Those which can be done without God's consent include the casting out of devils, healings, and protection against poisonous substances.

Basically Mormon doctrine delineates two types of miracles. First there is the manifestation of the power of God in destroying the wicked. This is usually accomplished without the agency of man. The second kind of miracle is that which serves to protect, bless, or confirm believers in the faith. Mormons see an example of this when sea gulls destroyed a horde of crickets which threatened to devour the crops of the pioneers in the Salt Lake Valley. The supernatural abilities most spoken of when I was a Mormon involved healings, prophecy through visions, dreams, speaking in tongues, and raising the dead.

I was anointed and blessed for healing once when I was a Mormon, when appendicitis apparently threatened. The procedure was the same as is prescribed in all such cases. At the request of an ill person, an elder places consecrated oil near the crown of the head of the afflicted person and pronounces a blessing. Then two other elders "seal" that blessing.

In spite of belief in divine healing, Mormons teach it is wrong to reject medical aid. If all fails, though, it is sometimes the practice in the situation of a dying person who is suffering, with no hope of recovery, for a holder of the Melchizidek Priesthood to offer a "prayer for the release of the spirit."

The 19th century Mormons blessed for healing indiscriminately. Stories (largely undocumented) of divine healings in the days of Joseph Smith persist in Mormon folklore. One story tells how sick twins of five months of age were healed at the touch of a handkerchief belonging to Joseph Smith.[23] And every Mormon child has heard the story of how fallen oxen were blessed and healed by pioneers who were crossing the plains.

Almost every Mormon prophet has told of how a dream served as a message from God to him. A friend of mine who drowned in the Provo River reportedly dreamed of her imminent death a few days before it occurred.

Speaking in tongues was common in the early Mormon church. Brigham Young and others claimed that they could speak in the unknown or "Adamic" language that God speaks. In the past, speaking in tongues has been heard in ward testimony meetings but is almost nonexistent now. Today Mormons still claim the gift of tongues and interpretation and cite as evidence their missionaries' ability to learn foreign languages quickly. (Of course, the Language Training Mission's intensive schooling doesn't hurt anything, either.)

Raising from the dead was supposedly practiced by early Mormons, too. The wife of Wilford Woodruff reportedly died and was given the choice of staying in paradise or returning to earth.[24] Sidney Rigdon's daughter Eliza, whom a doctor pronounced dead, is reported to have resumed life after thirty-six hours.[25]

However, such phenomena belong to the past, and can be expected to disappear altogether. As Mormon Hector Lee noted:

> Casting out devils, having visions, receiving revelations, talking in
> tongues, and similar psychic phenomena are decreasing because the
> Church has either openly discouraged them or has avoided en-

couraging them, and because the appeal of the Church is shifting from the emotional (characteristic of the 1830's and 1840's) to the rational, scientific, social and cultural.[26]

Why don't Mormon buildings have crosses on the spires?

Mormons regard a cross as a symbol of death, and counsel members not to wear crucifixes, either.

Why do Mormons emphasize marriage so?

Mormons believe that unmarried men and women cannot be fully happy on earth nor exalted in eternity. Marriage is the ideal for all adults, and up until just recently it was truly said that "bachelors and spinsters have no status in Mormon society."[27] Lately, though, the church has been more sensitive to the needs of the unmarried, the divorced, and the widowed.

While the spinster is regarded as unlucky, the deliberate bachelor is still seen as selfish. Mormon leaders urge young men to marry before they begin to enjoy the single life. Mormon leader Le Grand Richards once quipped that if a man was thirty and still looking for a wife, when he found "the one" she'd probably be special for waiting for him. If not, reflected Richards, at least the man wouldn't have to live with her so long!

A Mormon magazine published a short story showing how one young man of the pioneer days chose a wife. He had narrowed his choice down to three prospects, and decided to go to their homes and watch them make biscuits. One girl threw away the leavings, the second fed them to the chickens, and the third, whom the young man chose, kneaded them into the dough so that none was wasted.

This emphasis on thrift is certainly justified in view of the fact that many LDS couples marry before the husband finishes school, and no birth control is practiced. A married friend of mine at BYU had two children while her husband was finishing his education. He was in the Air Force, too, and in order to support his family he worked nights at a gas station and gave music lessons in addition to carrying a full class load and fulfilling his military responsibilities.

Mormons recognize civil marriages only as the legalization of sexual relations. However, it seems that the further the distance away from a temple, the less the stigma of a civil or ward marriage ceremony. Mormon youth in Salt Lake City, for instance, are expected to marry in the temple, whereas a poor couple in Mexico might be excused for marrying for time now and for eternity later.

Temple marriages have a high success rate claimed for them—the *Church News* claims as high as 90 percent.[28] However, a Mormon official once remarked at a meeting I attended that less than 30 percent of LDS youth marry in the temple.

Of course there are failures in temple marriages. A temple divorce ("cancellation of sealing") is preceeded by a civil divorce, and must be signed by the prophet himself. It is only granted where infidelity is involved.

Since Utah has so many Mormons, does it have a lower crime rate?

According to the Statistical Abstracts of the United States Department of the Census for 1982, Utah had 5,334 (per 100,000 population) offenses known to the police, very close to the national average of 5,586. However, in the same year Utah had a higher divorce rate than the national average, and an appalling suicide and teenage pregnancy rate.

How can the church keep track of its 5.8 million members?

Every member of the Church of Jesus Christ of the Latter Day Saints has information such as his birthdate, place of birth, names of parents, date of marriage, names of spouse and children, and positions held in the Mormon Church recorded on floppy computer disks. Information retrieval terminals around the country can call up this data, when needed, at a moment's notice. A member's life story is never more than a pushbutton away.

Do Mormons celebrate Christmas and Easter?

Even though Mormons believe that Christ was born on April 6, they still celebrate his birth on December 25th. They decorate trees, exchange gifts, and participate in Yuletide activities much like Gentiles. Christmas is for them a religious holiday as well. Special Christmas programs are presented in Sunday school. On Easter Sunday the emphasis is also on the religious background of the holiday.

Why do Mormons store food?

Many Mormon leaders have taught that the time will come when food and household goods may be unavailable for long periods of time. Mormons are encouraged to keep at least a one year's supply of food, paper products, toiletries, medicine, and other necessities in their homes, and to rotate their use for freshness. Often a bishop will tell his congregation at Sunday services to go home and refrain from buying anything for perhaps a month as a drill to check storage deficiencies.

Most Mormons, though, do not keep a year's supply of food.

Do the Mormons claim to know when Christ will return?

Mormons believe that the rising generation of 1843 was promised that some of their number should not taste death until the return of the Savior. A man's newborn child in 1843 could conceivably have half-brothers and sisters born sixty years afterwards, and such children, if they lived to be about one hundred, would be alive "in the beginning of the Seventh thousand years"[29]—about A.D. 2000. This is the approximate date when Mormons believe Christ will return. The exact time would be marked, said Joseph Smith in his *History of Joseph Smith,*[30] by a year in which there were no rainbows on earth.

NOTES

[1]*Doctrine and Covenants* 110:11; 133:25-34.

[2]Ibid., 133:26.

[3]Hymn #322 by Eliza R. Snow in 1891 edition of *Sacred Hymns.*

[4]*Doctrine and Covenants* 20:77. See also Moroni 4:3.

[5]*Doctrine and Covenants* 20:79. See also Moroni 5:2. (Water is now used instead of wine—see *Doctrine and Covenants* 27:1-3.)

[6]N. B. Lundwall, comp., *Inspired Prophetic Warnings (Publisher's Press, n.d.), 6th edition, p. 46.*

[7]*Doctrine and Covenants* 38:18-20.

[8]Ibid., 63:27.

[9]Ibid., 63:48.

[10]Fife, *Saints of Sage and Saddle,* p. 283.

[11]*People,* April 17, 1978.

[12]*People,* October 31, 1977.

[13]*Doctrines of Salvation* 2:87, 1960 edition.

[14]*Doctrine and Covenants* 59.

[15]Felt, *What It Means to Be a Latter-day Saint,* p. 69.

[16]Whalen, *The Latter-day Saints in the Modern-day World,* p. 79.

[17]Moses 7

[18]*Companion to the Book of Mormon, op. cit.,* p. 191.

[19]AP wire story December 11, 1977.

[20]See also 1 Nephi 13:16-19; 2 Nephi 1:7; Ether 2:8-12.

[21]As quoted in Anderson, *Inside Story of Mormonism,* p. 127.

[22]*Church News,* January 7, 1978, p. 2.

[23]Wilford Woodruff, *Leaves From My Journal,* 2nd edition, 1882.

[24]Fife, *Saints of Sage and Saddle,* p. 186.

[25]Joseph Smith Jr., *Documentary History of the Church,* V, pp. 121-124.

[26]Lee, *The Three Nephites,* p. 120.

[27]Whalen, *The Latter-day Saints in the Modern-day World,* p. 207.

[28]*Church News,* June 17, 1978.

[29]*Doctrine and Covenants* 77:6, 12.

[30]Joseph Smith, *History of Joseph Smith,* March 10, 1844. As quoted in *Principles of the Gospel,* p. 82.

Bibliography

Abbate, Francesco, general editor. *Precolumbian Art*. London: Octopus Books, 1972.

Anderson, Einar. *Inside Story of Mormonism*. Grand Rapids, Michigan: Kregel Publications, 1977.

(Anonymous.) "Jerald and Sandra Tanner's Distorted View of Mormonism: A Response to *Mormonism—Shadow or Reality?*" Salt Lake City, 1977. (LDS.)

Bailey, Jack Stephan. *Inside a Mormon Mission*. Salt Lake City: Hawkes Publishing Company, 1976. (LDS.)

Bales, James D., Ph.D. *The Book of Mormon?* Rosemead, California: Old Paths Book Club, 1958.

Bennion, Lowell. *An Introduction to the Gospel*. Teacher's supplement. Salt Lake City: Deseret Sunday School Union Board, 1964. (LDS.)

A Brief Statement of the Principles of the Gospel: Based Loosely Upon The Compendium (Richards-Little.) Church of Jesus Christ of Latter-day Saints, 1953. (LDS.)

Brodie, Fawn McKay. *No Man Knows My History*. New York: Alfred A. Knopf, 1946.

Budvarson, Arthur. *The Book of Mormon—True or False?* Concord, California: Pacific Publishing Company, 1974.

_____. *A Rebuttal to "The Problems of the Book of Mormon."* La Mesa, California: Utah Christian Tract Society.

Caswall, Henry. *The City of the Mormons, or Three Days at Nauvoo, in 1842*. London, 1842.

Cherry, Alan Gerald. *It's You and Me, Lord!* Salt Lake City: Bookcraft, 1970. (LDS.)

Conference Reports of the Church of Jesus Christ of Latter-day Saints. Various volumes. (LDS.)

Cowdrey, Wayne L.; Davis, Howard A.; and Scales, Donald K. *Who Really Wrote the Book of Mormon?* Santa Ana, California: Vision House Publishers, 1977.

Deen, Edith. *Family Living in the Bible.* New York: Harper and Row, 1963.

Felt, Marie F. *What It Means To Be a Latter-day Saint.* Teacher's manual. Salt Lake City: Deseret Sunday School Union Board, 1963. (LDS.)

Fife, Austin and Alta. *Saints of Sage and Saddle.* Bloomington, Indiana: Indiana University Press, 1956.

Fraser, Gordon. *Is Mormonism Christian?* Chicago: Moody Press, 1977.

_____. *A Manual for Christian Workers: A Workshop Outline for the Study of Mormonism.* Hubbard, Oregon: Gordon H. Fraser, Publisher, 1978.

_____. *What Does the Book of Mormon Teach?* Chicago: Moody Press, 1964.

Gerstner, John H. *The Theology of the Major Sects.* Grand Rapids, Michigan: Baker Book House, 1960.

The Gospel in Principle and Practice. Textbook. Provo, Utah: BYU Printing Service, 1966. (LDS.)

Guthrie, Gary Dean. "Joseph Smith as an Administrator." Unpublished Master's thesis, BYU, 1969 (LDS.)

Hougey, Hal. *Archaeology and the Book of Mormon.* Concord, California: Pacific Publishing Company, 1976.

_____. *Latter-day Saints—Where Did You Get Your Authority?* Concord, California: Pacific Publishing Company, 1977.

_____. *"A Parallel"—The Basis of the Book of Mormon.* Concord, California: Pacific Publishing Company, 1963.

Journal of Discourses. Twenty-six volumes. Liverpool, 1854-1886. (LDS.)

Kirkham, Francis J. *A New Witness for Christ in America: The Book of Mormon.* Independence, Missouri: Zion's Printing and Publishing Company, 1951. (LDS.)

Layton, Melanie. "Can the Descendants of Ham Hold the Priesthood?" Concord, California: Pacific Publishing Company,

_____. *I Pray That The Eyes of Your Heart May Be Enlightened.* Privately printed.

Lee, Hector. *The Three Nephites: The Substance and Significance of the Legend in Folklore.* Albuquerque, New Mexico: University of New Mexico Press, 1949.

Ludlow, Daniel H. *A Companion to Your Study of the Book of Mormon.* Provo, Utah: BYU Press, 1969. (LDS.)

Lundwall, N. B., compiler. *A Compilation Containing the Lectures on Faith,* and related works. Salt Lake City: N. D. Lundwall. (LDS.)

_____. *Inspired Prophetic Warnings.* Publisher's Press, 6th edition. (LDS).

McConkie, Bruce R. *Mormon Doctrine.* Salt Lake City: Bookcraft, 1966. (LDS.)

McElveen, Floyd. *Will The "Saints" Go Marching In?* Glendale, California: Regal Books Division, B/L Publications, 1977.

Mulder, William, and Mortensen, A. Russell, editors. *Among The Mormons: Historic Accounts by Contemporary Observers.* Lincoln, Nebraska: University of Nebraska Press, 1958. 1973 edition.

Nibley, Hugh. *An Approach to the Book of Mormon.* Salt Lake City: Deseret News Press, 1957. (LDS.)

Petersen, La Mar. "Problems in Mormon Text." Salt Lake City: La Mar Petersen, 1957. 1976 edition

Pratt, Orson. *Works.* Liverpool, 1851. (LDS.)

_____. *The Seer.* (Periodical—1852.) (LDS.)

Pratt, Parley P. *Key To Theology.* Liverpool: J. H. Smith, 1883. (LDS.)

Price, Lewis. "The Testimony of a Former Mormon Missionary." (Tract—no date or publisher.)

Richards, LeGrand. *A Marvelous Work and a Wonder.* Salt Lake City: Deseret Book Company, 1963 edition. (LDS.)

Roberts, Brigham H. *A Comprehensive History of the Church of Jesus Christ of Latter-day Saints.* Six volumes. Salt Lake City, 1930. (LDS.)

Root, Orrin. *Training For Service: A Survey of the Bible.* Student edition. Cincinnati: Standard Publishing, 1964.

Shook, Charles A. *The True Origin of the Book of Mormon.* Cincinnati, 1914.

Slade, Styne M. *The Mormon Way.* With photographs by James A. Warner. Englewood Cliffs, New Jersey: Prentice-Hall, Inc., 1976.

Smith, Lucy Mack. *Biographical Sketches of Joseph Smith the Prophet and His Progenitors for Many Generations.* Liverpool, 1853. (LDS.)

Smith, John L. *Brigham Smith.* (Fiction.) Marlowe, Oklahoma: Utah Missions, Inc., 1969.

_____. *Witnessing Effectively To Mormons.* Marlowe, Oklahoma: Utah Missions, Inc., 1975.

Smith, Joseph Jr. The *Book of Mormon.* Church of Jesus Christ of Latter-day Saints. (LDS.)

_____. *Doctrine and Covenants.* Church of Jesus Christ of Latter-day Saints. (LDS.)

————. *History of the Church of Jesus Christ of Latter-day Saints.* Six volumes. Introduction and notes by B. H. Roberts. Salt Lake City: Deseret News, 1902-1912. (LDS.)

————. *Inspired Version of the Holy Scriptures.* Independence: Herald Publishing House, 1955. (LDS.)

————. *King Follett Discourse.* Notes and references by B. H. Roberts. Salt Lake City: Magazine Printing Company, 1955. (LDS.)

————. *Pearl of Great Price.* Church of Jesus Christ of Latter-day Saints. (LDS.)

————. *Teachings of the Prophet Joseph Smith.* Selected and arranged by Joseph Fielding Smith. Salt Lake City: Deseret News Press, 1956 edition. (LDS.)

Smith, Joseph Fielding. *Answers To Gospel Questions.* Salt Lake City, 1958. (LDS.)

————. *Doctrines of Salvation.* Salt Lake City: Bookcraft, 1954-56. (LDS.)

Spalding, Reverend F. S. *Joseph Smith Jr. As a Translator.* Salt Lake City, 1912.

Sperry, Dr. Sidney. *Ancient Records Testify in Papyrus and Stone.* Salt Lake City: Bookcraft, 1938. (LDS.)

————. *Doctrine and Covenants Compendium.* Salt Lake City: Bookcraft, 1970 edition. (LDS.)

Talmadge, James E. *A Study of the Articles of Faith.* Salt Lake City, Utah: Church of Jesus Christ of Latter-day Saints, 1952. (LDS.)

Tanner, Jerald and Sandra: Their publishing company, formerly called Modern Microfilm, is now called Utah Lighthouse Ministry (Box 1884, Salt Lake City Utah, 84110.) Their following books can be ordered from them: *Mormonism, Shadow or Reality?; The Changing World of Mormonism* (Moody Press); *The Bible and Mormon Doctrine; Mormon Scriptures and the Bible; A Look at Christianity; Mormonism, Magic and Masonry; Joseph Smith and Money-Digging; Archaeology and the Book of Mormon; Tracking the White Salamander* (about Mark Hofman and the forging of documents); *The Tanners on Trial; Book of Mormon "Caractors' Found!; 3913 Changes in the Book of Mormon; Did Spalding Write the Book of Mormon?; Can The Browns Save Joseph Smith?; Mormon Spies, Hughes, and the CIA; Unmasking a Mormon Spy; Joseph Smith's Successor; Joseph Smith and Polygamy; Mormonism Like Watergate?; Mormons and Negroes; The Mormon Kingdom, Vols. 1 & 2; The Case Against Mormonism, Vols. 1, 2, 3; Changes In Joseph Smith's History; A Critical Look—A Study of the Overstreet "Confession" and the Cowdery "Defense'; Answer-*

ing Dr. Clandestine; Falsification of Joseph Smith's History; Changes in the Key to Theology. In addition, they publish photo-reprints of important Mormon documents. All are highly recommended.

Teachings of the Living Prophets. A compilation. Provo, Utah: BYU Press. (LDS.)

Terry, Keith, and Whipple, Walter. *From the Dust of Decades: A Saga of the Papyri and Mummies.* Salt Lake City: Bookcraft, 1968. (LDS.)

Turner, Wallace. *The Mormon Establishment.* Boston: Houghton Mifflin Company, 1966.

Wallace, Irving. *The Twenty-Seventh Wife.* New York: Simon and Schuster, 1961.

Walters, Wesley P. "Joseph Smith Among The Egyptians." Reprint of an article published in *The Journal of the Evangelical Theological Society,* volume XVI, No. 1, Winter 1973. Salt Lake City: Modern Microfilm, 1973.

Whalen, William J. *The Latter-day Saints in the Modern-day World.* University of Notre Dame Press, 1967.

Whitmer, David. *An Address to All Believers in Christ.* Reprint. Searcy, Arkansas: Bales Book Store, 1960.

Widtsoe, John A. *Gospel Interpretations: More Evidences and Reconciliations.* Salt Lake City: Bookcraft, 1947. (LDS.)

————. *Joseph Smith, Seeker After Truth.* Salt Lake City: Bookcraft, 1951. (LDS.)

Whitte, Bob. *Mormonism and the Negro.* Tape.

————, compiler. *Where Does It Say That?* Scottsdale, Arizona: COUP.

————. *Witnessing to Mormons Using "Where Does It Say That?"* Scottsdale, Arizona: COUP.

Young, Kimball. *Isn't One Wife Enough?* New York: Holt, 1954.

Mormon Chronology

December 1805	Joseph Smith Jr. born
Spring 1820	"First Vision" of Joseph Smith
1826	Joseph Smith, "The Glass-Looker," tried and convicted of being "disorderly and an imposter"
September 1827	Joseph Smith receives the golden plates; translation of *Book of Mormon* begins
March 1830	First edition of *Book of Mormon* published
April 1830	Church organized in New York with eight members
June 1830	Book of Moses "revealed" to Joseph Smith
1832	Joseph Smith receives "Civil War" revelation; United Order established; Brigham Young converted to Mormonism
1833	United Order collapses when Mormons are driven from Jackson County, Missouri; "Word of Wisdom" revealed
May 1834	"Zion's Camp" troops set out to redeem Jackson County
Summer 1835	Joseph Smith buys Chandler (*Pearl of Great Price*) papyri, begins to translate
1835	Compilation of *Book of Commandments* (later *Doctrine and Covenants*) completed
October 1838	"Extermination order" issued by Missouri Governor Boggs
August 1840	Doctrine of baptism for the dead first preached by Joseph Smith
1841	First vicarious baptisms performed; Joseph Smith commanded to publish new translation of Bible

1842	First published written account by Joseph Smith of "First Vision"
March 1842	Relief Society organized
1843	Kinderhook plates translated
July 1843	"Eternal marriage" (polygamy) revelation recorded
June 1844	Joseph Smith killed
February 1846	Mormons begin to migrate west
July 1846	Mormon Battallion leaves for Fort Leavenworth
July 1847	Mormons arrive in Salt Lake Valley
December 1847	Brigham Young becomes president of church
June 1848	Sea gulls save crops
September 1850	Territory of Utah organized with Brigham Young as governor
1853	Salt Lake Temple begun
November 1867	Young Women's Mutual Improvement Association formed
June 1875	Young Men's Mutual Improvement Association formed
August 1877	Brigham Young dies
August 1878	Primary Association organized
October 1880	John Taylor becomes president
1887	John Taylor dies
April 1889	Wilford Woodruff becomes president
October 1890	"Manifesto" issued
January 1896	Utah becomes a state
1898	Woodruff dies, Lorenzo Snow becomes president
1901	Snow dies, Joseph F. Smith becomes president
1907	Church pays off all debts
1918	Smith dies, Heber J. Grant becomes president
April 1936	Welfare Plan introduced
1946	Grant dies, George Albert Smith becomes president
1951	Smith dies, David O. McKay becomes president
1970	McKay dies, Joseph Fielding Smith becomes president
1972	Smith dies, Harold B. Lee becomes president
1973	Lee dies, Spencer W. Kimball becomes president
1976	"Vision of the Celestial Kingdom" and "Vision of the Redemption of the Dead" added to the *Pearl of Great Price*.
June 1978	Blacks allowed to receive Mormon priesthood.
1985	Kimball dies, Ezra Taft Benson becomes president

Subject Index

Mormon Scripture Index

273

Scripture Index